IER UNIVERSITY LEARNING INFORMATION SERVICES

STANDARD LOAN

w this item by the last date shown.

Reviews
for
Brand Spirit

"This is an in depth look at a vital and growing area of marketing. It is possible to synthesise the needs of a good cause and the objectives of a commercial company. Both parties have to understand the hearts and minds of consumers in the context of society. This ground breaking book describes how and why in a commendably readable way."

Nick Phillips, Director General, IPA, London

"Want to inspire your people? Want to build trust with your potential customers? Want to build a lasting positive reputation? Read *Brand Spirit*."

Robin Buchanan, Senior Partner, Bain & Company, Inc.

"*Brand Spirit* makes an eloquent case for CRM. The case studies demonstrate how CRM builds long-term differentiated brand equity and illuminates the personal benefits of the self-realisation and self-esteem for those contributing. An antidote to millennial anxiety. A really useful book for our times."

Fiona Gilmore, Springpoint

"If, as I believe, we are organizing the zeitgeist around sustainability versus progress, the *Brand Spirit*, more than brand personality or brand essence, will drive business success in the future. The fastest way to self-esteem is to stand up for what you believe. Pringle and Thompson have written a fabulous primer for the future of branding based upon self esteem and Cause Related Marketing."

Watts Wacker, Futurist, First Matter, USA

"The Kellogg's/Kids Help Line partnerships is a wonderful example of a CRM program that delivers benefit to the brand, the charity and the community. I believe that its success is down to the strategic way that Kellogg's went about finding the right partner – one that enhanced their image and appealed to their prime target audience, rather than choosing one based on a personal contact. CRMs formed on a CEO's pet cause do not work. The Kellogg's/Kids Help Line partnership is a shining example of a win win partnership."

Hayley Cavill, Cavill + Co, Australia

"At a time when the ethical standards of business are increasingly called into question and society looks for concrete evidence that business leaders are socially responsible, *Brand Spirit* shows in a clear and simple way how companies can be more ethical and responsible while still making money."

Professor Stephen Hill, London School of Economics

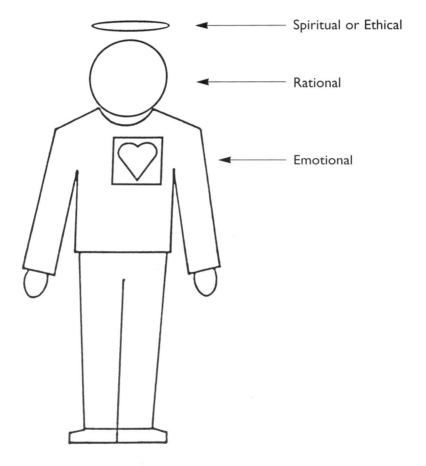

Spiritual or Ethical

Rational

Emotional

'*Anthropomorphy in branding: '50s Rational, '70s Emotional, '90s Spiritual*'

Brand *Spirit*

How cause related marketing builds brands

Hamish Pringle and Marjorie Thompson

JOHN WILEY & SONS
Chichester • New York • Weinheim • Brisbane • Singapore • Toronto

S 658.8 PRI

Copyright © 1999 by John Wiley & Sons Ltd,
Baffins Lane, Chichester,
West Sussex PO19 1UD, England
National   01243 779777
International   (+44) 1243 779777
e-mail (for orders and customer service enquiries):
cs-books@wiley.co.uk
Visit our Home Page on http://www.wiley.co.uk
or http://www.wiley.com

All Rights Reserved. No part of this publication may be reproduced, stored in a
retrieval system, or transmitted, in any form or by any means, electronic, mechanical,
photocopying, recording, scanning or otherwise, except under the terms of the
Copyright, Designs and Patents Act 1988 or under the terms of a licence issued by the
Copyright Licensing Agency, 90 Tottenham Court Road, London, UK W1P 9HE,
without the permission in writing of the publisher.

Other Wiley Editorial Offices

John Wiley & Sons, Inc., 605 Third Avenue,
New York, NY 10158-0012, USA

WILEY-VCH GmbH, Pappelallee 3,
D-69469 Weinheim, Germany

Jacaranda Wiley Ltd, 33 Park Road, Milton,
Queensland 4064, Australia

John Wiley & Sons (Asia) Pte Ltd, 2 Clementi Loop #02-01,
Jin Xing Distripark, Singapore 129809

John Wiley & Sons (Canada) Ltd, 22 Worcester Road,
Rexdale, Ontario M9W 1L1, Canada

Library of Congress Cataloging-in-Publication Data
Pringle, Hamish.
    Brand spirit : how cause related marketing builds brands / Hamish
Pringle and Marjorie Thompson.
        p.   cm.
    Includes bibliographical references and index.
    ISBN 0-471-98776-X (alk. paper)
    1. Social marketing.   I. Thompson, Marjorie, 1957–
II. Title.
HF5414.P75   1999
658.8–dc21
                                                                99–13354
                                                                CIP

British Library Cataloguing in Publication Data
A catalogue record for this book is available from the British Library

ISBN 0-471-98776-X

Designed and Typeset by Wyvern 21 Ltd, Bristol
Printed and bound in Great Britain by Biddles Ltd, Guildford and King's Lynn

This book is printed on acid-free paper responsibly manufactured from
sustainable forestry, in which at least two trees are planted for each one
used for paper production.

Dedications

To my Mother, Pamela Ann Pringle, and in grateful memory of my Father, Robert Henry Pringle; they gave me my value system, my education and the best possible start in life.

Hamish Pringle

For my parents, who encouraged me by their example to be an active citizen; for the AIDS and Breast Cancer Nurses and all those working for racial equality from whom I learned so much; and, most importantly, everyone campaigning for nuclear disarmament: without you there would be no world to make a better place.

Marjorie Thompson

Contents

And now abideth these three, faith, hope and charity,
but the greatest of these is charity.

I Corinithians, King James' Bible

Every gift has a price tag.

Renate Olins, London Marriage Guidance

Nothing is impossible

Saatchi & Saatchi

Acknowledgements and Thanks

Brand Spirit has been the product of a great team effort and particular thanks are due to the following people.

For sharing the dream of creating Saatchi & Saatchi Cause Connection: Claire McMaster and Christopher Lusty, and for helping to make it happen Tamara Ingram, Joint Chief Executive Officer and Simone Forster, Board Account Director, Saatchi & Saatchi.

For endorsing the idea and supporting the initiative: Alan Bishop, Vice-Chairman, International.

For inviting us to write the book in the first place: our editor Claire Plimmer, for tenacity in the pursuit of pictures Liz Benson, assistant editor and Jenny Mackenzie, our production editor at Wiley's.

For her invaluable contribution as our researcher, Elspeth Noble, Joey Gardiner for his diligent work on the case studies and Joshua Achene for all his assistance.

For valuable input: Roland Wales, Jon and Sue Thompson, Ellene Felder and the Rev. David Urquhart.

For typing the manuscript, Julie Dawson, and for preparing it for publication, Lee-Anne Harlow.

For feedback on the work: Marilyn Baxter, Steve Chinn, Avi Dan and Myra Stark.

We would also like to acknowledge all the other people who have volunteered their time for Saatchi & Saatchi Cause Connection and believed in it, including Dominic Burch, Kathryn Cunningham, Alasdair Fraser, Chris Gwyther, Hema Kotecha, Shirley Haw, Angus Jenkins,

Carin Lavery, Betsy Lucas, Ron Mateljan, Thuc Nguyen, Anne Ridgeon, Wendy Roy, Christina Ruiz, Jamie Thompson and Joanna Yarrow.

There is also a significant debt owed to the pioneers in this field who have been so generous with their advice and permissions to reproduce their research and case studies. We are particularly indebted to Jerry Welsh, the founding father of cause-related marketing, and the man who coined the phrase! He developed the first ever CRM campaigns for a symphony and local arts programmes in California and Texas with American Express in 1981 and additionally was responsible along with James D Robinson III and Lou Gerstner (now of IBM) of American Express for the 1983 Statue of Liberty campaign. Mr. Welsh has been generous with his time and his comments and like all the best 'ideas' people, wants his idea to be spread as far and widely as possible.

We would like to thank Hayley Cavill of Cavill + Co in Australia and Carol Cone of Cone Communications in Boston for their equally generous and helpful contribution in assisting us to promote the cause for which they have done so much. One unsung hero is Northern Ireland's Bob Doyle who came up with the original HelpAd idea of cross-branding; he too has been generous with his time and material, and most crucially put us in touch with Jerry Welsh.

Finally, Sue Adkins of Business in the Community, the Henley Centre, the Future Foundation and British Telecom deserve our gratitude.

We also acknowledge the following companies for their case studies and the extra input they have given us in many instances: American Express, Anchor, Andrex, Austin Reed, Avon, Birds Eye, BMW, British Airways, Cadbury, Co-operative Bank, Daddies Ketchup, Dollond & Aitchison, Flora, Liz Claiborne, Norwich Union, Procter & Gamble, Reebok, Tesco, VISA and WHSmith.

Publisher's Note

The publisher wishes to thank the following who have kindly given permission for the use of copyright material. The destination of the reproduced material is indicated in square brackets.

The Advertising Archives for: [p. 192] Flora tub/British Heart Foundation and Princess Diana

American Express for: [p. 9] 'Charge Against Hunger' advertisement

Anchor for: [p. 208] Hovis loaf with Anchor Butter image on wrapper

Apple Computer Ltd for: [p. 77] 'Big Blue' 1984 advertisement

Asda for: [p. 90] 'Pocket Pat' advertisement

Austin Reed Ltd for: [p. 202] Shelter 'National Suit Exchange' campaign image

Avon Products Inc. for: [p. 35] Avon Breast cancer 'pink ribbon'

Barclaycard and BMP DDB for: [p. 61] Rowan Atkinson and Henry Naylor in credit card advertisement

Bayer Plc and Abbott Mead Vickers for: [p. 73] Alka Seltzer 'Meatballs' advertisement

BiTeC and Research International for: [p. 117] 'Social Issues' survey; [p. 122] and [p. 123] 'Consumer Awareness' surveys

BMW (GB) Limited for: [p. 126] 'The Ultimate Driving Machine' logo

The Body Shop International Plc for: [p. 83] 'Against Animal Testing' posters/image

British Airways/UNICEF for: [p. 131] 'Change for Good' donation envelope

British Telecom/The Future Foundation for: [p. 117, 118 & 123] Charts 4.1, 4.9, 4.10, 4.11 and 4.16 from *The Responsible Organisation*

Cavill + Co./Worthington Di Marzio for: [p. 102] 'Combating Consumer Cynicism' table

Commission for Racial Equality for: [p. xiii] 'Brains' advertisement

Cone Communications for: [p. 122] 'The Cone/Roper Cause-Related Marketing Trends Report 1997'

The Co-operative Bank and Representation Joyce Edwards for: [p. 86] 'Making a Bank Statement' advertisement; [p. 87] 'The Impact of Ethics on Employees' Co-operative Bank employee survey

Dolland & Aitchison for: [p. 140] 'Old Man/Spectacles' press advertisement

Esso Petroleum Co. Ltd for: [p. 63] Esso Tiger image

Gallagher Ltd and CDP for: [p. 80] 'The Dawn of Surrealism in advertising' Benson & Hedges 'Pyramid' advertisement; [p. 81] 'Art in advertising' Benson & Hedges Silk Cut advertisements

The Henley Centre for: [p. 30] Figure 12.2 from '1999 Planning for Consumer Change' and '1998 Planning for Social Change'; [p. 31] Figure 12.3 from '1999 Planning for Consumer Change' and '1996/7 Planning for Social Change'

HP Foods Ltd for: [p. 104] Daddies Ketchup/NSPCC image

Imperial Chemical Industries Plc for: [p. 62] Dulux dog photograph

Johnson & Johnson for: [p. 68] 'Band Aid' advertisement

Kimberly Clark Ltd for: [p. 55] Andrex puppy photograph

Leagas Delaney for: [p. 70] Timberland 'Stole their Shoes' advertisement

The LEGO Group for: [p. 69] 'Kipper' advertisement

Lever Brothers for: [p. 65] Old 'Rinso' advertisement from *The 100 Greatest Advertisement*, New York, 1949, p. 80

Liz Claiborne Inc. and Patrice Tanaka & Co, New York for: [p. 230] 'Women's Work' campaign image

McCann Erickson and Shillons for: [p. 76] McCann Erickson/Levi's 'Route 66' advertisement

Michelin Tyre Plc for: [p. 58] Image of Michelin Man

Norwich Union for: [p. 246] Storyboard from Norwich Union/St John Ambulance campaign

PA News for: [p. 41] 'Diana in Angola' photograph; [p.42] 'Sea of flowers' at Kensington Palace photograph

Peter Lavery for: [p. 79] Castlemaine XXXX advertisement

The Pillsbury Company for: [p. 57] 'Green Giant' image

Pizza Express for: [p. 100] Menu

Reebok International Ltd for: [p. 46] Poster from 'Reebok Human Rights Now!' campaign

RNLI for: [p. xx] 'Austin Motor Company letter of 1942'; [p. 59] 'Lifeboat collection box' image

Rolls-Royce Motor Cars Limited for: [p. 67] 'Silver Cloud' advertisement

Sainsbury's Supermarkets for: [p. 81] 'Mince' poster

Tesco and Bell Pottinger Good Relations for: [p. 17] 'Computers for Schools' campaign poster

VISA, USA for: [p. 109] 'Visa Read Me a Story' campaign image

Volkswagen and BMP DDB for: [p. 72] Volkswagen 'Lemon' image

WHSmith for: [p. 135] Logo image from WHSmith 'Ready Steady Read!' campaign

Preface

Saatchi & Saatchi Cause Connection came about because of my long experience in the voluntary, trade union and public sector. I worked with a number of good causes ranging from the Campaign for Nuclear Disarmament to the Royal College of Nursing, and latterly at the Commission for Racial Equality which was a Saatchi & Saatchi client.

During the latter period with the CRE, I became increasingly aware of the need to communicate important issues in a more effective way. Rather than scramble around finding donated media space, and asking for pro bono work, it occurred to me that with the kind of careful targeting and planning which goes into the normal promotion of brands, one could actually change social attitudes more effectively. Then images such as the one below could really make an impact.

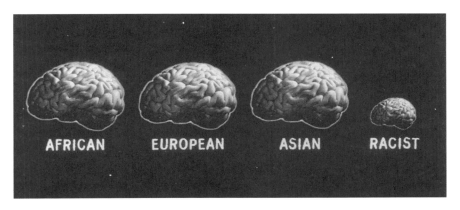

'Attacking small-mindedness globally.'

Inspired by the pioneering work in this area in the USA, I therefore approached Tamara Ingram of Saatchi & Saatchi in London, who agreed to set up the first specialist Cause Related Marketing unit inside an advertising agency, on either side of the Atlantic. Saatchi & Saatchi Cause Connection was launched at the Media Trust Conference in June 1997, and began operating in September of that year.

After almost a year spent influencing UK corporate culture, and finding a very keen charitable sector, we sponsored a conference in May 1998 in conjunction with the *Independent* newspaper and Learning in Business. We were inspired by speakers such as Maria Kalligeros of Patrice Tanaka & Company, talking about Liz Claiborne, the American women's retail clothing group and their campaign, which has taken on the very difficult issue of domestic violence. Doug Bauer of SmithKline Beecham, the major pharmaceutical company, also challenged us with SKB's visionary goal of eliminating an entire disease.

Hearing the quality of these and other presentations, many with outstanding results in terms of sales and attitude shifts, convinced us that they should be brought to a wider audience. One way of doing this would be to draw together all the examples of best practice, and thus we were ready and willing when the call came from Claire Plimmer, our Editor at John Wiley & Sons.

We hope that this book will go some way into making a contribution to society at large by encouraging the development of Cause Related Marketing in building brands and improving the quality of people's lives. Many activists from the environmental and peace movement in the 1980s are now in governments across Europe, others are advising companies about their social responsibilities in this area, and as we have all learned we can achieve more together than separately.

Marjorie Thompson, Director
Saatchi & Saatchi Cause Connection

Having worked in UK advertising agencies for 25 years, including Ogilvy & Mather, Boase Massimi Pollitt, Publicis, Abbott Mead Vickers, Leagas Delaney, KHBB and a spell in my own company, Madell Wilmot Pringle, I had become reasonably confident of being up-to-date with new thinking and developments in the industry.

I was therefore somewhat taken aback to discover the world of Cause Related Marketing in June 1997, no more than three months after joining Saatchi & Saatchi. I exaggerate to make a point, because on reflection I was aware of programmes such as Tesco's Computers for Schools, but the issue was certainly not at the top of my mind, nor was it a current topic of conversation in the UK communications industry at large.

The more I learned about the subject, the more excited I became. Here was a genuine new development in marketing, which did not appear to have been properly recognized. As I read the case histories and the research reports from the likes of Business in the Community and Cone Communications, I became increasingly convinced that the whole subject of Cause Related Marketing needed to be presented in the context of our wider understanding of the nature of brands and branding. Only if this were done would it be taken seriously by professional marketers and the top management of companies at large.

I was also excited by the creative possibilities presented by this new way of thinking about brand values. Saatchi & Saatchi have produced so many award-winning campaigns for social issues and good causes that we have a whole exhibition featuring them, which is currently touring the world. Much of this work has been done by the agency's offices on a pro bono basis and outstanding images have so often had too little money behind them to achieve their full impact. Imagine the potential for these world-changing ideas if they could be harnessed by mainstream brands as part of their total communication mix!

In a sense I have provided the commercial theory to support Marjorie's activist instincts. This book is designed to embrace her vision of commercial and charity partnership and bring together for the first time in one volume some of the best case histories of CRM campaigns and the most interesting research so far. But more importantly it explains not only how the concept fits in to the history of post-war advertising and communications, but also into the longer-term history of philanthropy and charitable giving. In this sense Cause Related Marketing has something of an historical inevitability about it, and I am convinced it is here to stay.

Hamish Pringle

A Foreword by Edward de Bono

Every business is all about 'value creation'. Value creation is so fundamental to success that it deserves a name of its own. In my book *Surpetition* I suggested the term 'valufacture' to capture this idea.

Many people are coming to the conclusion that valufacture in the future is increasingly going to become a commodity sold on price alone.

Cause Related Marketing is all about such synergies and alliances. All three parties involved benefit and that is why CRM is very much of the moment and has so much potential.

The charitable cause benefits because it gets so much publicity far beyond what it could otherwise afford to buy. In most cases there is also a direct financial benefit as a portion of profits or price resulting form the trading aspects of the partnership arrangement.

The vendor benefits because the commercial company involved is seen as making a social contribution through giving prominence and money to the cause. The vendor also benefits if the association leads to positive image attributes and increased sales of the brand.

The consumer benefits because of the double reward of obtaining the product and also benefiting the charity or cause. The customer feels better because, at no extra cost, he or she is doing good.

Some might think that Cause Related Marketing is simply a cynical exploitation of public sympathy for the sake of profits. There will always be people who take it upon themselves to make these sorts of judgements on behalf of others. However, consumers always have the power of the final choice and if most of them felt it was cynical, then CRM would cease to exist. Clearly this is not the case, but certainly the integrity of the idea is the basis of its successful future development.

Thus whether Cause Related Marketing is an expression of the social conscience of an organization, or simply an effective marketing tool may be difficult to distinguish from the outside. At one level this is unimportant. A person who gives to charity may do so for at least three reasons: the person genuinely wants to do good; giving money makes the person feel good; giving money makes the person look good in the community.

However, as far as the individual or organization receiving the financial support is concerned, the money is the same in all three cases. Once you get into analysing motives or assuming motives, there is no limit to what you can surmise. The question to ask is: 'What is the real value in the end?'

In the future I see commercial communication moving very much in the direction of Cause Related Marketing and further ideas beyond that. Communication is all about communication: it is the perceived outcome that is important, not the motives that are ascribed to it. What is put through the communications channel can have a multiplicity of values – all of them worthwhile.

I see the outcome of these new synergies and alliances in CRM as being a powerful force for good and very much bound up in the future economic culture of valufacture.

Edward de Bono

Introduction

One of the most appealing things about Cause Related Marketing (CRM) is that it is not a completely new idea. Rather it is an idea whose time has truly come. Blue chip marketing companies such as American Express, Avon, Procter & Gamble and the Co-operative (Co-op) Bank have already proven for themselves the power of CRM in sales and image terms. Now is the time for all marketers to assess its potential for their brand.

Nor is CRM a 'flash in the pan' or just another short-term marketing fad. Reviewing the history of charity and philanthropy it is clear that the driving motivations towards altruistic behaviour in pursuing commercial gains have precedents going back centuries.

Indeed we have evidence of marketers in the early part of the century carrying out what we today would see as Cause Related Marketing programmes – the charming letter dated 1942 from the Austin Motor Company to the Royal National Lifeboat Institution illustrated on the next page is evidence of this.

But as we approach the Millennium, and as Western economies mature, there is growing evidence that consumers are looking for new sorts of brand values. These go well beyond the practical issues of functional product performance or rational product benefits and further than the emotional and psychological aspects of brand personality and image. Consumers are moving towards the top of Maslow's Hierarchy of Needs and seeking 'self-realization'.

People are also asking more and more questions about the role of commercial organizations in society and are looking for demonstrations of

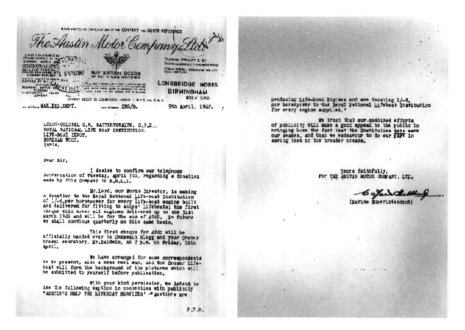

'Austin Motor Company letter of 1942 – the earliest evidence of cause marketing?'

good corporate citizenship with an awareness of the needs of all the stakeholders involved. Social and sustainability audits are becoming part of the corporate reporting landscape.

In an anthropomorphic sense, if consumers know how a brand functions and how it 'thinks' and 'feels', then the new question that has to be answered is 'what does it "believe" in?'

This development has profound implications for our thinking about brands and branding. In order to remain competitive, marketers are going to have to find ways and means of adding new sorts of values to their brands in order to satisfy the emerging consumer demand for 'higher order' image attributes.

Fortunately for their owners there are some very successful brands which already have powerful belief systems or corporate ethics which will drive them forward in this new era. The likes of Marks & Spencer or McDonald's have such clarity of mission and strength of purpose that they will easily be able to answer the challenge raised by consumers in this new era.

However, there are many more companies and brands which lack a 'credo'. For these companies a Cause Related Marketing campaign can provide them with a 'higher order' benefit to offer their consumers and stakeholders. While this may look like a potentially cynical exercise in image manipulation the truth of the matter is that if it is approached in that way, then it will be. In order to deliver a true CRM campaign there has to be a genuine commitment on behalf of the corporation, at its highest levels, to the cause.

The objective of this book is to describe all the factors that are involved in developing a Cause Related Marketing relationship, either with a charity, or directly with a cause and the many considerations that have to be taken into account in the process. It then goes on to describe how a CRM campaign can be created involving the use of research techniques and strategic planning tools. There are discussions of media usage and 'corporate body language' in the approach to a brand's CRM campaign in the context of the rest of its communications portfolio.

Within the body of the text there are many of the best CRM case histories that are currently available and these should give marketers plenty of ideas which can be applied to their own brands or companies.

Finally we summarize the historical and social trends which have led us to the point in the evolution of brands and branding where belief systems and credos have become part and parcel of the marketer's armoury, and then forecast some future developments.

Thus the overall purpose of this book is to explain the concept of Cause Related Marketing, its place within the historical context of thinking on branding, and how a marketer can harness its power for a product, service or corporate brand in its communications to consumers.

Hopefully the reader will come away from *Brand Spirit* with two main things: first, a thorough understanding of what Cause Related Marketing is all about and how to apply it in their situation to add distinctive and motivating new values; and secondly, a belief that it is the responsibility of the professional marketer nowadays to consider the wider role of the brand or the company in society, and to ensure that something relevant and of mutual benefit is being done for good causes in the course of achieving their business objectives.

PART I
Cause Related Marketing

1

Cause Related Marketing Defined

Cause Related Marketing (CRM) can be defined as a strategic positioning and marketing tool which links a company or brand to a relevant social cause or issue, for mutual benefit.

A Cause Related Marketing programme can be delivered via a strategic alliance between a company and a charity or voluntary organization committed to the defined area of concern, or by directly addressing the 'cause' itself. Adopting a 'cause' in either way can give a brand a 'credo' or 'belief system' and result in significantly improved consumer perceptions and purchase intentions. CRM can also create valuable relationships with a whole series of other important stakeholders in a company such as employees, suppliers and governmental agencies.

As Sir Dominic Cadbury, Chairman, Cadbury Schweppes plc said in 1996, when he was Chairman of the Business in the Community Cause Related Marketing Leadership Campaign:

> CRM is an effective way of enhancing corporate image, differentiating products and increasing both sales and loyalty.

However one of the keys to doing this successfully is to ensure that the brand and the cause share the same 'Territory'. Thus the old-fashioned 'charity promotion' whereby a brand simply donated money to any worthy cause, or where a company's corporate affairs department sponsored a range of strategically unrelated charities, is increasingly seen as empty patronage or even exploitation, rather than a living, altruistic partnership for mutual benefit.

Thus marketing's understanding and interpretation of a brand's 'Territory' needs to be extended beyond functional performance and emotional or aspirational imagery into that of 'ethics' and 'beliefs'. One way in which this can be done is through the development of a Cause Related Marketing relationship which 'fits' very well with these other core aspects of the brand to create a truly holistic persona.

An interesting issue for marketers in developing their CRM thinking is the consideration as to whether it would be better to 'go direct' to the cause, or to use a relevant charity as the 'vehicle' for the brand's involvement. Pizza Express, perhaps the godfather of CRM in the UK with Peter Boizot's 20-year-old levy on sales of Veneziana pizzas, directly addressed the problems of Venice in Peril. Tesco also went 'direct' with their highly successful 'Computers for Schools' programme which has become the best-known CRM campaign in the UK with a prompted awareness amongst all adults of 48%. SmithKline Beecham also intend to go straight to the heart of the matter with their visionary campaign to eliminate lymphatic filaria, the source of elephantiasis, a grotesque disease which afflicts literally hundreds of millions of people.

The benefit of the 'direct' approach is that the 'ownership' of the CRM campaign is unequivocally the company's or brand's, and there is a clarity in this which is of great value in the increasingly cluttered media environment in which consumers live.

On the other hand partnering with a respected charity can bring significant benefits in terms of credibility, distribution and the help of volunteers, all harnessed by an existing organization with considerable degrees of expertise in its area of operation. It is also the case that many charities are powerful brands in their own right and thus can be a valuable asset in attaching new values to commercial products and services.

This happened in the case of Norwich Union and St John Ambulance, where the company, operating in the insurance sector (not an industry best loved by consumers), clearly benefited from the association with the well-known and well-liked charity provider of first aid in a clear link to a key aspect of the company's business – 'protection'.

Harley Davidson, a brand with negative imagery of 'Hell's Angels' in its history, has gained positive attributes by supporting charities fighting against the immobilizing disease of muscular dystrophy. The appearance of sufferers in their wheelchairs at Harley Davidson's mass rallies has been a poignant reminder of the bike rider's freedom of the road while focusing on the need for more medical research and motivating the fund raising effort.

Andrex, the UK brand of toilet paper with its famous advertising icon of a golden labrador puppy, has made an enhancing link with Guide Dogs for the Blind whose highly trained labradors are the seeing eyes and companions for so many people. Austin Reed has given its menswear more 'street credibility' through its 'Suit Exchange' campaign in partnership with the campaigning charity, Shelter, whose mission is to reduce the plight of the homeless who are so visible on our city streets.

Either way, building and sustaining a Cause Related Marketing relationship is not always easy as it operates between two very different worlds – the commercial and the voluntary. Both parties need to come to the table in a spirit of transparency and with the intention of committing to a long-term partnership, signposted by publicly adopted goals.

In doing this it is vital that all the stakeholders involved gain ownership of a shared agenda and attainable targets. Key to this is the championing of the commitment to the cause at the very top of the company and the dedication of meaningful resources to the campaign.

The mixed history of marketing partnerships in the affinity credit card sector shows how important it is to develop the background strategic thinking, explore the range of potential partners in depth and have the chosen Cause Related Marketing relationship enshrined in a proper contractual agreement.

Perhaps the quickest and most effective way to demonstrate the potential for CRM in developing brand values and sales results, as well as indicating the wide range of stakeholders that a well-run programme can engage, is through the famous case of American Express' powerful 'Charge Against Hunger' campaign.

Case History: AMERICAN EXPRESS: 'CHARGE AGAINST HUNGER'

Inspired by their original and highly visible campaign to renovate the Statue of Liberty, which generated $1.7 million in funds, a 27% increase in card usage and a 10% jump in new card member applications (Mintel Marketing Intelligence, February 1998), American Express and agency Ogilvy & Mather moved on in 1992 to develop a new and longer ranging CRM programme with an even closer strategic link to their business.

At the time American Express was facing some difficulties with its restaurant partners. The restaurant representatives were disputing American Express' fees, which were perceived as high, and were questioning their commitment to merchants and local communities. Therefore the company needed a vehicle to create better relationships with individual restaurants and also to establish links with new ones in the locality.

As always there was a desire to increase overall card membership and usage. Wider acceptance of American Express was the key to greater consumer usage: consumers did not want to encounter a negative reaction when they proffered their card. In a highly competitive market place, with the average user carrying two or three cards, American Express did not want any barrier to customers choosing to use American Express cards.

Meanwhile Share Our Strength (SOS), a non-profit organization focused on tackling the problem of hunger in the USA, was seeking a long-term corporate partner for its food and wine campaign 'Taste of the Nation'. After establishing American Express as the national co-sponsor of 'Taste of the Nation' the two organizations joined together in a strategic alliance and created one of the USA's best known and most successful Cause Related Marketing campaigns – Charge Against Hunger. The project was designed to last for three years, but in fact was carried over for a fourth. It raised in excess of $21M and benefited over 600 anti-hunger groups nationwide.

The mechanics of the CRM campaign were very straightforward. During November and December of each year American Express undertook to donate 3 cents per card purchase – and other transactions and contributions – from every other single Card Member transaction to Share Our Strength's campaign to reduce hunger. This added up to an annual donation of up to $5M. Equally importantly, and beyond the invaluable fundraising aspect, Charge Against Hunger increased America's awareness of the extraordinary problem of people suffering from a severe lack of food in its very midst, and challenged the community to become involved in reducing it.

The obvious link between one of the prime usages of the American Express Card, namely paying for meals in restaurants, and an anti-hunger campaign through a major charity, created great impact and resonance with Card Members. They identified strongly with the Charge as a way to fight hunger in their communities while alleviating perhaps a little of the guilt involved in an expense account lunch. A typical quote from an American Express Card Member is as follows:

> It made me proud to present my American Express card during the holiday season, knowing that every purchase I made would contribute to anti-hunger efforts.

Throughout the campaign American Express made as complete a corporate commitment to the project as possible. Employees were engaged as volunteers and joined in with local Share Our Strength grant recipients, with the Taste of Nation committees helping to organize additional fundraising events and in this way became effective spokespeople for anti-hunger awareness. Literally hundreds of American Express staff joined the Charge committing creative resources and many hours of unpaid work.

David House, President of the Establishment Services Worldwide Division of American Express Travel Related Service Company, Inc. said at the time:

> I am particularly proud of our employees around the US who have volunteered their time and services to host events, staff soup kitchens and co-ordinate food drives in their communities. Additionally, we believe that the partnerships we have established and continue to enrich with Share Our Strength, our merchants and Cardmembers are model programmes for how business and non-profit organizations can work together to solve problems that affect us all.

In the first year of the partnership 100% of American Express' advertising during November and December promoted Charge Against Hunger and this included heavyweight TV exposure. Subsequent campaigns maintained this high profile. In 1994 Stevie Wonder's song 'Take the Time Out' was the campaign anthem and his 11-city tour, sponsored by American Express, took the message to tens of thousands of fans. That year also saw the CRM programme exposed in perhaps the most prestigious TV advertising environment of all, namely during Super Bowl XXVIII. One of the biggest audiences was therefore woken up to the social problem of hunger in the USA through the partnership between American Express and Share Our Strength.

In 1996 the agency Ogilvy & Mather managed to secure the support of Yoko Ono in using the music of John Lennon's 'Imagine' as the theme for TV and radio commercials. The voiceover for this campaign read:

> Imagine . . . if every time you bought groceries, gas, gifts . . . anything . . . with your American Express Card, you helped feed someone who's hungry. You can. With the American Express Charge Against Hunger, we can all do more.

Thus the advertising for the specific CRM campaign was tied in closely and synergistically with the umbrella American Express global advertising theme of 'Do More'. It also included an onomatopoeic toll-free number, 1-888-8TOGIVE to enable consumers to obtain more information about the programme and how to make their contribution.

As John Hayes, Executive Vice President of Global Advertising for American Express said:

> American Express hopes to make a difference with the funds raised through Charge Against Hunger. In a country with so many resources, some people find it hard to believe that there is a hunger crisis in America. Our goal with the 1996 Charge Against Hunger campaign is to increase public awareness and to encourage those who can, to do something for someone who's hungry.

There was a further ripple effect in the corporate commitment of American Express and its partners. Scores of restaurants, many travel companies and retailers such as K-Mart joined in the programme. Along with Campbell's Soup, Williams-Sonoma, Hertz and Delta Airlines their combined donations added nearly $1M in one year alone to the core American Express contribution of $5M. An example of the special Charge Against Hunger decal distributed by American Express to merchants who provided additional funds is shown opposite:

We Support

CHARGE AGAINST HUNGER

AMERICAN EXPRESS **Cards Welcome**

'Giving as you eat: one way to help.'

Public relations also formed an important part of the communications mix. For example for the launch of the 1994 campaign First Lady Hillary Rodham Clinton was involved in a nation-wide breakfast event designed to kick-start that year's programme while also educating kids as to the importance of a healthy meal to begin their day.

The Harvard Business Review in 1996 said:

> American Express found that as a result of the programme, transactions with the card have increased and more merchants now accept the card. Furthermore, Card holders have expressed strong support for the Charge Against Hunger and greater satisfaction with American Express, and thousands of the company's employees have volunteered their time to fight hunger.

In fact Card member usage quantifiably increased overall in direct attribution to the Charge campaign.

Share Our Strength was elevated to a new and higher level as a charity as a result of this major and famous campaign. The relationship between SOS and American Express was very positive and the charity never felt that they were being exploited for purely commercial gain. SOS's co-founder and Associate Director Debbie Shore consistently praises American Express' attitude towards the charity, saying:

They treated us as corporate partners, which went a long way to ensuring the success of the campaign.

While this specific programme has now run its course both partners are still working together and are at present developing new concepts for future action. For the marketer intending to mount a CRM campaign the American Express example demonstrates the key success factors:

- shared 'Territory' between the brand and the cause
- simple mechanic and motivating consumer involvement
- top management commitment
- an open and mutually beneficial relationship with a charity
- volunteering by employees
- engagement of suppliers and strategic partners
- significant advertising and communications budget
- creativity and synergy between the CRM campaign and other brand advertising
- celebrity endorsement and PR events
- depth of commitment and longevity of relationship
- measurable results.

PART II
The Pre-Conditions for Cause Related Marketing

Summary

Following the broad definition of CRM and the American Express Charge Against Hunger campaign case history described in Part I, this second section takes a step back to deal with the specific consumer attitudinal and behavioural contexts which have established the pre-conditions for Cause Related Marketing.

During the latter half of the century intense competition between manufacturers, the power of multiple retailers, and the speed of leap-frogging technological advances have made it increasingly hard for brands to communicate clearly differentiated positions and sustain the necessary price premiums. 'Disintermediation' (cutting out the middle-man) via the Internet will compound these problems for brands.

This problem has been exacerbated by the fragmentation of media and audiences at the same time as there has been a phenomenal increase in the sheer volume of commercial communications directed at the market. Consumers have responded by becoming ever more adept at 'screening out' irrelevant messages. How can marketers create new messages that will get through these filters?

Many observers of mature markets have come to realize that new customer acquisition is an increasingly expensive way to attempt to build share, because it is usually at the expense of profitability. At the same time the true appreciation of the lifetime value of a loyal customer has led to a much greater concern with customer retention. Hence the plethora of loyalty schemes that have been launched over the past few years (although slightly less extensively in the USA than in Britain) which have effectively discounted sales permanently by up to 3%. However, there is an increasing realization that real loyalty cannot be 'bought', it has to be 'earned' by brands. Indeed Jim Taylor and Watts Wacker, in their book *The 500 Year Delta*, speak of the need for companies to be loyal to their customers, rather than the other way around. By what means can this be done?

'Buying' loyalty is not only very expensive, it is becoming harder because consumers in Westernized economies have acquired material wealth that could not have been dreamed of three generations earlier. There is strong statistical evidence that consumers really are ascending towards the pinnacle of Maslow's Hierarchy of Needs. This means that material wealth is decreasingly relevant to personal happiness as the desire for 'belonging', 'self-esteem' and self-realization' become more important.

At the same time there has been an alarming decline in the levels of trust in the traditional institutions, the pillars of the community such as the Church, government, and the police to which people had been accustomed to 'belonging' or from which many had gained their sense of social direction and moral authority.

The extraordinary global response to the untimely death of Diana Princess of Wales was absolutely indicative of the powerful need to 'belong' that exists in societies and perhaps further confirmation of the relative lack of things to belong to. Looking back we may see the seeds of this desire in the huge success of fundraising 'telethon' events such as the global Live Aid concert and the UK's Red Nose Day.

Thus a series of factors have combined to present brands with a threat and an opportunity: the threat of global competition and commodity markets co-exists with the opportunity to harness a new form of communications to cut through the clutter and add desirable new brand values: Cause Related Marketing.

2

The Commodity Threat and the Importance of Loyalty

One of the major problems facing brands in mature Westernized economies is the inexorable trend towards commodity. Each new technological innovation or exciting piece of new product development is rapidly 'me-tooed' by rival brand manufacturers and demanded as own label by retailers. This is the difficulty that marketers face in sustaining an adequate price premium over retailer own brands to continue to invest in creating the very brand values that differentiated their product in the first place.

The growing sophistication with which retailers have exploited their buying power and indeed their relationships with their branded suppliers to develop their own brand versions has progressively undermined the traditional manufacturers' position. Indeed in many market sectors it has reached the point where it is the retailer brands which are the true innovators and by comparison the manufacturer brands can appear staid and 'off the pace'. Examples of this abound but are particularly prevalent in prepared meals such as those produced by Marks & Spencer in the UK and Boston Market in the USA.

Clearly there are two main constituents to a brand's authority: its rational or performance benefits, and its emotional or image ones. If retailer own brands manage to gain the ascendancy in the former and if the manufacturer brand finds it progressively unaffordable to build the latter, then this can leave the traditional brands without a raison d'être. Thus in many market sectors the roster of manufacturer brands stocked has been rapidly reduced over the last 20 years and typically the brand leader and perhaps one other will be stocked alongside the store's own offering. The latest data from Taylor Nelson Sofres shows the own label share of trade within UK packaged groceries is now up to 47%.

It used to be the case that retailer's brands or more pejoratively 'own labels' were not really regarded as true brands but as poor alternatives to true brands. However as a result of the sustained level of innovation by the supermarkets and the enormous investment they have made in new store formats and in promoting both these and their expanded product range through advertising and other communications, they have now achieved the status of true brands.

Perhaps most significantly J. Sainsbury has recently announced that for the first time it is going to make its branded products available through small independent stores in outlying regions of the UK, with the clear implication that they have the power to reverse a long-term trend towards superstores. Now while this is presented as a quasi altruistic move in that their declared motive is to help preserve these outlets, which perform a valuable local service, it is ironic as they have been endangered by the expansion of the very likes of Sainsbury.

The result of all this is that manufacturer brands are stuck between a rock and a hard place. On the one hand they have to continue to cohabit with their major multiple customers and to continue to supply them with their retailer brands (there are very few companies like Heinz or Kelloggs which have withstood the demands for this and many more such as Cereal Partners who have successfully provided both). On the other hand they must continue to find the resources, within squeezed margins, to continue to invest in new product development and build their emotional brand values. If they do not, they will embark on a downward spiral of reduced margins, lack of budget to invest in brand values, diminution of consumer franchise, evaporation of retailer reason to stock and disappearing sales.

In younger developing markets the priority for marketers and brands is to achieve rapid gains in consumer penetration and market share. The battle is all about acquiring new customers before the competition does. On a global basis there are still many opportunities of this sort and they are being seized by the increasing numbers of multinationals which are bringing their historical expertise to bear in these emerging markets.

However, back home in the more mature markets where growth is slow and steady if at all, marketers have realized that new customer acquisition strategies can be very expensive and that the pursuit of brand share is often at the expense of profitability. Respected authors such as Frederick F. Reichheld in his book *The Loyalty Effect: The Hidden Force Behind Growth, Profits, and Lasting Value* have demonstrated that the true life-time value of a customer can be much more significant than is realized in the typical short-term view. Indeed, some of his calculations suggest that a 5% increase in customer loyalty can result in between 50% and 75% improvement in bottom line profit.

There are many industries, for example the automotive and the mortgage markets, where repeat purchase to the same marque or provider can be as low as 40%. Given the cost of acquiring a customer in these relatively infrequently purchased markets the loss of up to 60% of them when they come to renew is extraordinarily wasteful.

Accordingly, in these Westernized markets, practitioners have increasingly focused their attentions on retaining their customers and building loyalty to their brands. This explains the intense interest in the direct marketing industry, its dramatic growth over the past decade, and the preoccupation with 'one-to-one' relationships. It also explains the plethora of customer loyalty schemes that have been launched and the emerging power of data marketing.

There is no doubting the potential power of database marketing – for example in 1997 Tesco claimed that 70% of all pregnant mothers in the UK became members of the Tesco Baby Club. However, apart from almost drowning in data the supermarkets have effectively discounted their sales on a permanent basis, by up to 3%, through their loyalty schemes. If having a loyalty scheme becomes a 'hygiene factor' across a market, then the only winners are the companies who get in first with a pre-emptive strike within their sector as Tesco did against Sainsbury in the UK and as Walmart did against K-Mart in the USA. For everyone else it becomes a costly zero sum game.

Meanwhile consumers have become very familiar with these schemes and are quite expert in playing the loyalty 'game', and in trading off one set of benefits against another. The latest research suggests that actually true loyalty cannot be bought but has to be earned. The brand has to demonstrate more than just a mechanistic or purely monetary commitment to its customers. If true customer loyalty now has to be earned by brands how is this to be done? Clearly more powerful brand values are required as opposed to simple bribery no matter how targeted.

Case History: TESCO:
'COMPUTERS FOR SCHOOLS'

The fact that the Tesco Computers for Schools scheme is about to enter its eighth year speaks volumes about the success of the campaign. It is by far the best known Cause Related Marketing activity in the UK with a prompted awareness of 48% among the adult population and the brand has moved quickly up the league table of those enjoying public 'trust'. Given the level of expenditure involved by the company, this represents excellent value for Tesco.

Since the scheme's inception in 1992, £44M worth of computer equipment has been delivered to UK schools amounting to 34 000 computers – equivalent to one for every school in the country. Acres of good publicity have been generated and the campaign has been regarded as a powerful contributor to the 'Every little helps' positioning for the Tesco brand. During this same time period Tesco's business has done extremely well and the previous brand leader in the UK supermarket sector J. Sainsbury has now been overtaken by Tesco.

The Tesco Computers for Schools campaign has been included within the 'Every little helps' campaign, which featured other innovations such as wider aisles, baby changing facilities in-store and a commitment to stopping long waiting times on till queues. An example of the print advertisement is shown opposite.

The mechanics of the CRM campaign are very straightforward. Tesco now gives its customers a voucher for every £10 spent in-store (reduced from £25 initially, making the value even greater). Shoppers donate their vouchers to the school of their choice, which exchanges them for brand new computer equipment. Parents in schools have clubbed together to increase the numbers of vouchers collected, and school governors and parent–teacher associations have become involved as well. It has become very much a local community effort and promotes excellent links between the

'Every little helps, at school too.'

individual store and its locality which may contain between 40 and 100 schools within its catchment area.

The results for Tesco in sales terms have been reported as extremely successful, but very hard to isolate from all the other promotional activity running simultaneously. The chain certainly regards it as having contributed significantly to a brand reputation as a 'responsible corporate citizen'.

The campaign has gone from strength to strength with the equivalent of £10M worth of computer equipment delivered in 1998 alone. It has been further leveraged by a link with Coca-Cola which used a multi-pack promotion to enable customers to collect more vouchers. Staff in Tesco have become very involved in the programme and have reacted very positively to it.

The Tesco Computers for Schools scheme has naturally led Tesco to develop Tesco SchoolNet 2000 – the largest schools' Internet project in the world. Thousands of schools nation-wide are taking part in this curriculum based initiative, which runs over four school terms and which began in autumn 1998. The project will be showcased in the Learn Zone of the Millennium Dome from 1 January 2000. This is funded entirely by Tesco as a further commitment to providing quality technological equipment for schools and to enhance its reputation with its customers for this kind of extensive commitment.

Overall then the Tesco programme has been a great success and has been strategically closely aligned to its objective of being 'Number 1 locally' in the areas it serves.

An intriguing footnote in business terms is that in 1998 Tesco began selling computer hardware for the first time in direct competition to the more specialist chains. It also announced that it was going to become an Internet Service Provider, i.e. offering its customers a gateway to the Internet through its own website which has already been set up as part of its Tesco Direct homeshopping initiative.

Thus the 'fit' between their brand 'Territory' and the cause, which was only really linked via a shared target audience at its inception as essentially a sales promotion, is getting much closer. Perhaps this is the first time a Cause Related Marketing campaign has influenced what the company actually sells!

One of the most interesting things about the Tesco Computers for Schools programme is that it is one which goes direct to the 'cause' and does not use a charitable organization as a strategic partner. Tesco, as one of the most powerful brands in the UK, clearly has the authority to do this, which avoids the accusation of 'hi-jacking' the goodwill already created by a chosen charity's branding. The clarity of ownership of the project is therefore a major benefit to this retailer. It is also clear that the customer loyalty engendered by this CRM programme has been truly earned rather than just 'bought'.

3

Communications Clutter and Expert Consumers

Once upon a time media life was relatively straightforward. In the United States as far as television was concerned there were the major networks, ABC, CBS, NBC and the local stations, and PBS. However in the UK a much more restricted situation obtained with BBC1, BBC2, ITV and Channel 4 constituting the choice of television channels. A similar picture could be found, often of an even more restricted nature in the European TV market, for example in Germany.

What a difference a decade makes! The wave of deregulation and the advent of cable and satellite TV has led to an explosion in all sorts of broadcast media. In the United States, by the early 1990s the consumer could access dozens of TV channels. A similar fragmentation has taken place in the UK where there were over 40 TV channels available through cable or satellite.

The next wave of expansion, of almost mind-boggling potential, is that of digital television. With the UK launches of Sky Digital, and On Digital in the autumn of 1998 with Cable & Wireless to follow in 1999, the viewer is faced with well over 100 channels. It is widely expected that by the turn of the Millennium there could easily be 1000 digital channels available to the TV viewer and at least that many in the USA. Niche channels such as Manchester United TV will appeal to special interest groups and broadcasters such as Sky will scour the markets for these sorts of famous sports club brands and other 'content providers' to fill their schedules and deliver pay-per-view revenue streams.

Ironically this extraordinary proliferation of TV media has not significantly reduced the price of airtime. This is counter-intuitive in that an economist would expect an increased supply for a relatively fixed demand to result in falling price. However, due to the particular circumstances within the TV media market most of the money still chases scarce prime time. There is still much lower demand for the micro ratings offered by the niche cable or satellite channels.

The paradox then for the brand marketer is that while the digital revolution theoretically raises the prospect of being able to target its consumer audience with ever greater precision and relevance, the actual cost of doing so shows no real sign of diminishing.

The 'double whammy' is produced by the fact that the almost geometric increase in the number of commercial communications that the average consumer receives on a daily basis – currently estimated by Zenith Media Worldwide at around 1300 – means that the same advertising dollar buys a fraction of the 'stand out' that it did 10 years ago.

Clearly TV is the most powerful of all the media available to the advertiser and its exploitation in the context of the deregulation of the markets has gone far beyond simple advertising. Marketers and their agencies have worked hard to counteract these adverse trends and the wheel has been turned full circle in the USA where commercial television had its birth in sponsored programming or 'soap operas'. We have returned to a situation where programme sponsorship has once again become a major feature of the media landscape. The same has happened even in European countries like the UK and Germany, which have been very tightly regulated hitherto in this respect.

Product placement, once largely the preserve of Hollywood and feature films, has increasingly been extended into television programming. *Men Behaving Badly*, one of the most popular sit-coms in the UK, would not be the same without its cans of Stella Artois lager, while *Friends* has done wonders for Oreo Cookies and Gateway Computers have achieved similar product exposure by placing their computers and 'cow' logo in the hospital drama *ER*.

The use of famous personalities in advertising for brands is as old as the art of publicity itself – Ronald Reagan was an early star of advertisements for Marlboro – but nowadays the situation has become more complex. Many TV commercials are pastiches of TV programmes and use shorthand versions of characters which have been established at length in a series to great effect in commercials for a brand. This technique enables a brand campaign to be established on many fewer ratings because the advertisements trade off the consumer communications asset already created by the programme.

Harry Enfield and Paul Whitehouse's myriad of characters have formed the basis of many a UK TV campaign for brands as diverse as Mercury, Hula Hoops and Holsten Pils. In the United States Jerry Seinfeld has been the inspiration for campaigns by American Express, while Paul Reiser has been used as the face of AT&T.

Moving to the other end of the spectrum, media providers have become increasingly ingenious with their use of surprising opportunities to attract the consumer's attention with a timely message. The backs of subway tickets and store receipts are old hat, nowadays we have ads on gas station petrol pump handles – what could be more appropriate for an ad for car insurance than that?

But how does the consumer react to this almost overwhelming 'communications clutter'? Research evidence suggests that people are becoming increasingly adept at screening out unwelcome, irrelevant or unnecessary messages. They can see an ad coming, and they have the opportunity to duck it. Peak time breaks in the highest rating TV programmes have been known to be destroyed by the audience exodus to make a cup of tea, as evidenced by the data from electricity generators which shows the enormous surge in demand for power at the end of major TV programme events. Zapping with the ever-present remote control has become endemic especially in multi-channel homes.

Whole pages in broadsheet newspapers are flicked past in their millions by readers who are simply not in the market for that particular product or service on that particular day. By contrast when the consumer is actually in buying mode they become amazingly perceptive in their information-gathering role. Hard core retail ads with their apparent jumble of typefaces and starbursts suddenly become the most engaging of communications. Tiny ads can pull as powerfully as whole pages – headlines such as 'Pregnant?', 'Impotence', 'Baldness' or 'Hearing Problems' garner coupons in their thousands from such small spaces and off-the-page marketers know the cost-efficiency of quarter pages as opposed to the glamour of whole ones.

Unfortunately for the mass marketer the statistical likelihood of their target audience being 'in the market' at any given time is small and therefore the sort of communication referred to above can only ever be a part of a programme. The challenge is to produce communication of a sort that will appeal to people who may be customers at some point in the future and who will have to be sufficiently 'rewarded' in order to gain their attention when they are currently not.

Accordingly, the use of entertainment in its widest sense has become a staple of the advertising industry. New product information, a joke, a famous personality, beautiful photography, a wonderful special effect, or stirring music can all reward the viewer for their attention and a selling message can be slipped under the radar.

But what if these traditional selling techniques start to lose their effectiveness? What if the tendency to commodity renders them increasingly neutral in a competitive sense? What if consumers become dissatisfied with advertising which just plagiarizes programming or worse is aridly self-referential to other advertising?

The most powerful medium, TV, is not getting any cheaper and indeed may actually be becoming relatively less effective as a result of the fragmentation and clutter that it creates. Retailer brands have an unfair advantage in their guaranteed presence on shelf in front of the consumer. If manufacturer brands have scarce resources with which to produce genuine product innovations or to continue to invest in their brand equity, then the challenge is to find new and affordable messages which can cut through and be heard. Cause Related Marketing messages can achieve this for marketers.

Another problem in the more sophisticated and increasingly cluttered markets is that consumers have become increasingly adept at playing the marketing 'game'.

Many a product manager has sat on the other side of a one-way mirror watching a focus group and been astonished at how transparent a well worked brand positioning and communications strategy has become under the scrutiny of consumers.

It used to be the case that it was predominantly younger children and teenagers who exhibited the levels of interest and enthusiasm required to dissect the meaning and symbolism of a TV commercial. Nowadays it is common to find consumers at all life-stages in the market who are able to do this with ease. Perhaps it is hardly surprising, as the communications industry has been educating the population in marketing and advertising for most of the post-war period. The media in general have also become so much more pervasive that people are almost compelled to take an interest in it.

Apart from the obvious implication that flawed arguments, unsupported propositions and exaggerated claims are given short shrift by the consumer, judge and jury, it has forced marketers and their agencies to become ever more inventive in the ways in which compelling communications are put together. It is not surprising that the cost of TV production has escalated to minor movie levels in some market sectors, for example financial services. Here the interchangeability and low interest of most of the products and services on offer requires a huge injection of production values to gain attention and add value.

A more challenging implication is that the staples in the marketer's cupboard of 'new improved', 'new flavour', 'new feature', 'extra free' are all relatively un-newsworthy nowadays. That is not to say they can't be effective in the short term but it is unlikely that these sorts of communications alone can build genuine brand values and really motivate customers.

Clearly this dilemma and the search for newsworthiness has led many advertisers to favour form over content. For a while during the late 1980s and 90s this did seem to hold some sway with consumers as brands successfully constructed ravishing imagery, enlisted psychological tricks and built aspirational style on TV.

But in the 'morning after' decade of the 90s the consumer pendulum has swung back to a concern with intrinsic values and the market is less convinced by cosmetic displays. Again this is not to say that exciting brand imagery or evocative lifestyle statements are not viable routes to brand building, it's just that it seems to be harder and more expensive to achieve them nowadays.

In the search for a distinctive and motivated communication strategy many advertisers have become increasingly self-referential in their communications. Commercials contain 'in jokes' which are only meaningful if the viewer understands the reference to another advertiser's spot which in turn may depend on familiarity with a TV programme. This sort of approach may be involving to a relatively small 'in group' but is likely to be relatively obscure to a wider target audience and in the end may come across as self-indulgent 'navel gazing' by the brand.

Perhaps in CRM there are new sorts of values and themes brands can adopt which will relate very closely to their intrinsic values and which are highly newsworthy in the current climate? A good example of this is in one of the toughest consumer markets, namely detergents and the partnership between P&G's Dash and ACTIONAID in Italy.

Case History: PROCTER & GAMBLE: 'DASH AND ACTIONAID'

In the developed world we take fresh water supply absolutely for granted. We think nothing of having showers, baths and using automatic washing machines to do our laundry, whereas in other parts of the word just a cup full of the same precious liquid could mean the difference between life and death.

Procter & Gamble Italy used this shocking dichotomy to great advantage as the link in their campaign for the Dash brand of detergent in partnership with the charity ACTIONAID.

Their joint mission was to raise money to help supply water to Dalocha in Ethiopia, an area with limited water supplies and all the associated problems.

The mechanic took the form of a sales promotion where an in-pack leaflet carried by Dash asked purchasers to donate L1000 ($0.57) to the ACTIONAID programme. The scheme was also promoted on television using a weekly 15-minute prime time TV programme *Domenica In* presented by leading TV personality Pippo Baudo.

Dash buyers received an on-pack 'thank you' gift – a music cassette tape carried on bottles of liquid, an LP in large soap powder packs or a CD with the Ultra powder variant. Well-known Italian pop stars donated all the songs on these cassettes, LPs and CDs.

During the campaign Procter & Gamble (P&G) took its own crew to Ethiopia so it could film its charitable activities in partnership with ACTIONAID in reality. Footage was generated which was subsequently used in Dash advertising and thus produced a very different sort of commercial for a washing powder brand.

'P&G helped give water for life, not just for washing.'

The results of this Cause Related Marketing activity were extremely good and a testimony to the appropriateness of the 'fit' between Dash as a washing powder brand and the issue of water shortage in Ethiopia. Over the 6-year period of the campaign more than 170 000 people responded with an average gift of L10 000 ($5). The total amount raised was the equivalent of $1.8M. Some donations were even made by viewers of *Domenica In* who did not actually buy a Dash product. Dash sales in Italy rose over the period of the campaign by 5%.

Overall then the initiative was a great success and formed part of the company's social and human welfare policy. It was also designed to enhance Dash's brand image and to promote the parent company, P&G, among consumers. While TV was the key medium, the use of sponsored programming as well as spot advertising clearly helped generate more newsworthiness and 'cut-through' to consumers in a market that has constant pressures towards commodity. It clearly engaged shoppers who were perhaps less motivated by the traditional 'new improved' sort of message.

4

Maslow's Hierarchy of Needs and the Loss of Trust

In the early 1940s, as an academic working at Brooklyn College, A.H. Maslow produced his now famous 'Hierarchy of Needs'. At the time it seemed to many to be a rather fanciful theory but there is now concrete evidence that he was uncannily accurate in forecasting the evolution of consumer behaviour. His hypothesis is symbolized by the pyramid graphic illustrated on the next page.

Maslow suggested that human beings have a progressive series of needs, which they seek to fulfil, starting with the most basic ones, which are to do with survival itself: that is the requirement for food, shelter, warmth and sex.

His idea was that as these basic or subsistence needs were progressively satisfied, people would lift their eyes to broader horizons, and address needs which were more to do with their role in relationship to others, and their standing within the community.

Again, he hypothesized that once a person had achieved their 'image' in their relationship with others, they would move on to higher order concerns. These are to do with the degree to which they enjoyed self-esteem as a result of their 'belonging' in society, and beyond that, whether they might achieve 'self-realization' in a more spiritual sense.

There is now a good deal of evidence to suggest that consumers have indeed followed the path set out by Maslow. For example, in relation to material wealth there is now relatively little difference between upmarket and downmarket consumers in terms of the durable goods that they own.

Maslow's hierarchy of needs

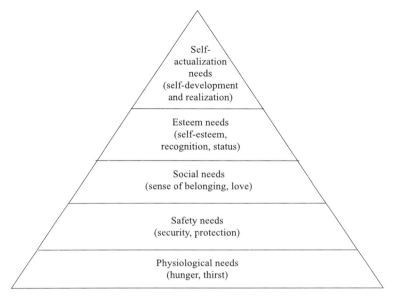

'We're getting to the top of the pyramid.'

This is evidenced by the chart below which shows the relative penetration of TV, video recorders and cars between ABC1s and C2Ds (upper and lower socio-demographic groupings) in the UK.

EVEN TRADITIONALLY LOWER INCOME HOMES NOW HAVE
COMPARATIVE MATERIAL WEALTH

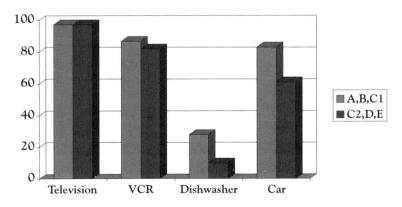

'We've got the material wealth we want.'

A similar picture can be seen in the United States as the material gap has closed between white and blue-collar workers as it has done in Western Europe. In 1960, 45.7 million American households had televisions, with an average one set per household, now 95 million homes have 213 million TV sets.

Another indication that people are moving up Maslow's pyramid is that they are beginning to take action over issues concerning money, which suggest motives other than simple profit. An example of this has been the growth of so-called ethical funds in both the USA and the UK. As the graph below shows, while small in the context of the total market for investment funds, there has been an almost exponential growth in the amounts of money put into funds which have declared themselves clean of investments in companies which behave in an antisocial or unethical way – for example those active in munitions.

What is striking about this consumer investment behaviour is that it is reasonably well known that ethical funds have under-performed the market by as much as 27% over the last five years according to EIRIS/NOP (Oct. 1997).

Further, when the same organization asked people whether they felt

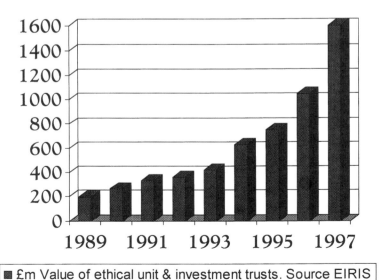

'*Sticking to ethical principles is costing people money.*'

that their pension should be invested 'ethically' 73% said that they thought it should be. When, in the same survey, the respondents had it pointed out to them that the fund would be likely to under-perform the all share index 29% still said they wanted their pension to have an ethical policy.

One of modern advertising's founding fathers, Bill Bernbach, once said 'a principle is only a principle if it costs you money': this consumer behaviour certainly looks pretty principled.

The implications of the apparent realization of Maslow's theory of the Hierarchy of Needs is that marketers now have a new area of human preoccupation to consider when developing their brand propositions to the consumer. It must be possible for brands, which have always had a powerfully anthropomorphic aspect, to incorporate in their 'human' personification the growing consumer need for 'self-realization'.

Meanwhile, for many people, one of the most disturbing phenomena of the past decade has been the apparent collapse in the regard with which traditional institutions are held. Government, church, police and armed forces, all once the pillars of society and the means by which people orientated themselves, seem to have lost large amounts of authority and credibility. In Britain this has also extended to the monarchy.

The Henley Centre has monitored this decline and the table on p. 30 shows it in graphic detail between the years 1983 and 1996.

There have been many theories as to why this should have happened and indeed why it appears to be continuing to do so. The increased intrusiveness of the media and its penchant for aggressive investigative journalism has undoubtedly played a very significant part. What were once slightly distant, opaque and apparently 'holier than thou' institutions have been remorselessly exposed as having the same human failings as the rest of us.

One such organization is the Church of England, which has always had its divisions, but these were, if not suppressed, not that widely debated. Now the Church has been publicly revealed as being riven with contradictory beliefs at the highest levels, and has been afflicted by a series of public failures to resolve issues of pressing public concern such as contraception, abortion, celibacy, homosexuality and women priests.

These very public debates and disagreements allied to forms of service

The Henley Centre

Confidence in institutions (% answering 'a great deal' or 'quite a lot')

Institutions	1983	1993	1998
Armed Forces	88	84	71
Police	83	70	59
Royal Family	25	18	30
The Church	52	37	30
Legal System	58	36	26
Civil Service	46	36	20
Trade Unions	23	26	17
Parliament	54	30	16
Press	32	18	7

Source: This data is a compilation of '1999 Planning for Consumer Change' and '1996/7 Planning for Social Change'

'Pillars of society are crumbling.'

which have been increasingly regarded, rightly or wrongly, as lacking the entertainment value of competing attractions have led to dwindling church attendance and a diminution of the role of traditional religion.

This is ironic given what Maslow had to say about 'higher order' needs – one might have expected the Church to be very much in the ascendant as a result. Similar processes have undermined other established institutions. The Presidency in the United States has been tarnished on a number of occasions, most recently with 'Zippergate' which has done so much damage to what in other respects might have been perceived as one of the most successful incumbencies since those of John F. Kennedy and Ronald Reagan.

In the UK, the last Conservative government was dogged by an apparently never-ending series of revelations about the private lives and peccadilloes of senior politicians. Even the New Labour landslide victory has been quickly pulled up short by the scandal over Bernie Ecclestone, the founder and owner of Formula One. His notorious £1 000 000 'donation' to party funds came rather too close for comfort to the Government's highly controversial decision not to include motor sport sponsorship from the otherwise total ban on cigarette advertising. Since the dust settled on that incident we have had a whole new series of allegations of cronyism and lobbyists' offers of 'access for cash'. 1998 finished with the resignations of two Government Ministers over conflict of interest and a mortgage loan.

Perhaps by contrast, but more likely on merit, some other sorts of 'institutions' have been gaining ground in terms of public trust. The Henley Centre has also been measuring over time the degree of confidence in companies. Their data shows that many of them have significantly increased their standing in the public regard and as the table below illustrates several of them have actually overtaken the likes of the Church and the police in terms of 'trust'.

These companies, which are of course also brands, have earned their spurs in the intensely contested market place and, despite the same intensity of media scrutiny, have stood up for their codes of practice and consumer values to their justifiable reward.

What this means is that some leading companies have achieved such positions of authority that they are probably better placed nowadays than virtually any other institution to take convincing positions with the public at large.

Recent UK government research into voting behaviour is indicative of the implications this might have. On investigating reasons why there is such a poor turnout for local elections and indeed why a surprising proportion of the electorate – 28.5% in 1997 – doesn't even bother to vote

The Henley Centre

Trust companies to be honest and fair (% answering 'a great deal' or 'mostly')

Companies	1994	1998
Marks & Spencer	73	80
Boots	78	78
Cadbury's	75	77
Sainsbury	59	69
Asda	46	65
Nestlé	57	58

Source: This data is a compilation of '1999 Planning for Consumer Change' and '1998 Planning for Social Change' reports

'A new set of authority figures.'

in general elections, the Department of the Environment, Transport and the Regions research found that many voters simply didn't like the places in which they were asked to cast their vote. The turnout in British elections however is still relatively high compared with other European countries and especially the USA where turnouts for presidential elections are consistently below 50% of the population.

Often obscure and perhaps even potentially intimidating routes to rarely visited village halls and community centres were a strong disincentive to many. By contrast the possibility of casting a vote at the checkout of a local Safeway was very much more attractive and seen as bringing voting into the mainstream of daily life. It will, however, take a great deal more than that to effect a change in the USA, where the turnout in the congressional elections is regularly under 40%.

While traditionalists may regret the demise of the previous pillars of society, the exciting prospect for the corporate beneficiaries of the situation is the possibility to leverage their well-earned degrees of consumer trust and confidence to their commercial benefit. This can be done through the technique of Cause Related Marketing while not doing anything to undermine their position. If the sense of 'belonging' which is so important to consumers according to Maslow's theory, becomes reality, and there's not much left around to belong to in terms of traditional institutions, then perhaps newer ones, even brands, can step into the breach.

Across the spectrum of distribution the person-to-person sales channel is one of the ones that requires a very high degree of trust and integrity. A global brand such as Avon has built its market position by recruiting, training and motivating a vast and evolving army of representatives. In the process it has created valuable relationships with millions of women. As such Avon has had the authority to embark on an ambitious CRM campaign focused on a highly personal issue, namely breast cancer. This campaign from a trusted brand has probably done more than any governmental organization to demystify, educate and help prevent this debilitating and often fatal disease.

Case History: **AVON:**
'BREAST CANCER AWARENESS CRUSADE'

Avon is the world's leading direct seller of beauty products with sales of $5bn world-wide and $2bn in the USA alone. Avon products are sold globally in more than 130 countries, and there are approximately 2.5 million Avon sales representatives world-wide, with at least 440 000 in the USA.

The historical popular involvement with the brand is truly enormous: more than 40 million women world-wide and 25 million in the USA alone have sold Avon products since the company was founded 112 years ago. Given its business system and its target audience, it is hardly surprising that Avon boasts more women in management positions at 86% than any other Fortune 500 company. Indeed 17 of Avon's 54 officers are women, and Avon's main board of directors has five women in its ranks.

Quite apart from the intense competition in the beauty and cosmetic markets in which Avon trades, from competitors such as P&G's Oil of Ulay, Avon faces a particular challenge as a result of its home selling distribution channel. There is the continuing problem of recruiting and maintaining the representative sales force. Clearly it is essential that these ambassadors for the brand are enthused and motivated in order to be productive. As anyone who has done direct selling knows, this is easier said than done.

At the same time, the direct selling concept is in itself surrounded with some historical 'baggage'. In many more 'mature' markets, such as the UK, it is perceived as a relatively old fashioned and possibly downmarket way of doing business and one that may be superseded in many people's minds by the greater attractions of shopping at retail outlets.

Thus Avon was a prime candidate for the addition of brand values on top of the existing core ones of outstanding product performance and aspirational imagery, which can be created through the use of catalogue advertising and of course by the representatives' personal presentation of themselves.

Avon's Breast Cancer Awareness Crusade in the USA was launched in 1993 after the link being pioneered in Britain in 1992. Its aim is to support breast cancer education and to enable access to early detection services. Avon has done an excellent job of documenting all aspects of the Crusade and full details on it can be found in their website located at http://www.avoncrusade.com.

The key mechanic for fundraising in the campaign, which has also created engagement by sales representatives and customers, has been the sales of pink ribbon products as part and parcel of the process of selling toiletries and cosmetics. The symbol was originally chosen by the International Breast Cancer community to represent awareness of and hope for women affected by the disease. Proceeds from the sales of Avon's pink ribbons products are used to fund the breast health programmes supported by the Crusade. Since 1993 Avon's 450 000 sales representatives in the USA have raised over $32M by this means.

In delivering the campaign Avon has partnered with a number of other organizations in both the private and non-profit and public sectors – for example the YWCA of the USA, the National Alliance of Breast Cancer Organizations (NABCO) and the National Cancer Institute (NCI).

Avon's partnership with the YWCA was established with assistance from the Federal Center for Disease Control and Prevention (CDC) to create and fund ENCORE *plus*. This programme was made available to qualified YWCA associations that wish to offer women a structured programme of education, early detection and post-diagnosis services for breast and cervical cancer. So far grants totalling $14.5M have been made by Avon's Crusade to ENCORE *plus*.

Avon specifically wanted to highlight the fact that early detection of breast cancer was the key to defeating it and so set up the 'Avon Pledge'. Women were asked to buy a pen with which to sign the three-step recommendation for early detection, proceeds of which went to the cause.

Another innovative aspect of Avon's Crusade is the way in which it has used the Internet to spread the word. From their website you can download the pink ribbon logo ('Post the pink ribbon online') and apply it to your own website to indicate support for the cause. This has been highly successful and since its 1997 launch 25 major corporate websites, 200 commercial sites and numerous individual sites have worn Avon's pink ribbon on their home pages, creating over 2 million impressions of the symbol throughout the Internet during Breast Cancer Awareness Month alone. A copy of this logo is illustrated below.

AVON'S
BREAST
CANCER
AWARENESS
CRUSADE

'Wearing virtual pink ribbons with pride.'

Apart from the vast amount of money raised – over $32M making Avon's Crusade the largest ever contributor to non-profit healthcare programmes in the USA, it has also had a big impact in other ways. Avon calculate that they have transmitted over 900 million impressions through print and broadcast media giving multiple opportunities for people to read, watch or hear about the Crusade.

Avon sales representatives have distributed more than 60 million educational brochures about breast cancer in door-to-door campaigns since 1993. Apart from the grant to the ENCORE programme, Avon's Crusade has also awarded $8M to community based breast health programmes through NABCO. The campaign has also been extended to include a new target audience: kids.

In 1997–98 the 'Avon Kids Care' essay contest invited young people to submit original 100 word essays about why and how they would encourage a favourite female adult to take good care of her health. The 16 winners, who represented elementary school, junior high, high school and college categories, each received a $1000 savings bond. Then, on their behalf, Avon's Crusade awarded a $50 000 'Avon Kids Care' grant, $800 000 in total, to 16 not-for-profit breast health programmes that were matched geographically to individual contest winner locations.

In another newsworthy development Avon has mounted the Avon's Breast Cancer 3 day event, an outdoor empowerment fundraising activity in October 1998. Two and a half thousand walkers undertook an extraordinary journey, which had them walking 60 miles over 3 days. Each person was required to raise at least $1700. The net proceeds of $5 million raised by the participants will be awarded to non-profit breast health programmes nation-wide through the Avon Breast Health Access Fund administered by Avon and NABCO.

All in all Avon's Crusade is a most impressive Cause Related Marketing campaign. It is one which is steadily adding extremely valuable additional brand values to ensure that Avon remains contemporary and absolutely in touch with both its customers and its sales representatives, and their concerns as active healthy women. The key to the success of this campaign was the resonance that the issue of Breast Cancer had with both the majority of Avon's sales people and the majority of their customers. This cause was chosen because in research, it was overwhelmingly favoured by Avon customers, showing that campaigns such as these benefit enormously from planning and research in advance.

In the UK the campaign has until recently been more low key in its relationship with the charity Breakthrough Breast Cancer. The sale of a different promotional item each year through Avon reps has however still raised £5.6 million since 1992 when Avon first produced a lapel badge for the price of £1, all proceeds going to Breakthrough Breast Cancer.

As in the USA the commitment is a long-term one and in Britain it is one that is ever-expanding and becoming more high profile. This year Avon chose to become the official sponsor for Breakthrough Breast Cancer's 'Fashion Targets Breast Cancer' campaign, which involved a much more ambitious advertising campaign.

This is a scheme in which T-shirts with the 'target' logo are promoted for sale all through the fashion industry, and it involves every area from major high street shops to important high-fashion models and designers. By becoming the main sponsor for this Avon deepens and re-affirms its commitment to the Breast Cancer issue amongst its existing customers. In addition the direct association with high fashion adds to Avon's 're-branding' as an organization that is very much keeping up with the times and appealing to younger more fashion-conscious consumers.

'Confronting the issue and contemporising the brand.'

As a result of this campaign people who might not normally see or be interested in Avon products will be aware of their presence as a 'fashion' company which cares about its customers. For example the campaign has secured the support of prestigious supermodel Yasmin Le Bon, who then appeared in the Avon catalogue, and who has not previously been prepared to appear in Avon advertising. The scheme has been widely promoted through a poster advertising campaign from which a key image is shown on the previous page.

5

The Diana Effect and the Opportunity for Brands

The American culture has always been one that has been regarded by Northern Europeans as much more overtly demonstrative, emotional and even sentimental. Its advertising history has always reflected this and the use of powerful emotions and appeals to the heart have been used in every sector, from automotives to breakfast foods.

But even American commentators have been taken aback at the rise of so called 'victim TV' in the shape of programmes such as Oprah, Jerry Springer, Geraldo, Montel Williams, and Jenny Jones, in which extra-ordinarily large numbers of ordinary citizens seem prepared to expose themselves physically, emotionally and psychologically to their fellow participants and the national audience.

This desire for self-revelation seems to go far beyond Andy Warhol's prediction that everyone will have their 15 minutes of fame. Clearly the mass audience that these shows attract find the vicarious experience personally cathartic and great entertainment to boot.

In the UK the arrival of emotion in advertising in any mainstream way has been much more recent and perhaps dates back to the early 1980s with the Abbott Mead Vickers campaign for Yellow Pages in which an elderly gentleman goes on a tour of old bookshops seeking a particular title called *Fly Fishing* by J.R. Hartley. Arriving home exhausted and unsuccessful, his sympathetic daughter suggests he look for other bookshops in Yellow Pages. Sure enough he finds a place over the phone that has a copy and when asked for his name so that it can be reserved for him, he gives it as 'J.R. Hartley' with a beam of pleasure.

Previously such a sentimental approach would have been deemed inappropriate and indeed the memory of the previous campaign, 'Let Your Fingers Do The Walking' to the tune of 'Yellow River', did take a while to fade. However the fact that David Abbott's 'J.R. Hartley' commercial is still being used over 15 years later is a testament to its success.

If the rising tide of emotionalism has been at differing levels depending on national culture and tradition, the globalization of TV on the one hand and the seismic event of the untimely death of Diana Princess of Wales on the other has probably brought it very much closer together across the world.

While Diana had been established as a global celebrity for some years it was more as a denizen of the gossip and society columns than as a serious personality. This all changed when she resigned her position as patron of her many charities and focused her efforts on just a few major commitments and in particular her campaign against landmines. The image of her wearing a perspex mask and protective clothing in order to walk through a real minefield became an incredibly powerful metaphor for her own life. It was a truly dramatic demonstration of her commitment to the cause which set her at odds with some extremely powerful vested interests at the military industrial complex and governmental levels.

It was when she stuck her head above the parapet and took on a cause which was personally and politically dangerous and nailed her royal colours to its mast that she achieved global celebrity of a very much more profound sort.

In fact the United Nations had been touring the world with a very well produced exhibition as part of its own campaign against landmines but with remarkably little practical effect on international opinion or individual governments' policies. The Princess of Wales' intervention crystallized public opposition and galvanized political action. Within a year of her death legislation was passed by the British Government enabling Britain to comply with the Ottawa Convention outlawing the manufacture and sale of landmines which came into force on 1 March 1999.

All this goes some way towards explaining the extraordinary global outpouring of grief at the news of her tragic and accidental death, but it does not explain quite the extent of it all. Obviously the death of a

'Diana ascends to a higher level.'

woman in the prime of her life is tragic in itself, but when she is a star the event becomes all too easily identified with the individual. Marilyn Monroe makes more headlines 36 years after her death in 1962 than she ever did when alive and the same will be true of Diana.

However, despite the best efforts of the revisionists such as Anthony O'Hear who have condemned what they see as a mawkish descent into exaggerated sentimentality, they have not convinced the vast majority of

'An overwhelming need to be there, to belong.'

the people that this was anything other than a phenomenal event in their lives with very significant implications for the future emotional climate.

Literally millions of people in the UK alone and many millions more world-wide felt an overwhelming need to 'belong' with the mourners who instinctively congregated at Kensington Palace, Buckingham Palace and Althorp. They 'paid' for their membership of this 'club' with bouquets of flowers and in the act of doing so subscribed to a person and a set of beliefs and behaviours which seemed to them to be one of the great goods in national and international life.

As the first anniversary of the death of the Princess of Wales approached, the *Sunday Times* commissioned a poll through NOP which was published in August 1998, and one of the questions was, 'Some people talk of a post-Diana Britain – would you say the country is more caring and compassionate since her death?' In fact, 41% of the population agreed, 'yes', things have changed, 52% said, 'no', people are no different, 4% said neither and 3% said 'don't know'.

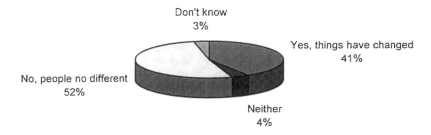

'Diana's legacy – a more caring society?'

The magazine *Hello* also commissioned an anniversary telephone poll carried out by Audience Selection. This revealed a similar paradox, that 60% of those interviewed agreed strongly with the proposition that Diana's life will have left a positive effect on the world, yet at the same time clearly believed that people themselves have not changed, only 12% agreeing strongly and 13% agreeing slightly, with the suggestion that the experience of Diana's death and its aftermath has made a permanent difference to the way they see life.

This suggests that people are prepared to conceive of a change in a public dimension that they do not necessarily have to identify in themselves. Taken together with the results of the Saatchi & Saatchi survey on attitudes towards the Millennium, this indicates that consumers' expectations of others, and in particular of companies and government institutions, will be higher in future.

Nevertheless, it seems to be confirmation of the power of the Diana Syndrome and the sense of loss reaffirming people's desire to 'belong' that as many as 41% believe that her death has actually had a huge impact on the dimensions of caring and compassion as far as the country as a whole is concerned.

Nor has the public reaction to Diana's death been an isolated event of its sort. In March of 1998 the Countryside Alliance organized a march on London which attracted nearly 300 000 people and again captured the imagination of millions more. What was surprising about the event was that it comprised a most unlikely alliance of otherwise disparate groups of people only loosely linked by an over-riding allegiance to country life, who were also historically almost totally undemonstrative in a political sense.

Obviously they were united by a series of grievances and feeling that the 'townies' at the centre of government were not taking full and proper account of the issues facing the countryside, but there was also a sense of people wanting to belong to a movement and they gained enormous emotional reward as a result of doing so.

In the United States the Million Man March and the gatherings of the Promise Keepers confirms that the phenomenon is a transatlantic one. The Million Man March took place on 16th October 1995, when hundreds of thousands of black men from all across America marched into Washington DC and gathered in front of the Capitol, in something like an attempt to recreate the spirit of Martin Luther King's 'I have a dream'. It was the culmination of a year-long move to raise awareness of black issues which had begun with the Nation of Islam, led by Louis Farrakhan, but had spread far wider, gathering the endorsement of the NAACP (the National Association for the Advancement of Colored People) and over 200 other black groups. The Promise Keepers describe themselves as a 'national Christian men's ministry', but again they exist almost entirely through the power of the desire to be part of a massed group, holding regular rallies where they affirm their promises to be good men and to be faithful to Christ. Their largest was a gathering on the Mall in Washington DC in 1997 called 'Stand in the Gap: A Sacred Assembly of Men', where the idea of men standing together in a march was almost enough reason in itself to constitute the goal of the march.

This end-of-century desire to belong is absolutely as predicted by Maslow's Hierarchy of Needs and the strength with which so many people have expressed it is at once confirmation of the singular lack in their lives of other institutions to which they want to belong, and the continuing need for human society to generate groups with which they can identify.

Given what the Henley Centre has demonstrated about the degrees of trust enjoyed by some of Britain's best companies, is it too fanciful to think that these sorts of organizations can in part fulfil the need to belong? If they align themselves to great causes in the way that Diana did, then they are likely to create a focal point in people's lives which will be far more potent than that represented by a simpler buying and selling relationship.

If they really want to become a rallying point for consumers, then the cause they adopt needs to be high profile, even controversial by nature.

Reebok achieved this with its campaign for human rights in association with Amnesty International, a campaigning and often radical charity.

Case History: REEBOK:
'HUMAN RIGHTS NOW! TOUR'

In 1988 Reebok was a young company growing rapidly in the massive sportswear market with $1.8 billion in global sales, but facing intensifying competition. The company was looking for a way to make a bold statement about themselves which would have a global impact and a universal relevance. In particular Reebok wanted to maintain a youthful and meaningful image among its key market of high school and college students. Reebok knew that young people had contributed to their growing success, and wanted to give something back. Amnesty International came to Reebok with a proposal for the Human Rights Now! Tour, and Reebok made the decision that the cause of human rights fitted the image they wanted to project, with research showing that Amnesty International was a very highly regarded organization with a large and loyal membership.

Reebok wanted to make a statement which went beyond short term fund-raising campaigns to become a defining idea about Reebok as a company, really setting it apart from its competition. Cone Communications designed a multi-tiered public relations campaign promoting the 16-country tour 'Human Rights Now!' which was promoting the 40th anniversary of the UN Universal Declaration of Human Rights. This was funded by Reebok as a perfect vehicle to get their brand's message across, worldwide. Thus the concept embraced sport, music, aspirational figures and individual human rights – a perfect combination for a youth market audience.

The objective was to make a statement about themselves as a company and not primarily to generate sales. The link with the company was philosophical – people should be free to do what they want and wear what they want. Many of the rights included in the Universal Declaration of Human Rights had a resonance with Reebok: from freedom of expression and freedom of assembly to rights over personal identity. There was a natural link through to the issue of human rights and areas of concern for young people around the world.

'A rock'n'roll declaration of human rights.'

The commitment from Reebok to the project was massive and comprehensive. The company spent in excess of $10 million to produce and promote the tour and Reebok's association with it, which in that year was approximately 90% of the entire marketing budget. The tour featured rock stars such as Bruce Springsteen, Sting, Peter Gabriel, Tracy Chapman and others who performed with the objective of raising awareness for the leading international organization dedicated to the preservation and enhancement of human rights, namely Amnesty International.

The tour, in 1988, was on a global scale and was particularly focused on countries in which human rights was an active issue, playing in places as diverse as Buenos Aires, Moscow, São Paulo and Zimbabwe. In each country 'Human Rights Now!' produced a translation of the United Nation's Universal Declaration of Human Rights in the local language to ensure that it had the widest possible understanding and coverage. Press conferences were also held in each country by Amnesty International aimed at generating publicity to increase awareness among young people and to raise issues of human rights in countries where these are by no means guaranteed.

Thus the event managed to transcend the level of the average rock concert, being fundamentally about creating awareness as well as raising money.

Reebok have continued their investment in human rights to this day and following the tour they set up their own Human Rights Award, giving a $100 000 grant each year to four young people who have had an innovative or courageous approach to extending this basic human requirement. Famous politicians and personalities have participated as members of the Awards board and through this association with people such as former President Jimmy Carter, Senator Edward Kennedy, Richard Gere and Ted Turner, valuable PR coverage was added to the campaign. Over and above the Award somewhere in the region of $1M a year is given through The Reebok Human Rights Foundation and thus well over $10M has been donated to date on top of the original investment on the tour.

Reebok's commitment to the cause has manifested itself in many ways since the tour of 1988. For example Reebok in partnership with Peter Gabriel and the Lawyers Committee for Human Rights founded Witness, a programme which puts video cameras in the hands of human rights activists, with the goal of 'making the truth visible'. Human rights issues are now written into Reebok's corporate culture. They have a rigorous corporate code of conduct to ethically govern their supplier relationships, and they benefit from better relations with their employees who have pride in working for a company that makes this kind of statement.

From the early bold step in partnering the brand with an important and potentially controversial cause in some markets, Reebok remain a massive player in the world-wide sportswear industry with real credibility among its core target audiences. Reebok benefited from the fact that they were seen to be taking a totally relevant 'cause' seriously, with a philosophical commitment backed up by a large investment.

The preceding chapters have ranged across a number of the preconditions for Cause Related Marketing. At one end of the equation there is the marketer faced with an increasing series of obstacles to effective communications with consumers: the commodity threat, communications clutter and 'disintermediation'. At the other end of the equation lie increasingly expert consumers, the value of whose loyalty is at last becoming fully recognized.

Consumers have moved well beyond the lower slopes of Maslow's Hierarchy of Needs but face a prospect of decaying traditional institutions at the same time as they feel an increasing need to belong and experience self-realization. In part by default, but also as a result of their own efforts, consumers display a rising respect for companies.

A potential solution for these related problems is that of a powerful unifying idea, which a brand can own. Cause Related Marketing can be that idea and it represents a newsworthy opportunity for brands to move onto higher ground, the ground on which consumers in the post-materialist era increasingly want to live their lives. For them CRM is a way of increasing personal commitment to others without an increase in conventional taxation.

PART III
The Third Wave in Branding

Summary

Most thinkers about the nature of branding have come to the view that brands are largely 'promises' in the minds of consumers i.e. the anticipation of their value can, in the short term at least, exceed the reality of their delivery in practice. Good brands therefore have 'the benefit of the doubt' working in their favour, and truly strong brands actually reward the consumer with both a functional and emotional over-delivery in the usage situation.

Over the history of modern, post-war marketing of brands there is evidence to suggest that the nature and scope of the brand 'promise' has evolved from an essentially rational basis such as 'washes whiter', to more of an emotional one like 'that'll do nicely'.

The advertising industry has codified these first and second 'waves' of branding and used theories such as Rosser Reeves' USP (Unique Selling Proposition) and Bartle Bogle Hegarty's ESP (Emotional Selling Proposition) to explain them. Often their practical manifestation in terms of advertising ideas has been anthropomorphic, with the product or service being personified by a brand 'icon' such as Bibendum, the Michelin Man, or the Esso Tiger.

Most recently we are witnessing the emergence of the third wave in branding in which the 'promise' has been extended into hitherto uncharted territory, namely the 'ethical' or 'spiritual' dimensions of a brand. Nowadays it seems that it is no longer enough for consumers to know what a product or service does, or what imagery it bestows upon the purchaser: now they need to understand what the brand they buy 'believes' in.

There is an emerging body of quantified market research, as will be detailed in Chapter 11, which supports this. Interestingly these findings tie in with other data indicating the power of companies and brands which have strong 'belief systems', which are not necessarily, but often are, ethical, e.g. John Lewis Partnership, 3M, Body Shop, McDonald's and the Co-operative Bank.

The problem for many companies as they acknowledge this new dimension of branding is that while they may have a 'mission' and a 'vision', these are rarely more than a series of undifferentiated 'motherhood' statements and do not have the status of a genuine 'belief system' which will engage and motivate not just their direct consumers, but all their stakeholders. If done with integrity and commitment, Cause Related Marketing can provide such companies with a solution to this emerging branding challenge.

6

Brands and Anthropomorphy in Branding

At one level brands are very simple things. From the first day on which a tanner burned the letter K onto a sheepskin with a red-hot iron to denote that it was destined for the factory in Kendal in the Lake District, which subsequently came to denote the K-Shoe brand, or from the first use of the red triangle on casks of Bass beer (generally accepted as the oldest logo in the world), it has been clear that a brand is a proprietary version of a commodity product.

Brands are an entirely relative concept. In India today a brand may be created by as rudimentary a technique as putting loose rice in a bag and labelling it. The act of doing so, with its implied selection and endorsement, gives the customer some increased guarantee of quality and convenience no matter how slight that may seem.

It is worth reminding ourselves of this basic truth about brands because the concept has become encrusted with jargon and complex theories, which often obscure the hard reality of branded life.

Brands may well be largely 'promises' created in the minds of consumers but these promises have to be made and kept, and every time that they are reneged upon there is a diminution in credibility and thus brand value.

The power of branding can be demonstrated most dramatically by comparative pricing research allied to, for example, taste tests. It is easy to demonstrate that in blind taste tests version A may achieve only the same level of price expectation as version B. But when the exercise is

NAPIER UNIVERSITY L.I.S.

repeated with branding visible, the price premium of A over B can easily be 10%, 15% or even more. Thus the visual signals which emanate from a brand name, a logo, a colour scheme and a packaging format and design can all, taken together, connote a whole realm of promise from the manufacturer to the consumer. Peter Doyle, Professor of Marketing and Strategic Management at the University of Warwick Business School examines this phenomenon in much more detail in his book *Marketing Management and Strategy*.

One of the reasons for the frustration often expressed by manufacturer brand owners is at the way in which retailer own brand producers have stolen their 'clothes'. In retailers producing their lower priced own brand 'copycat' versions, manufacturer brand owners know that their hard earned 'promises', as represented by their brand aesthetics, are being passed off by good imitations without anything like the same investment in product development, packaging research and design or consumer communications having been made.

Another important general characteristic of brands is that they can only truly exist in the public domain. In a sense being a consumer of a particular brand is like being a member of that brand's 'club'. Because the act of purchasing and using the brand is in so many cases a conspicuous consumption the act has clear implications for the personality of the buyer. Thus each time a customer uses a brand they are reaffirming their sympathy with what that brand represents in terms of its promise.

However, it is not enough for the individual consumer to understand and be aware of that promise. It is as important a function of the compact that is made between brand and buyer that other people, who may well not be buyers, or members of the 'club' are aware of what that compact represents.

As Jeremy Bullmore, one of the leading British thinkers on branding, so eloquently put it, 'what is great about being an owner of a BMW is knowing that all the other people who can't afford one know what it's like to have one'. On this basis he argued quite cogently that the dictum often attributed to Lord Leverhulme that 'fifty per cent of my advertising is wasted but I don't know which 50%' is actually untrue. If half the money addresses the actual target audience which is going to belong to the brand 'club', then the other half which addresses the people who are not is just as valuable. This is because it explains to them the meaning of club membership and ensures that everyone knows the value of belonging, both inside and out.

Groucho Marx's statement that he 'didn't want to belong to any club that would have him as a member' has such resonance because it goes to the heart of what clubs are all about. Clubs have members and non-members and there are clear criteria for each, which are known to all. In the same way that there are no clubs which anyone wants to belong to if no-one knows what they stand for, there are no brands that can exist exclusively on a one-to-one basis. This is the reason why direct marketing alone, which is essentially a private communication, can never build a brand. Brands are created by broadcast media, and this includes not just television and radio but also ubiquitous mass media such as posters and editorial coverage generated by public relations.

The promise that a brand makes has to be made in public. As we shall see, a corporate or brand commitment to a cause is akin to taking marriage vows: it is a highly personal matter, which is enhanced by being undertaken in front of witnesses.

From this it can be seen that enhancing the promise as the manifestation of a brand is a key role for communications and most of the investment in advertising and public relations is designed to do this. CRM is another, perhaps more powerful way to do this per pound or dollar of precious marketing budget. Andrex, the leading brand of toilet tissue in the UK, enlisted this technique in its never-ending battle to justify its premium over retailer own brand alternatives and to leverage its historical adstock, established in better times.

Case History: ANDREX:
'GUIDE DOGS FOR THE BLIND'

The UK toilet tissue market is a very competitive one with a significant share of the business being accounted for by own labels – 43% in 1996, a growth of 19% in just 4 years (MINTEL Market intelligence July 1997). Given the nature of the product it obviously has very strong tendencies to commodity and the challenge for Andrex, the leading brand, is to continue to reassure its customers that it is worth paying that little bit more for their product.

One of the major assets that Andrex has is a very long running campaign originated by J. Walter Thompson and now continued by

Foote Cone & Belding, featuring the famous 'Andrex Puppy', a golden labrador which charms the audience every time it appears in a commercial.

The core theme of the advertising is that Andrex toilet tissue is 'soft, strong and incredibly long'. The format of the commercials is effectively a product demonstration usually entailing the Andrex Puppy unravelling enormous lengths of toilet tissue from the roll and ending up tangled in a gloriously soft pile of unbroken tissue. As such the Andrex Puppy has become one of the classic 'brand icons' in UK advertising.

It therefore has great potential for campaignability and extension into other media and other communications channels, so the move into Cause Related Marketing was natural. In fact the association between the Guide Dogs for the Blind Association and Andrex goes back over 10 years but the 25th anniversary of the Andrex Puppy in 1997 crystallized the thinking which resulted in the launch of a Cause Related Marketing programme to celebrate the anniversary. In that particular year it was one of the largest Cause Related Marketing programmes in the UK and involved an on-pack consumer promotion that resulted in over £263,300 of donations being made to Guide Dogs for the Blind.

The 'Territorial' fit between the brand and the charity is self-evidently good, so it is surprising to learn that Kimberly-Clark nevertheless surveyed its customers just to double check that it was deemed to be an appropriate link. Reassuringly the response was overwhelmingly in support of Guide Dogs for the Blind. The company's objectives in the CRM campaign were primarily sales-driven, but also to celebrate the anniversary of their brand icon and to elevate Andrex to a new level of prominence in local news coverage. It was also to help position the company as a good corporate neighbour.

The mechanic of the campaign was an on-pack promotion which ran during April, May and June 1997. The packaging featured tokens, the number depending on the size of the pack, that could be collected and sent back to Andrex resulting in a 5 pence donation per token being made to the charity. Alternatively these tokens could be sent in with a payment of £4.99 to buy a limited edition 25th anniversary Andrex Puppy. In the event 400 000 soft toys were sold and this of course was a valuable physical enhancement of an already famous brand icon.

As well as being featured at a point of sale via packaging the campaign was publicized by vigorous PR campaign targeting local media in line with the overall strategic objective of making this high profile national brand more approachable and familiar at the grass roots level.

The campaign was also leveraged by the enlistment of the help of the Girl Guides Association and the Brownies. They helped with the collection of tokens, with the added incentive that the Guide or Brownie pack that succeeded in collecting the most in each region would be awarded a cash prize by Andrex.

'Not just cute and cuddly, a guide dog too.'

Guide Dogs received £263,300 worth of donations, which was obviously a very significant benefit to them. In addition they also benefited from the television advertising for the Andrex brand which was effectively communicating their issue to a vast public. Thus an enduring benefit to the charity was the greater understanding that the scheme created of their work among the public at large, for example that they are responsible for over 6750 dogs which are blind people's all-important guides in their daily lives.

All parties involved regarded the campaign as a very great success. Kimberly-Clark were particularly pleased with the 15% sales increase of the Andrex brand and also the massively increased press coverage – up to five times the normal level that they received during the period. This settled down to a continuing level twice that of the previous one, due in large part to the better links that had been created with local media during the campaign itself.

Of course Andrex were beneficiaries from the sales of the 400 000 soft toys, to say nothing of the long-term effect of having those in so many people's homes around the country.

But perhaps the most important benefit to the brand was that, as a result of the public link between the Andrex Puppy and GDBA, there is now an extra dimension to their brand icon. Every time the puppy is seen there will be a subliminal connection in people's minds between that particular puppy and the labrador dogs that are most often used as guides for the blind. Thus what was already a very successful mass market advertising device has now an extra layer of 'credo' or ethical value. The Andrex Puppy has a 'soul'.

As the Andrex campaign demonstrates, one of the endearing characteristics of human beings is their strong desire to imbue inanimate objects, animals and other aspects of their surroundings with human characteristics. Anthropomorphy and animism seem to be a fundamental part of the way we think about things and view the world: why is this?

In the best sense of the word human beings are almost totally preoccupied with themselves and the people or things around them that have a direct effect on their lives. So perhaps it is this constant process of appraising these environmental factors and their impact and implications for the self which leads to people thinking so often in anthropomorphic terms.

Unsurprisingly the language about brands is full of human references. It is also full of references to brands as 'icons' almost as if they were gods to be revered and worshipped.

The degree to which marketers and indeed consumers have viewed brands as being anthropomorphic has developed progressively over time from the original, rather prosaic focus on practical benefits through the era of behavioural psychology and its concerns about emotions, personality and self-image.

All this can be summed up very simply. People very often look at brands either literally 'as people' or as having personality characteristics with which they interact as if they were a person. In any focus group research it is very easy to get consumers to project a brand's attributes in human terms and this feedback is very often the basis for key decisions about reinforcements or shifts in positioning and communications strategy. Is the brand 'unfriendly', 'cold' and 'unwelcoming', or is it 'sociable', 'your best friend' and 'someone to rely on'? This is the common parlance of customers about inanimate products and services which have become brands.

What this means is that a brand can be analysed as if it were a living being. What a brand is called (named), its line extensions or variants (relatives), the way it looks (the 'clothes' it wears), what it says (on its packaging label, in its advertising), what others say about it (in editorial created by PR), what it does (its behaviour) and its reputation (its character and person-ality) are all legitimate ways of defining it in consumer terms.

A fully rounded brand will have an underlying positioning strategy, which will be manifested in all these dimensions as if it were a character in a play. The marketer as the impresario of this actor brand must ensure that the character is consistent with the needs of the audience (customer) and evolves over time to reflect the changing nature of the drama (their life demands and aspirations).

While there are many executional typologies in advertising, some of the most prevalent and successful are those which exploit brand anthropomorphy to the full. There are many examples of this such as the Green Giant, 'Bibendum' the Michelin Man, and the Pillsbury Doughboy, to name but a few.

'Personification of the brand comes naturally.'

'Icons never age, they can even get younger.'

These examples are ones in which the brand comes to be represented symbolically, often by an invented being. The attractions of these are that they are totally under the control of the brand owner and can be manipulated at will to say precisely the things that need to be said. They can also evolve subtly over time in a continuing process of 'make over', as has happened to Bibendum on his 100th birthday from which celebrations he has emerged slightly slimmer!

The same thing has been done with one of the oldest invented brand characters in UK marketing and advertising, namely Captain Birds Eye, the eponymous spokesman for the Unilever frozen food brand. The

Captain's brand and its charity partner the Royal National Lifeboat Institution are also some of the earliest recorded practitioners of CRM as the following case history shows.

Case History: BIRDS EYE:
Royal National Lifeboat Institution

Great Britain as an island has a very close relationship with the sea and at no point in the UK are you further than 70 miles from it. With the proud nautical tradition of a seafaring race there is a natural affinity for the water but also due respect for it. The RNLI is a charity which operates lifeboats on behalf of the community and has its basis in an appeal by Sir William Hillary to set up a comprehensive national lifeboat service as long ago as 1824. Since then it has saved the lives of over 131 400 people and has 300 lifeboats situated in 222 stations up and down the coastline of Britain and the Republic of Ireland.

The RNLI distinctive collection box in the shape of a lifeboat is a regular fixture around the country and the link with Captain Birds Eye as a trusty old seadog with a friendly twinkle in his eye was a natural one.

But well before the modern era of marketing the RNLI was involved with CRM. The charming letter reproduced in the introduction from The Marine Superintendent of the Austin Motor Company Ltd. (which subsequently became part of British Leyland and then eventually Rover) confirms an arrangement dating back to 9th April 1942, in the depths of the Second World War and the submarine assault on Allied shipping.

Under it the RNLI received one shilling for every lifeboat engine built and delivered for fitting to ships' lifeboats. There were also plans made for a 'photo opportunity' featuring the Cromer lifeboat at the handover ceremony of the first cheque for £240! The letter's final paragraph sums up the CRM sentiment

'Collecting for those in peril on the sea.'

very well with its emphasis on mutuality, publicity and a good cause. 'We trust that our combined efforts of publicity will make a good appeal to the public in bringing home the fact that the Institution <u>does</u> save our seamen, and that we endeavour to do our part in saving them on the broader oceans.'

Another of the earliest examples of CRM in the UK is from an RNLI initiative that took place in two separate promotions in 1969 and 1970, both with Birds Eye Fish Fingers. Again the RNLI have realized the need in a scheme such as this for a coherent 'match' between the company and the charity involved, and this is a long time before CRM existed formally as a defined marketing concept.

The mechanic was very simple – RNLI tokens were printed on packets of Birds Eye Fish Fingers which consumers collected and sent in to create funding for a new lifeboat. For the first promotion 5p was paid by Birds Eye for every token sent in and the project achieved a top selling rate of over 500 tons a week for Birds Eye which was their most successful ever promotion. The going rate increased by 11% as a direct result of the promotion and £4711 was raised for the RNLI, which enabled them to buy another boat.

The second promotion was run over a 4-week period in July of 1970 and this was run on a similar basis with the offer being extended to include Battered Fish Fingers. In addition to a donation on behalf of the RNLI, customers of Birds Eye were also sent a 24-page book about the activities of the RNLI and how to help its charitable work. The tokens appeared on 10 million packs of Fish Fingers with Tesco running extension promotions on top. Again sales were up, this time by 8.5% on the same period the previous year, which represents a similar increase in going rate as that achieved in the first promotion. In addition the redemption of the vouchers was 50% up on 1969 and 2.5 times the applications were received for the scheme, all of which benefited the RNLI directly and of course Birds Eye through its association. The promotion in 1970 raised £29242 11s 4d for the RNLI.

The RNLI continues with CRM programmes to this day – it currently has several partnerships ranging from a branded Lifeboat

Tea retailed through Sainsbury's to a credit card with the Royal Bank of Scotland which itself has raised more than £800 000 and created considerable awareness at point of sale. This is testament to the role that CRM campaigns continue to play in their corporate strategy.

However, in many ways a more powerful although riskier route is to personify the brand with a real person and thus the characteristics of the personality involved, if shrewdly cast, both reflect and reinforce the core characteristics of the brand. A good example of this technique would be the old, but still well-remembered advertisements for Mr Coffee coffee brewer featuring the all-American hero Joe DiMaggio. Paul Reiser and Bob Hoskins have been used in the USA and the UK for phone companies AT&T and BT respectively. Also memorable are Rowan Atkinson for Barclaycard, and Burt Reynolds for Dollond & Aitchison.

'Rowan Atkinson in a credit card classic.'

The power that famous stars bring to the communication can generate very significant levels of advertising awareness. But there is often a question mark as to whether they 'vampire' the video – British consumers are still unsure whether Joan Collins was acting for Cinzano or Martini in the famous series with Leonard Rossiter (it was Cinzano!).

There is also the risk that the star may do something which is not 'in character' with the 'part' or they may say something embarrassing. Pepsi's use of Michael Jackson ran into this problem.

Another, closely related technique is to represent the brand as an animal. Again the personality of the chosen creature needs to be closely allied to the desired characteristics of the brand. The catalogue of marketing campaigns is littered with examples, but among the best of them are McCann Erickson's Esso tiger and FCB's Dulux sheepdog (man's best friend again).

'A shaggy dog story that's still being told.'

Like the human icons, these animal versions can move with the times. If the homely values of the English Sheepdog are hardy perennials, so much the better, but the challenge facing an oil company in these environmentally sensitive times means the icon needs to evolve to reflect them. Thus the Esso tiger, which started life as an image of undiluted natural power, has softened to become a caring creature with a family and in harmony with its surroundings.

If brand anthropomorphy is as powerful a continuing theme in brand advertising communications as it appears to be, then it seems quite natural to pursue the analogy to its logical conclusion. If I know what a brand does in practical performance terms, and if I also know what it means in psychological, emotional and image terms, then am I not also entitled to know what it believes in and what its values are? Nowadays consumers need more rounded and holistic brand personalities to relate to: a Third Wave brand needs to evidence these higher order issues to reflect their customers' concerns in a fully anthropomorphic sense.

'The tiger family goes green.'

7

The Three Waves in Branding

The first wave: rational

In trying to put the evolution of Cause Related Marketing and its role in brand building in context we can see that theories of branding, and their outcomes in terms of executional approaches in advertising, can be divided into two main 'waves' so far. Now there is clear evidence that we are entering the third 'wave' as we approach the new Millennium.

Taking our starting point as the post-war period and the advent of commercial television we see that a large proportion of the advertising that appeared fell into what we would describe as the 'Rational' school, led by copywriters such as Claude Hopkins (see illustration on p. 65).

Hardly surprisingly, their approach to communication was heavily influenced by the direct marketers who had evolved the art of 'off-the-page' selling to virtually that of a science. Relentless copy testing through the use of 'split runs' (two slightly different versions of the same advertisement published in two halves of a newspaper edition with different identification, or 'key' numbers to track the source of coupons) had refined the cost-efficiency of the print medium in an era when the vast expanse of the USA made home shopping from catalogues a key distribution channel (see illustration on p. 66).

This is not to say that there were not many examples of early attempts at 'lifestyle' advertising, but in retrospect these look remarkably unsophisticated and unconvincing and the best of them still depended on key facts to make their impact (see illustration on p. 67).

Who else wants a *whiter* wash — *with no hard work* ?

HOW would you like to see your wash come out of a simple soaking—whiter than hours of scrubbing could make it!

Millions of women do it every week. They've given up washboards for good. They've freed themselves *forever* from the hard work and reddened hands of washday.

Now they just soak—rinse—and hang out to dry! In half the time, without a bit of hard rubbing, the wash is on the line—*whiter than ever!*

Dirt floats off—stains go

The secret is simply Rinso—a mild, granulated soap that gives rich, lasting suds even in the hardest water.

Just soak the clothes in the creamy Rinso suds —and the dirt and stains float off. Rinse—and the wash is spotless.

Even the most soiled parts need only a gentle rub between the fingers to make them snowy. Thus clothes last longer, for there's no hard rubbing against a board.

Safe for clothes, easy on hands

No laundry soap is easier on clothes or on hands than Rinso. Contains no acids, harsh chemicals or bleaches—nothing to injure white clothes or fast colors.

Rinso is all you need on washday. No bar soaps, chips or powders. Get Rinso for small cost from your grocer. Follow easy directions on package.

Use in washing machines

Rinso is wonderful in washers. Recommended by 23 leading washing machine makers for safety, and for a whiter, cleaner wash.

Guaranteed by the makers of Lux
Lever Bros. Co.

"Rinso suds soak everything clean, so I have no more boiling to do, no hard rubbing on a washboard. Little wonder that my clothes last a lot longer. And Rinso isn't hard on my hands, either. I have used all kinds of laundry soaps—bar soaps and chip soaps—for a good many years, but nothing but Rinso for me, now. It makes my washday so easy and my clothes so white and bright. Rinso deserves to be the Boston woman's very own laundry soap."

MRS. GEO. N. TAPP
13 Haviland St.
Boston, Mass.

Millions use Rinso. Thousands write us letters like this.

Mrs. G. N. Tapp, a Hub woman, says:

Rinso

The Granulated Soap that Soaks Clothes Whiter

2 sizes— most women use the big package

'Salesmanship in print'

The real TV successes of this phase were achieved by, for example, Band Aid and Alka-Seltzer who pioneered broadcast versions of the product demonstration and the 'hard sell' to produce some great advertising. A typical example of such work is shown in the storyboard on p. 68.

This was also the era of 'show and tell' advertising in which one typical housewife would talk to another, usually in a kitchen, about a superior product that the one would like the other to try in preference to her usual brand – Folger's ran some brilliant coffee ads of this variety in the USA. As with product demonstrations this 'two housewives in a kitchen' style of advertising is still valid today and indeed commercials such as the

'Advertising as a science, not an art.'

'Kipper' commercial for Lego and the recent male/female role reversal campaign for Flash are excellent pieces of advertising within their own genres (see story board as illustrated on p. 69).

The great attraction of advertising for brands based on a rational appeal is that it is by definition a pretty straightforward one, but it does depend on having genuine news to communicate. David Ogilvy, another doyen of the rational school, believed that the most powerful words in

The Rolls-Royce Silver Cloud—$13,550.

"At 60 miles an hour the loudest noise in this new Rolls-Royce comes from the electric clock"

What __makes__ Rolls-Royce the best car in the world? "There is really no magic about it— it is merely patient attention to detail," says an eminent Rolls-Royce engineer.

1. "At 60 miles an hour the loudest noise comes from the electric clock," reports the Technical Editor of THE MOTOR. The silence of the engine is uncanny. Three mufflers tune out sound frequencies — acoustically.

2. Every Rolls-Royce engine is run for seven hours at full throttle before installation, and each car is test-driven for hundreds of miles over varying road surfaces.

3. The Rolls-Royce is designed as an owner-driven car. It is eighteen inches shorter than the largest domestic cars.

4. The car has power steering, power brakes and automatic gear-shift. It is very easy to drive and to park. No chauffeur required.

5. There is no metal-to-metal contact between the body of the car and the chassis frame — except for the speedometer drive. The entire body is insulated and under-sealed.

6. The finished car spends a week in the final test shop, being fine-tuned. Here it is subjected to ninety-eight separate ordeals. For example, the engineers use a stethoscope to listen for axle-whine.

7. The Rolls-Royce is guaranteed for three years. With a new network of dealers and parts-depots from

Coast to Coast, service is no longer any problem.

8. The famous Rolls-Royce radiator has never been changed, except that when Sir Henry Royce died in 1933 the monogram RR was changed from red to black.

9. The coachwork is given five coats of primer paint, and hand rubbed between each coat, before fourteen coats of finishing paint go on.

10. By moving a switch on the steering column, you can adjust the shock-absorbers to suit road conditions. (The lack of fatigue in driving this car is remarkable.)

11. Another switch defrosts the rear window, by heating a network of 1360 invisible wires in the glass. There are two separate ventilating systems, so that you can ride in comfort with all the windows closed. Air conditioning is optional.

12. The seats are upholstered with eight hides of English leather — enough to make 128 pairs of soft shoes.

13. A picnic table, veneered in French walnut, slides out from under the dash. Two more swing out behind the front seats.

14. You can get such optional extras as an Espresso coffee-making machine, a dictating machine, a bed, hot and cold water for washing, an electric razor.

15. You can lubricate the entire chassis by simply pushing a pedal from the driver's seat. A gauge on the dash shows the level of oil in the crankcase.

16. Gasoline consumption is remarkably low and there is no need to use premium gas; a happy economy.

17. There are two separate systems of power brakes, hydraulic and mechanical. The Rolls-Royce is a very safe car — and also a very lively car. It cruises serenely at eighty-five. Top speed is in excess of 100 m.p.h.

18. Rolls-Royce engineers make periodic visits to inspect owners' motor cars and advise on service.

ROLLS-ROYCE AND BENTLEY

19. The Bentley is made by Rolls-Royce. Except for the radiators, they are identical motor cars, manufactured by the same engineers in the same works. The Bentley costs $300 less, because its radiator is simpler to make. People who feel diffident about driving a Rolls-Royce can buy a Bentley.

PRICE. The car illustrated in this advertisement — f.o.b. principal port of entry — costs $13,550.
If you would like the rewarding experience of driving a Rolls-Royce or Bentley, get in touch with our dealer. His name is on the bottom of this page. Rolls-Royce Inc., 10 Rockefeller Plaza, New York, N.Y.

JET ENGINES AND THE FUTURE

Certain airlines have chosen Rolls-Royce turbo-jets for their Boeing 707's and Douglas DC8's. Rolls-Royce prop-jets are in the Vickers Viscount, the Fairchild F-27 and the Grumman Gulfstream.
Rolls-Royce engines power more than half the turbo-jet and prop-jet airliners supplied in or on order for world airlines.
Rolls-Royce now employs 42,000 people and the company's engineering experience does not stop at motor cars and jet engines. There are Rolls-Royce diesel and gasoline engines for many other applications.
The huge research and development resources of the company are now at work on many projects for the future, including nuclear and rocket propulsion.

Special showing of the Rolls-Royce and Bentley at Salter Automotive Imports, Inc., 9009 Carnegie Ave., tomorrow through April 26.

'Giving a product a first-class ticket through life.'

Voice over: Here's proof of the amazing sticking power of the new Band Aid plastic strips with super-stick

And it stays stuck – even in boiling water.

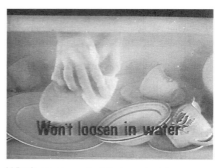

Band Aid plastic strips stick to you better than any other bandage.

What's more practical it stays stuck to you – better than any other bandage. In the hottest, soapiest dishwater your Band Aid plastic strip stays snug and neat – it won't loosen in water.

Look – No-other bandage before super stick could lift an egg just by touching it. *Other plaster shown to fail.* A Band Aid strip can.

No other bandage gives you super stick – no other stays on so well.

And here's proof – of the amazing sticking power of the new Band Aid plaster strips with super-stick.

Made only by Johnson & Johnson – the most trusted name in surgical dressings. Band Aid plastic strips with super-stick.

'Hard sell with a hard-boiled egg.'

Voice over (Tommy Cooper): You see I was standing outside my mousehole the other day,

And then, and then he turned into a submarine I then turned into a submarine eating kipper – I said a kipper not a slipper – thank you very much. Hur hur hur.

when all of a sudden along comes this cat, so, quick as a flash I turned into a dog. A-ruff ruff.

But he turned into an anti-kipper ballistic missile, so I turned into a missile cruncher – crunch crunch crunch crunch crunch!

But the cat turned into a dragon so I turned into a fire engine – How's that? Hur hur hur.

Just in time to see him change into a very very big elephant. So do you know what I did then? I turned back into a mouse and gave him the fright of his life. Just like that. Ha ha ha.

'A magical product demo for Lego.'

'Intrinsic values and no frills created a classic.'

advertising were those such as 'new' and 'free', and exhorted clients and copywriters alike to use them relentlessly.

Tim Delaney of Leagas Delaney has inherited this mantle and produced many persuasive campaigns built essentially on product information or the 'way we make it' approach. When he combines it with his combative 'Who's the enemy?' copywriting slant, then it can result in outstanding advertising as in the celebrated series for Timberland.

Otherwise, within the context of television as an entertainment medium, this approach will simply not engage the audience's attention. Because at any given point in a brand's life there may not be rational news to impart, it means that there are relatively few that can depend solely on this technique. It is no accident that the marketers such as Procter & Gamble, who excel at this approach, are heavily committed to R&D as a core part of their activity.

It is probably also the case that rational advertising appeals are most effective when the viewer or reader is actually in buying mode and actively seeking this sort of practical information. For a homeowner in search of a mortgage an interest rate can be genuinely interesting, but for everyone else it is one of the dullest things imaginable.

There is a tendency for marketers to adopt positions around the various types of communication and there are those who will only countenance 'rational' approaches to communication. These professionals will find the USP (the Unique Selling Proposition theory originally proposed by Rosser Reeves in 1961 in his book *Reality in Advertising*) a complete explanation of their model of how to go about their business.

While it is very true that nearly all successful brands have a rational side to them and this needs to be communicated to the consumers as the foundations of the brand's promise that is not all there is to it by a long way.

Most marketers nowadays would view the branding process in a less compartmentalized and unidimensional way. In particular they have been increasingly concerned about the emotional, psychological and image attributes of their brands. This trend was already well under way when Vance Packard wrote his pot-boiling attack on Madison Avenue, the *Hidden Persuaders*, in 1957.

The second wave: emotional

It is difficult to pinpoint the onset of the second wave in advertising but it probably dates from the 1960s when behavioural psychologists started to become involved in the business in a big way and Marshall McLuhan wrote *Understanding Media*, published in 1964.

It probably also coincided with the ascendancy in creative terms of ad agency Doyle Dane Bernbach which broke the mould of the established way of doing advertising. With the use of self-deprecating Jewish humour, irony and the clever use of the 'reverse sell' DDB managed to create a whole new advertising vocabulary. Perhaps their most famous single print advertisement. which shocked the industry at the time, was the famous 'Lemon' advertisement for VW, which is illustrated on p. 72.

'Less really was more.'

On television DDB used the same sorts of techniques and produced seminal commercials for VW and Avis, but also for Alka-Seltzer whose storyboard for 'Meatballs' is illustrated on p. 73.

Their use of humour in particular signalled the move away from the left-hand brain, rational approach which focused on product points alone, to a style designed to appeal as well to the right-hand brain in which the pill was sugared with an emotional coating. This 'softer' approach was the bridge into a whole new way of selling.

Advertisers became much more concerned with the emotional image and lifestyle benefits of their products and services. Advertising agencies started to talk about 'end end benefits' as opposed to just 'end benefits', meaning the final consumer satisfaction in emotional terms rather than the physical satisfaction to be gained on the way there. Copywriters started to say things like 'we're selling the sizzle not the steak'.

This development signalled a field day for the intellectuals and philosophers: the world of Freudian and Jungian psychology suddenly became all part and parcel of the consumer landscape. The rise of qualitative research in the shape of the focus group brought genuine consumer insight into the creative process.

Man: "Mama-mia that's a some-a specy ..."

Director: "Cut. Spicy Meatballs Jack."

Clapper.

Director: "Take 28."

Man: *unenthusiastically* "Mam-mia that's a some-a spicy meatball."

Director: "Cut."

Man: "What's wrong with that?"

Director: "The accent."

Next take. Burns mouth.

Next take. Spaghetti hangs out of mouth.

Next take.

Man: "Meecey-micey ballsy-ball ..."

Director: "Take 59."

Man looks sick from indigestion.

Alka-Seltzer fizz. Voice over: Sometimes you eat more than you should, and when its spicy besides mama-mia do you need alka-seltzer. Alka-Seltzer can help unstuff you, relieve the acid indigestion and help make you your old self again.

Man: *with relish* "Mama-mia that's a spicy meatball."

Oven door falls off – Man looks back.

Director: "Cut. Okay, lets break for lunch."

'Humour does sell.'

Would you be more careful if it was you that got pregnant?

Anyone married or single can get advice on contraception from the Family Planning Association
Margaret Pyke House, 27-35 Mortimer Street, London W1 N 8BQ. Tel. 01-636 9135.

'Not quite what he was expecting.'

Group discussion moderators, often qualified with degrees in sociology or psychology, spend an hour and a half with a carefully recruited group of respondents representing the target audience for the brand. As well as confirming basic purchasing patterns and usage behaviour (with reference to the more traditionally used quantitative data provided by, for instance, NOP Nielsen), projective techniques are used to dig beneath the surface. Questions such as 'If this brand were a car, what marque would it be?' and 'If this brand were to come alive, what famous person would it be?' can be remarkably stimulating to the consumer subconscious.

Other devices such as the production of collages from magazines and newspapers or de Bono derived lateral thinking processes are all harnessed to get to the deeper relationships between a consumer and a brand. These helped achieve the objective of understanding the unconscious motivations and drives that became the preoccupation of most marketers.

It was recognized that communication was not a one-way street. The rational school believed that the message sent was the message received, but the emotional school realized that the recipient filters the message not only through their perception of the sender, and the medium used to send it, but also their self-perception. This resulted in a much more complex model of communications and created a whole new world of opportunities in creative terms.

Again there are many different typologies of advertising which illustrate this point, but three of them are probably worth exploring in a little detail. The first of these can be described as 're-cast slice of life', the second 'brand attitude' and the third of these as 'surrealism'.

If people are primarily self-concerned then it is understandable that communications will be much more attractive to them if they are directly relevant to their own circumstances, buying behaviour and lifestyle aspirations. This is the reason that the housewives in the kitchen or the two men in the bar scenarios work, but clearly there are other layers that can be added to make the communication more powerful.

In recasting the slice of life in creative terms, the advertiser must first gain a deep understanding of the behaviour surrounding their brand and obtain as precise a description as possible of the demographics and psychographics of the target audience. This becomes the basic template or platform from which a truly creative leap can be made.

In the best examples the archetypal behaviour and psychology surrounding the brand can be clearly identified, but it is presented in a heightened way which adds values that are intrinsic to the brand in question and portrays an idealized, aspirational lifestyle for the consumer.

Perhaps a classic of this type is the McCann advertising for Levis in which young people can see themselves, but in a dramatized and addictively glamorous way. One of the earliest examples, 'Route 66', is storyboarded on p. 76. The music track, made famous by the Rolling Stones, and the iconic use of Americana as a backdrop to the ultimate trip across the States, presents the target audience with the ultimate of wish fulfilment. But stripped down, it is a just a bunch of kids wearing blue jeans.

'Route 66: the road to the American dream.'

There are many other variations on this theme such as Boase Massimi Pollitt's classic Cadbury's Smash 'Martians' created by the master of the genre, John Webster. They are a space age family who make fun of earthlings and their primitive habit of peeling potatoes, boiling them and then smashing them to pieces instead of using Smash as they did. Deconstructed, this is a family eating instant mashed potato but presented through the filter of an ultra-modern space age lifestyle.

An extension of this approach can be termed 'brand attitude'. This is where the advertiser identifies an approach to life or character trait, which is both true to heritage, and appealing to the target audience. The advertising then embarks on a series of narrative tales in which this particular attitude is acted out, often in a heightened or aspirational form.

'Taking a bite out of big blue.'

BRIDGE

Wife: Huh, I reckon we'll be alright if
we lose some weight off the back.

Stationhand: She's a good sport
your missus ....

M.V.O.: Australians wouldn't give a
Castlemaine XXXX for anything else.

'XXXX marks the Territory'

The target consumer, on viewing the advertising is able to indulge in a gratifying form of wish-fulfilment and often take cues in terms of verbal or gestural behaviour, which can be repeated, in a social context to great effect. Thus Apple Computer built its sales by espousing the laid-back West Coast attitude to life and extending it into business, turning a cold functional machine (IBM) into a distinctive lifestyle accessory. This culminated in the epic '1984' commercial with its attack on 'Big Blue', which only ran once, in the centre break of the Super Bowl, but has been talked about ever since (see illustration on p. 77).

A more recent example of this approach is the Saatchi & Saatchi campaign for Castlemaine XXXX in which the swearword pun on 'XXXX' becomes the centrepiece of the attitude statement which defines the 'Territory' for the brand: 'Australians wouldn't give a XXXX for anything else'. The advertising campaign captured the world of the straight-talking, beer drinking, male chauvinist, ruggedly individualistic Aussie for the soft Pommies, and they drank it in!

Once established on TV, such a powerful brand attitude can be easily short-handed on posters.

AUSTRALIANS WOULDN'T GIVE A XXXX FOR ANYTHING ELSE.

'XXXX shorthand.'

Another key typology in the era of emotional advertising is that of 'surrealism'. This is the use of powerful symbolism, often quite abstract, and often derived from references in the world of art to create a brand universe which at first sight may appear to be completely dreamlike and disconnected from reality. However, on inspection, it is sufficiently intriguing to lead the consumer to further enquiry and the realization that there are coded messages well worth deciphering.

Perhaps the classic example of this approach was that taken for Benson & Hedges Pure Gold by agency Collett Dickenson Pearce. The seeds of the campaign were sown in a more ordinary but nevertheless highly successful lifestyle campaign involving associated objects and the creation of an analogy between Benson & Hedges Pure Gold cigarettes and gold as a precious metal.

The breakthrough came when the gold pack, which by then had come to represent the valuable gold metal itself, was juxtaposed with the Great Pyramid of Cheops so that it created a third pyramid on the horizon – this is shown on p. 80.

This image stunned the advertising world for a number of reasons. Firstly, the advertisement contained no copy (apart from the mandatory government health warning) secondly, two-thirds of the packaging was obscured so it was relatively difficult to read the brand name. Thirdly the power of the image depended entirely upon viewers attempting to decipher its meaning and being 'rewarded' by the satisfaction of doing so.

MIDDLE TAR as defined by H.M. Government
H.M. Government Health Departments' WARNING: CIGARETTES CAN SERIOUSLY DAMAGE YOUR HEALTH

'The dawn of surrealism in advertising.'

'Pyramids' was but the first in a long series of brilliant advertisements, which became increasingly abstract, but because of the skill with which the progression was managed the attention of the consumer was fully retained. Indeed the appearance of a new poster in the series became a news event in itself because people knew that there was going to be another exciting puzzle to solve.

The apotheosis of the campaign was a poster without a pack shot at all, with just cigarettes raining down. In parallel with the poster campaign Benson & Hedges produced some astonishing cinema commercials and the epic 'Arizona' commercial featuring giant lizards, helicopters, sardine tins and divers was of almost Hollywood proportions.

The Silk Cut campaign created by Saatchi & Saatchi, with its purple silk imagery and references to the work of artists Fontana & Christo, has achieved something of the same level of intrigue.

Between the relative extremes of 'recast slice of life' and 'surrealism' with 'brand attitude' in between, there have been many variations on the theme of communications, which appeal to the emotions and the human desire for self-improvement through aspiration. But the fact that these sorts of values can be attached to brands of all sorts across virtually every market does not deny the need for a rational underpinning. Indeed the rational and emotional should be seen as mutually reinforcing.

Thus many successful brands produce both sorts of communication within an overall campaign. Retailers are good examples of this, where on

'Art in advertising'

the one hand they will produce thematic, almost corporate advertising talking about their retail attitude and the basis for their merchandise selection, while elsewhere they will be focusing on today's offers at attractive prices. One set of communications 'retails the retailer'; the other 'retails the products'.

In the UK the originator of the most powerful campaign embracing these two strands of communication was Sainsbury, the supermarket chain, through its agency Abbott Mead Vickers. Their use of double page spreads in Sunday colour magazine supplements talking about the quality of fresh produce without a price in sight was regarded as revolutionary at the time and certainly contributed hugely, especially in its subsequent television version, to the dominance of the chain in the marketplace.

'A supermarket becomes a true brand.'

Its chief competitor Tesco moved away from its 'pile it high sell it cheap' approach and aped the Sainsbury formula in order to compete, but also made a series of own label brand and in-store service innovations. All this was encapsulated in Tesco's 'Every Little Helps' campaign and has been so successful that it has now actually overtaken Sainsbury in the market. In the United States good examples of a harmonious relationship between emotional and rational advertising can be seen in the campaign for Little Caesars pizzas.

As we have seen there was still an underpinning of the rational appeal in many campaigns, but as of the late 1980s the 'state of the art' in marketing and advertising were campaigns that appealed primarily to the heart. These were developed as a result of a deep understanding of consumer needs and wants, and executed with a combination of powerful emotions and the dazzling use of imagery.

These approaches were perfectly suited to the Baby Boomer 'me' generation which thrived in this materialistic period. This was the time of the Yuppy (Young Upwardly Mobile Professionals), the Sloane Ranger (or the Preppie in the USA) and the Mayfair Mercenary. What it was less appropriate for was the vicious downturn into recession, which was to mark the end of the 1980s. This heralded the beginning of what came to be seen as the 'caring nineties', an era which would need different sorts of brand values and new ways to communicate them.

The third wave: spiritual

Perhaps it was Michael Douglas as Gordon Gecko in 'Wall Street' who finally pricked the 1980s' bubble. In the context of a severe world-wide recession yuppydom suddenly looked distinctly unfashionable and undesirable. Politically the heyday of right-of-centre political leaders such as Ronald Reagan, Margaret Thatcher and Malcolm Fraser seemed to be over, to be replaced by left-of-centre politicians who espoused a much more democratic, 'caring, sharing' manifesto. This trend has continued with the recent defeat of Germany's long-term leader, Helmut Kohl at the hands of Gerhard Schroder.

The news media were very quick to pick up on, and no doubt magnify, this shift in collective mood as we entered the '90s. There was a strong

'They bought ethics as well as cosmetics'

sense of 'the morning after the night before', a culmination of collective guilt at the excesses that had occurred, and a feeling of lack of fulfilment despite the material glut that had been experienced.

In this changed environment the seeds of the third wave in branding and communication flourished. For some time there had been one or two retail brands such as The Body Shop in the UK and Liz Claiborne in the United States, which had made an 'issue' central to their positioning. In the case of The Body Shop, Anita Roddick's passionate commitment to the environment and abhorrence of the idea of animal testing gave her cosmetics chain a raison d'être way beyond the provision of beauty treatments and toiletries, despite their undoubted inventiveness as products.

Thus the buyers of Body Shop products were not just purchasing efficacious shampoos, nor were they simply acquiring aspirational fashion and image values through colourful and stylish cosmetics. They were voting with their wallets for an ethical stance. This is the basis of the third wave in communications, that is, the development of a 'spiritual' dimension to brands.

If anthropomorphy is one of the fundamentals in branding then it was inevitable that sooner or later the analogy with human behaviour and psychology would be pursued to its logical conclusion. It would lead marketers to having to provide the ultimate dimension in brand personality and brand character in order to complete the presentation to the consumer: the brand's 'soul'. To pursue the acting analogy, brands had to adopt the Stanislavsky approach as described in 'An Actor Prepares', of really thinking themselves into the complete mind of the consumer.

Interestingly The Body Shop did not use any advertising or other paid-for media to disseminate its ideology. The brand managed to communicate its ethic via window displays, the staff and most importantly via public relations generated by Anita Roddick herself. Although The Body Shop has had its ups and downs in share price and profitability, overall it has been an astonishing success achieved without conventional advertising and this is a testament to the power of a 'higher order' set of brand values.

Looking back over the evolution of these three waves of advertising and communication for brands we can see that they tie in very closely with Maslow's Hierarchy of Needs. As consumers have ascended the pyramid in their fulfilment of subsistence needs and moved on to the higher order ones, so they have required their brands to reflect this progression themselves. Now that so many consumers have arrived at the levels of self-esteem and self-realization they want the brands they buy to be there with them too.

As we are still in the very early stages of this latest wave, it would be premature to talk about particular typologies of advertising or communications but perhaps the best example so far is the case of the Co-op Bank in the UK.

Case History: THE CO-OPERATIVE BANK

At the beginning of the decade the Co-op Bank was not really 'on the map' as far as the highly competitive banking, credit card and financial services industry was concerned. The Co-operative movement itself in banking and in retailing was a declining force and regarded as rather old-fashioned and irrelevant to today's consumer.

Following a fundamental strategic review it was decided that the best course of action was to go back to the mutual and ethical values at the root of the Co-op. It took two years for the Co-op Bank to set its house in order before it could declare its now famous 'ethical' stance. The reason why it took two years was because the institution had to disentangle itself from all sorts of investments and business arrangements set up under previous management regimes. Had they been left in place, the Co-op Bank would have presented their competitors with a glaringly obvious Achilles heel. In order to declare an ethical stance in public the Co-op Bank had to be squeaky clean in private.

By 1998 the Co-op Bank had become a major success story, declaring outstanding financial results based on very significant growth in number and quality of customers. The credit card business has also done extremely well. The award-winning case study is written up in detail in the IPA's Advertising Works 8 and the latest results, drawn from Leslie Butterfield's Admap article of April 1998, are summarized below.

Between 1991 and 1996:

- Co-operative Bank account closures reduced by over 30%
- Account openings increased by 6% per annum and average balances by nearly 20%
- 44% of new account openings were claimed as due to the Bank's ethical positioning
- The customer profile shifted up-market and to higher-net-worth individuals
- The Co-operative Bank is now the largest issuer of Gold Visa cards in Europe
- Deposits from personal customers have more than doubled, and from business customers, more than quadrupled
- Operating income is up by 47%
- Profits have gone from minus £7 million to £45 million plus
- Across this whole period advertising expenditure has never exceeded £5 million

From this the main lesson to be learned is that it was not just the practical banking transactions nor simply the image benefits of being associated with an unconventional bank that worked. It was the spiritual reward of knowing that your money was not doing any harm while it was doing you some good that has driven the success.

In an age when customer loyalty is so important and when the delivery of customer service via employees (and not just those in

What's the difference between the Co-operative Bank and other major banks?

Is it that we have the use of over 6,000 Link cash machines?

Is it that we have 24 hour telephone banking?

Or is it, that we promise never to invest our customers' money in countries with oppressive regimes?

Is it that we have a network of High Street branches?

'Making a banking statement.'

CO-OPERATIVE BANK EMPLOYEE SURVEY

- 97% satisfied with Bank's decision on ethical policies
- 97% believe stance has a direct affect on customer recruitment
- 89% believe it has a direct affect on customer retention
- 89% feel proud to be an employee of the Co-operative Bank
- 89% perceive the company to be a responsible member of society
- 87% feel business is mindful of its impact on the environment
- 82% believe stance has a positive affect on customer service

Source: Co-operative Bank Employee Survey March 1998

'*Truly mobilized and motivated staff.*'

face-to-face contact with the public, but the back office too) it is inspiring to see the results of the Co-op Bank's 1998 employees' survey.

There can not be many companies which can boast employee survey results of this sort and the full support of their staff is clearly enabling them to build their market share – no mean achievement for a financial institution which many had written off. It will be very interesting to see if their supermarket arm can achieve a similar result, working with its agency.

8

The Power of Belief Systems

It is interesting to note that some of the most successful companies in recent times have been those that, on inspection, have turned out not only to have outstanding products and services, and associated positive imagery, but have also been organizations with a clear vision or 'belief system'. For example, Marks & Spencer, perhaps the UK's most consistently successful retailer, has at its core one very powerful belief, which underpins its overall commitment to quality.

This is the unconditional guarantee that any item can be returned to the shop and a full refund given. Before banks made themselves available at the weekend, or the advent of cash machines, Marks & Spencer became the unofficial bank for many thousands of UK citizens. People knew that you could pay for a shirt by cheque, walk out of the shop, walk round the block and go back into Marks & Spencer and be assured of getting your money back, this time in cash.

M&S knew this, and no doubt had many internal debates as to the merits of continuing their policy, but to their lasting benefit they stuck to it. For them the returns policy has been 'immeasurably' important as a symbol of the profound trust that it creates between the company and the people who shop there. When M&S opens up for business in overseas markets it exports 100% of its operational philosophy, including the returns policy, often to the initial bemusement of the local management who cannot understand why a retailer would want to take something back it has just sold. Once the trading pattern is established they soon appreciate its benefits. Consistency of character is one of the cornerstones of successful branding.

Another UK retailer, which might have up until quite recently been regarded as operating to an old-fashioned or indeed outmoded concept, is the John Lewis Partnership. In a way the name of the company says it all – Partnership. All the employees are owners of the company and share in its success. Here again there is a very strong belief system which underpins their retailing philosophy and is encapsulated in their promise of being 'Never Knowingly Undersold'.

The recovery of the supermarket chain ASDA in the UK has also been largely driven by the rediscovery of its own belief system through a classical piece of 'brand archaeology'. ASDA started as a 'cut case discounter', i.e. a superstore in which there were no frills, just open cases of products stacked high on the shelves selling at aggressively low prices.

From its birthplace as an offshoot of Associated Dairies (hence ASDA) in the north of England, it expanded rapidly and started to make serious incursions into the southern part of the country. As it did so it lost focus on its core business strategy and values, becoming overly concerned with how it was going to compete with the quality platforms and more up-market, aspirational positionings of supermarkets such as Sainsbury and Tesco.

The original proposition, encapsulated as 'ASDA price, pocket the difference' (with a memorable graphic device of a housewife patting the purse in the rear pocket of her jeans to signify saving), became diluted with all sorts of messages in an attempt to wear the clothes of its competitors. By the time that Archie Norman took over as Chief Executive, the City (Britain's Wall Street) had lost faith in ASDA and most observers regarded it as a take-over candidate at best.

Archie Norman set about re-discovering ASDA's roots and did a few very simple things very well. He went back to a no-frills approach. He made many innovative changes, often as a result of advice from Julian Richer of Richer Sounds, an inspired hi-fi retailer (about whom more below). But the fundamentals of his strategy were to reassert the original belief system and this was manifested by his return to the original JWT Manchester advertising campaign and copy platform, which had built the business. Agency Publicis have continued the campaign with great success.

Today ASDA is regarded in the City as one of the great recovery stories and far from being a candidate for take-over it is now regarded as a predator in the market.

'Advertising archaeology helped resurrect the business.'

Julian Richer of Richer Sounds is a comparative minnow in the UK retailing world, but his hi-fi chain holds the distinction of having had the highest turnover per square foot of any retailer in the world and has an entry in the *Guinness Book of Records* to prove it. His ideas have become so influential that he has set up a consultancy business as a separate entity to capture the revenue stream that he derives from them.

Perhaps one of the most distinctive things about his business system is that, as he describes in his book, *The Richer Way*, it is almost entirely driven by an employee suggestion scheme which he personally supervises. What this means is that the business has an incredibly powerful belief system. The belief is that all employees can have a real and regular input into the way the business is run and know that good ideas will actually be put into practice, and will be rewarded.

Julian Richer therefore finds himself in the extraordinary position of having people on waiting lists to get jobs in his shops – how many retailers can come anywhere near to claiming that?

Perhaps one of the earliest examples of a company which decided to drive itself via a business ethic is Avis in the United States. Their adoption of the slogan 'We're number two, we try harder' was not just a slogan, it translated itself into a whole way of doing business within the company. It was an attitudinal shift which leveraged its underdog status vis-à-vis the brand leader Hertz and gave all its employees a distinctive and motivating approach to their work. Avis is now experimenting with 'time chits' – giving 5 or 10-minute chits to an employee every time the employee was particularly effective in the small details of their job, or performed in ways consistent with corporate strategy. These chits eventually added up to valuable periods of free time off work.

3M is another good example from the United States. 3M positioned itself as a company committed to innovation but in the mouths of many organizations that comes across as empty and platitudinous. In the case of 3M however there is a deep-seated belief system within the company which gives this claim real resonance.

3M is the company that invented the Post-It Note, almost by accident. The story goes that a scientist, working in his own time, invented a glue that didn't stick nearly as well as a glue should, and then realized there was actually an enormous benefit to be had in a glue that could stick again and again and again. Hence the Post-It Note which has become a multi-billion dollar business for 3M.

As a result of this scientist's marvellous piece of serendipity, one of the things that is now particular to the 3M culture is that every employee is encouraged to spend 15% of their working time in the company devoted to their own personal projects. At first sight this may not seem particularly revolutionary but if you calculate the aggregated salary cost opportunity of this policy it runs into millions of dollars annually.

However, the great benefit in practice is that the sorts of inventive and innovative people who work at 3M use this 15% of time for their own projects, but almost inevitably the projects that they work on feed back into the cycle of R&D innovation for the company's own ventures.

This is why 3M is so prolific in terms of new product development and over the last 5 years has introduced an astonishing 25 000 new products into the market. Indeed their annual reports suggest that up to 30% of the company's annual revenues are now generated by products or services which simply did not exist 4 years ago.

Employee support and feedback is integral to the way 3M operates, and results in a remarkably small staff turnover. Every year, an all-employee opinion survey is conducted and results are fed back at different levels: the large staff audience first. Then each business unit feeds back specific areas, along with an action plan for implementing the suggestions by the unit itself, at plant location level, by the human resources group or the company as a whole. Regular polls are conducted throughout the year and report-backs are made through newsletters or presentations and 'face to face', which the corporate communications managers indicate is always their preference.

Another American brand which is based on a powerful belief system is McDonald's. Its global success story is well known. With already over 23 000 restaurants in 109 countries, approximately 40 new McDonald's outlets open every week somewhere in the world. They are famous for their burgers, other fast foods and for the service that accompanies it. But have you ever noticed the little lapel badges that the employees wear behind the counter? Have a look at the stars that some have and some do not have; that little signifier is indicative of a whole structure of employee motivation, incentives and training. The belief system within the company is that ascending the rungs of the ladder to reach five stars is a goal worth striving for.

This ethos is inculcated in the famous McDonald's hamburger university in the United States. It was set up in Oakport, Illinois in 1972, and employees attend courses (usually lasting about a week) according to the level of training that they have reached, and can return for more courses when they reach higher levels within the organization. In the UK, as well as a training centre, which all levels of management staff attend, and a policy of promoting from within, McDonald's also run an education scheme, which includes 10 McScholarships per year. These effectively encourage university-level Business Studies students to fulfil the work-based elements of their studies at McDonald's. They also give McEducation cash awards, which employees are to use for tuition or books to assist their studies, and McBooks, another cash award to be spent specifically on books for study.

It is interesting to note how often these highly successful companies are the product of the imagination and vision of a driven entrepreneur: an entrepreneur such as Ray Kroc of McDonald's or Colonel Saunders of KFC, or a Kellogg or a Rowntree or even John S. Pemberton, the inventor of the secret formula for Coca-Cola, and Asa Chandler who turned it into a successful product.

Perhaps this explains why so many of the entrepreneurially led and driven companies falter when the founder dies. During their lifetime they literally walk the talk of the company culture: they're a one-man, or one-woman, PR machine which continuously tells us of the story that the company is based upon.

Howard Gardner, in his book *Leading Minds: An Anatomy of Leadership*, shows convincingly that the key to corporate leadership is the ability to be a great storyteller. The story needs to be simple, compelling, but above all continuously told, told and retold again to the company's employees and its customers. Sadly, when the leader departs or dies there is very often a vacuum left behind. During their lifetime there is a tendency for these dynamic leaders to be surrounded by people who are essentially sycophantic in their behaviour. Thus they often do not take the time or trouble to codify the leader's words or actions, and when the figurehead goes, the story ends.

Laura Ashley, the international fabric and housewear firm, is a classic example of this. Ever since the death of its eponymous founder the company has never really found its way. The same might have happened to Liz Claiborne's business, which she sold in 1989 after 15 years, had it not been for their CRM campaign, one of the key components of their recovery programme. This campaign gave the company an exciting new story to believe in and is detailed in a compelling case study later.

But what if the company doesn't have an entrepreneurial or visionary leader? What if it does not have a compelling vision encapsulated in a simple statement of its beliefs? What if it is a company which is simply based on the traditional combination of rational and emotional benefits? How does such a company face up to the latest stage, the third wave in communications? In short, how does a company acquire a belief system if it does not already have one?

For the past 10 years or so there has been a vogue for the corporate mission statement. Many consultancies of all shapes and sizes have made significant amounts of money by turning the same limited list of words into platitudinous motherhood statements for which chief executives of many major companies have paid vast amounts of money. Take away the letterhead or the name at the bottom of the page and these mission statements are virtually interchangeable from one company to the next.

They may look good on the page and indeed they may give the

audience a temporary frisson of excitement at an annual company meeting but in the day-to-day reality of the operation of most businesses they are simply irrelevant. Worse, because they are usually handed down from the mount of the chief executive's office, these mission statements written in their tablets of stone actually become an obstruction to developing a real and motivating belief system for the company.

One of the fundamental problems with most mission statements is they are general, not specific. They are safe, not risk taking. They are the language of corporate marketing speak, not of human conversation. They are all-inclusive and bland, not exclusive and exciting.

We have now reached the stage in the evolution of brand marketing where companies need more than this in order to move forward into the 21st century. Employees, customers and indeed all the stakeholders in a business need something far more profound and far more meaningful in order to motivate them.

The exciting thing about all this, and the lesson that needs to be learned from the examples that have been outlined above, is that for a belief system to be successful and to be something that is actually the guiding light of a company through its daily life it has, by definition, to be extremely simple and clear.

Most mission statements and indeed most corporate strategies fall into the trap of being multi-faceted: too many paragraphs, too many objectives, too many bullet points, and too many sub-clauses.

There is a now well known trick, originally used by David Abbott in the selling of single-minded advertising ideas. This is to throw a handful of tennis balls at the audience and defy the recipient to catch any of them – and of course they usually drop them all. Follow this by throwing them a single tennis ball and the tennis ball is always caught.

In the context of media clutter and media fragmentation this analogy becomes ever more true and ever more powerful. Consumers, employees, and stakeholders simply cannot hold as much information in their minds as many would like them to. The responsibility of the chief executive of a corporation is to edit, edit, edit.

The corporate mission (and the word mission should probably be banned because it has become devalued) must be distilled to a single compelling and distinctive commitment. The trouble is that most companies have simply too much they want to say to themselves, their employees and their customers. The temptation to over-elaborate is incredibly seductive and hard to resist.

By way of an example, consider the plight of the car manufacturer. The contemporary automobile is a miracle of electronic and mechanical engineering. Cars nowadays are bristling with features. How can a car as complex, as refined, and as imbued with technical miracles as this is be summarized in one sentence, let alone one word? And if that is hard to do with one model, how can we possibly do it with a whole range? This is why virtually all car advertising says everything and ends up communicating nothing.

Yet there are some car makes which have become associated with distinctive and singular values: BMW for performance, Volvo for reliability and safety, VW for idiosyncratic individualism. They chose a simple, common sense, consumer value, which was relevant to their product, and its heritage, then communicated it and stuck to it.

By analogy the same thing can be done with a cause and in the process a company or brand can acquire a belief system or mission. At one level it is as simple as that: identify a wrong that needs righting, make sure it truly connects to the business, commit to resolve it long term, and then put personal and corporate resources behind the campaign. This becomes the leader's 'story', the simple repeatable mantra, the trading rock upon which the brand will continue to be built.

PART IV

The Essentials of Cause Related Marketing

Summary

There are important differences between a genuine CRM campaign and the old-fashioned charity promotion. Perhaps the most striking is that the short-term promotion is less and less likely to generate the quick sales fix that is its primary motivation. This is because increasingly sophisticated and marketing-savvy consumers see through these sorts of programmes and recognize them for what they are. These exploitative attempts to 'buy' ethical values and customer loyalty are doomed to failure in an era when these valuable attributes have to be earned.

This increasing need for real commitment and integrity in a company's or brand's charitable involvement has a number of knock-on effects. The main one of these is the impetus towards a greater concentration of effort on fewer, more focused areas of activity, which have better relevance or 'fit' with the core brand values. Thus companies are becoming less promiscuous in their relationships with charities or good causes. This is a two-way street: charities have also been too ready to accept relatively small sums of money and levels of support from too many benefactors. This has meant a low intensity of relationship and a lack of true leverage of the full potential of two organizations working together for mutual benefit. Many charities are powerful brands in their own right and increasingly need to ensure that their commercial partners reinforce their values, rather than detract from them.

The history of corporate philanthropy has left another legacy which is problematical for today's marketers. This is the corporate foundation or trust set up as a separate arms-length entity specifically for the purpose of distributing the company's charitable donations to good causes. The difficulty arises when the commercial side of the business, which after all provides the money for the foundation or trust to dispense, feels that the direction in which it is spent ought to reflect the overall positioning strategy, perhaps against the views of the trustees. In a social context wherein people want to know more and more about how a corporation is fulfilling its role in the community, and expect good works to be publicized, this potential dichotomy of purpose needs to be resolved.

Another hang-over from the past is the nature of the 'good causes' that CEOs and Chairpersons have tended to pursue, which seem increasingly out of synch with what ordinary people deem worthwhile. Sponsorship of the arts and sports are high on many corporate lists of areas to support, whereas their customers are much more likely to favour health, education and environmental issues. The controversy surrounding The National Lottery Fund grant to re-build the Royal Opera House in Covent Garden is indicative of the strength of divergent views on this issue: at this point the habitués of the so-called 'Crush' bar there are under considerable pressure.

Fortunately, the marketer does not have to give the whole area up as a bad lot. There is increasing quantitative research data which can be used to build the business case for modern Cause Related Marketing campaigns to replace the serendipity of traditional corporate giving.

Once persuaded of the case for including CRM within the corporate or brand communication mix, the marketer still has a key issue to face before embarking on actually creating a programme. Is it better to be in partnership with a charity or is it better to address the cause directly? Is there a hybrid route between these two options, such as a tailor-made activity carried out under the umbrella of a corporate/charity partnership?

9

Differentiating CRM From 'Charity Promotions'

Peter Boizot started the Pizza Express chain of restaurants in Wardour Street London in 1965 and since then, primarily under his leadership but subsequently as part of the larger Belgo Group, Pizza Express has grown to some 180 outlets throughout the UK and has embarked on an international expansion. There are many very good things about Pizza Express as a restaurant but one of the best little details was Peter's original inspiration in starting what must be one of the earliest examples of Cause Related Marketing that is still running today.

If a customer goes into a Pizza Express restaurant they will see on the menu that there is a dish called Veneziana, and it states clearly that for every one of these pizzas sold a donation of 25p will be made to the Venice in Peril fund. The beauty of this promotion is its simplicity. Over the years it has resonated with their clientele because Venice is known to be a city in peril, with the historical and cultural treasures it contains in constant danger of deterioration due to pollution and loss as the city sinks back into the lagoon in which it was built. Further, the fact that it is in Italy and is one of the great cities of the world fits very neatly with the positioning of Pizza Express as a genuine Italian pizzeria.

Peter Boizot started his Venice appeal over 25 years ago and since then the total sum of money raised up to July 1998 has been £804 123.

At a very simple level that is the basis of Cause Related Marketing. A company, and often a committed individual within the company at the very top of it, believes in a cause, and sees a way in which their support

PIZZA EXPRESS

MENU

MARGHERITA	405p
mozzarella, tomato	
NAPOLETANA	450p
mozzarella, tomato, capers, anchovies, olives	
MUSHROOM	450p
mushrooms, mozzarella, tomato	
NEPTUNE	695p
tuna, anchovies, olives, capers, onion, tomato (no cheese)	
FIORENTINA™	535p
spinach, free range egg, parmesan, garlic, olives, mozzarella, tomato	
VENEZIANA™	455p
onions, capers, olives, pine kernels, sultanas, mozzarella, tomato	
(A discretionary 25p is included which is paid to The Veneziana	
Fund on your behalf.)	
MARINARA	530p
anchovies, garlic, tomato, olives, (no cheese)	
GIARDINIERA	615p
sliced tomato, mushrooms, olives, peperonata, leeks,	
parmesan, petits pois, mozzarella, tomato	
FOUR SEASONS	655p
mushrooms, peperoni sausage, capers, anchovies, olives,	
mozzarella, tomato	
CAPRICCIOSA	640p
ham, peperonata, anchovy, free range egg, capers,	
olives, mozzarella, tomato	
LA REINE	525p
ham, olives, mushrooms, mozzarella, tomato	
SICILIANA	640p
artichokes, anchovy, ham, olives, garlic, mozzarella, tomato	
AMERICAN	615p
peperoni sausage, mozzarella, tomato	
AMERICAN HOT™	650p
peperoni sausage, hot green peppers, mozzarella, tomato	
QUATTRO FORMAGGI	450p
four cheeses, tomato	
extra tuna, peperoni sausage *per item*	100p
any other pizza ingredients as an extra *per item*	85p
LASAGNE PASTICCIATE	615p
layers of pasta with Bechamel, cheese, bolognese sauce	
and parmesan	
CANNELLONI	615p
rolls of pasta filled with ricotta, spinach and parmesan	
HAM & EGGS *"PizzaExpress"*	450p
two free range eggs, ham, tomato, baked dough balls	
SALADE NICOISE *"PizzaExpress"*	650p
tuna, free range egg, anchovies, capers, olives, lettuce	
tomato, cucumber, dressing and baked dough balls	
MOZZARELLA & TOMATO SALAD	630p
with baked dough balls	

SIDE ORDERS

GARLIC BREAD *"PizzaExpress"*	135p
baked dough sticks brushed with garlic butter	
BAKED DOUGH BALLS	135p
MIXED SIDE SALAD	230p
MOZZARELLA & TOMATO SALAD	280p

WINES

HOUSE WINE - ZONIN	
BY BOTTLE 75cl *red or white*	965p
¹/₂ BOTTLE 37.5cl *red or white*	520p
BY GLASS 175ml *red or white* 12%/11.5% a.b.v.	260p
CHIANTI *Straccali* Litre Flask	1340p
CHIANTI *Frescobaldi* 75cl	1055p
VALPOLICELLA *Maso Laito* 75cl	1055p
¹/₂ VALPOLICELLA *Maso Laito* 37.5cl	590p
BARBERA D'ASTI *Ceppe Storici* 75cl	1095p
FRASCATI *Fontana Candida* 75cl	1055p
¹/₂ FRASCATI *Fontana Candida* 37.5cl	590p
CHARDONNAY *Araldica* 75cl	1110p
VERDICCHIO *Casal di Serra* 75cl	1100p
PROSECCO *Zonin* 75cl	1440p
CHAMPAGNE *Mercier* 75cl	2515p
PERONI BEER *Nastro Azzurro* 5.2% a.b.v. 33cl	240p
APERITIF	155p
SCOTCH 40% a.b.v. GIN, VODKA 37.5% a.b.v. 25ml	170p
BRANDY *or* LIQUEURS 40% a.b.v.	220p
tonic, dry ginger or bitter lemon	115p
TOMATO JUICE *"PizzaExpress"*	120p
ORANGE JUICE	120p
APPLE JUICE *Copella*	120p
MINERAL WATER *San Bernardo* 50cl	140p
Coca-Cola Coke 33cl	135p
LEMONADE 25cl	115p
MILK	80p
COFFEE *filter*	105p
cappuccino	155p
espresso	135p

DESSERTS

DUOMO DI BOSCO	305p
An Italian Summer Pudding	
FRESH FRUIT SALAD	285p
CHOCOLATE FUDGE CAKE	275p
PEAR TART	275p
CHEESECAKE	275p
all of the above are served with cream, ice cream or mascarpone	
TIRAMI SU	275p
ICE CREAMS:	
CASSATA 260p BOMBE 260p TARTUFO 315p	

PRICES INCLUDE VAT
THERE IS NO SERVICE CHARGE

All gratuities go to your waiter or waitress.
An optional service charge of 10% will be
added for parties of 7 or more.

PizzaExpress hopes that you have enjoyed your pizza
Your comments will be welcomed by
our Manager, or by the Directors at
PizzaExpress, Kensal Road, London W10 5BN
Telephone 0181-960 8238

© Copyright belongs to PizzaExpress PLC.   **PIZZAEXPRESS HOUSE DRESSING NOW AVAILABLE IN 200ml BOTTLES**   *PE1 PS010798*

'Veneziana and Venice in Peril – the longest running cause marketing campaign of all?'

of the cause will dovetail with the commercial development of their business and their brand positioning.

The formal definition of Cause Related Marketing by Business in the Community (the UK registered charity established in 1982 with the specific purpose of inspiring business to increase the quality and extent of their contribution to social regeneration, by making corporate social responsibility an essential part of business excellence) is as follows:

> A commercial activity by which businesses and charities or causes form a partnership with each other to market an image, product or service for mutual benefit.

The mission of Saatchi & Saatchi Cause Connection in developing the role of Cause Related Marketing is:

> To encourage a company to commit to a long term programme of activity in the charitable/voluntary sector which reinforces their brand 'Territory' and to develop their association with a 'cause' as an active ingredient in the consumer's perception of the company or brand, conveyed through advertising and communications.

But what is it that makes a true Cause Related Marketing campaign? For many years brands have produced what might be described as 'charity promotions' whereby purchases of products have resulted in a donation to a charity. Clearly brand managers and their agencies are not fools and when this has been done there has usually been an attempt to ensure relevance between the brand and the charity involved.

You could say that Peter Boizot's Pizza Express Veneziana campaign has only the status of a sales promotion. So what is it that elevates a charity promotion to the status of a true Cause Related Marketing campaign?

The distinctive thing about Cause Related Marketing campaigns is that they are themselves promoted. Given that the chain does not advertise at all, it is consistent that Pizza Express has done little to advertise its commitment to the Venice in Peril fund beyond selling Veneziana pizzas and stating on the menu that there is a 25p donation to the charity. Of course they have had some PR coverage of their efforts, but there has been no concerted attempt to publicize their support.

The key concept within CRM is that the brand should actively use its commitment to a charity or a cause as part of the brand communication that it makes to its consuming public. This extra layer of communication is in addition to that which continues to convey the rational and emotional values on offer, and should be seen to be synergistic with the total presentation of the brand.

The other distinctive characteristic of the true Cause Related Marketing campaign is longevity. Charity promotions are by definition short-termist both in the actual period during which they occur and also in the attitude that underlies them. The charity promotion is usually looking for a quick fix. The Cause Related Marketing campaign is looking for a fundamental and long-term change both in brand image and in the approach to the tackling of an issue or a cause: it is strategic not tactical.

There are very good reasons, rooted in consumer attitudes, why these two key aspects – longevity and publicity – are the cornerstones of CRM. The consumer research in the United States shows the remarkably low level of consumer cynicism in 1996, with general levels of doubt about company motives in getting involved in good causes having fallen from 58% to 21% since 1993. Thus this objection against publicizing corporate philanthropy seems decreasingly valid.

There is also research evidence that consumers actively want companies to advertise their charitable actions as indicated in the table below:

What Proves a Corporate's Commitment?

Showing tangible results	25%
Some media publicity	23%
Duration devoted to the cause	13%

Source: Cavill + Co. and Worthington Di Marzio 1997

'The need for a public commitment.'

However, there is clearly a danger that this trend could be reversed. In the case of McNeil Consumer Products (a subsidiary of Johnson & Johnson) and the Arthritis Foundation, it was misleading advertising that led to the abandonment of the partnership in the face of consumer rejection. Indeed, the campaign for a range of arthritis pain relief products, launched in 1994 with the Arthritis Foundation name and logo, provoked legal action from 19 US states for violating consumer law.

The advertising suggested that the products were entirely new and had been created with the help of the Arthritis Foundation, which was not true. It also implied that a percentage of each sale went to the Arthritis Foundation, instead of the flat annual donation from McNeil, regardless of sales. As a result, the company was perceived as having taken advantage of the Arthritis Foundation, and the particular range of pain relief products had to be withdrawn due to poor sales.

Two very simple ways of providing an antidote to the potential for this cynical response are for the company to commit in the long term to a cause – a true marriage not a one-night stand – and for the brand to be proud of the relationship and publicize it. If the consumer sees that there is a genuine commitment, manifested in these two very practical and observable ways, and if the fit between the company or brand or cause is appropriate then the chances of a negative reaction or cynical backlash from the public is minimized.

Perhaps one of the reasons that the Daddies Ketchup link with the NSPCC seems to have run its course in its initial incarnation has been to do with the fact that the relationship, despite its good 'Territorial' fit, had more of the status of a 'charity promotion' than a true CRM campaign.

Case History: DADDIES KETCHUP: 'NSPCC'

This campaign was a partnership between a very long-standing brand of sauce and its newer Tomato Ketchup product, and the NSPCC (National Society for the Prevention of Cruelty to Children), one of the UK's leading children's charities.

The UK sauce market is a highly competitive one with brands such as Heinz Tomato Ketchup having a dominant position. Daddies was a declining brand with under 5% share at the time of this campaign but now there is evidence that this decline has halted with market share stabilized and growing in the most recent period.

The key to success in the crowded UK sauce market is brand differentiation – in a market which consists of many supermarket own brand labels consumers have to be given an incentive to pay that extra penny for an independently branded product. Daddies Ketchup worked out that they could get this differentiation through a CRM campaign and at the same time enhance the whole brand profile.

'Daddies partner with a kids charity.'

For the NSPCC this was an attractive conceptual link because of the obvious implications of the brand name and the link to the children. It is also a way of raising awareness of the charity in a supermarket or retail environment.

The initial promotion was very simple in that each purchase of Daddies Ketchup created a 1p donation to NSPCC and over £250 000 was raised for the charity in this way – that is a lot of bottles! There was also copy about NSPCC on the Daddies Ketchup packaging.

That particular promotion has now ended. The reason given was that the promotion had simply stopped motivating consumers and had ceased delivering Daddies Ketchup or NSPCC the desired results. Perhaps this is another indication that the basic 'on-pack' promotion is not really enough to create a genuine CRM campaign. It can look to the consumer as if the level of brand commitment is low, perhaps to the point of being a little exploitative. However the basic relationship has remained solid and a new initiative is being developed which will explore different ways of making the link between Daddies and the NSPCC. The commitment to the new scheme is strong on both sides and there is a realization that the connection has great potential for both the NSPCC and the recovering Daddies Ketchup brand, particularly if it acquires the status of a true CRM campaign, with all that that entails in terms of brand advertising and communications support.

10

The Nature of Giving

Spreading too thin

As a result of the 'Chairman's Wife' syndrome, of which more later, and the historical tendency for corporate donations to be parcelled out in small bite-sized chunks to a whole range of good causes, there has inevitably developed an 'all things to all men' aspect to both charity' fundraising activity and to company donor behaviour.

For the last decade management consultants have been advising their corporate clients to 'leverage their supplier relationships', and the same recommendation should be made in the world of charity fundraising and giving. The objective at Saatchi & Saatchi Cause Connection is to help effect, in as painless a way as possible (and therefore gradually, over time), a move towards strategic alignment between the corporate or brand positioning and the company's or brand's charitable activities.

The current picture is of charities and companies with very long lists of donors and recipients. For example, Crime Concern in the UK has a corporate sponsor list numbering some 40 different companies. In the USA the Red Cross differentiates between those companies (about 15 at the moment) with which it has a 'marketing' relationship, and the very large and continually fluctuating number of companies which are purely philanthropic donors.

As a result of this promiscuity on both sides of the giving and receiving relationship, the corporation or brand rarely has any real sense of 'ownership' of the cause to which the charity is committed or indeed any particular special relationship with the charity. Nor on the other hand does the charity or voluntary organization have any particular allegiance to a particular donor, nor is there any benefit in really investing in a long-term partnership to mutual benefit and ultimately to the cause which it espouses.

The list of charities to which companies give has typically grown organically over time. Many commitments will have been inherited from chairmen or chief executives long departed or from sales directors with particular relationships in certain parts of the country. Thus there is neither an overall logic to their giving nor do the individual sums of money have any real impact. Worse, it is doubtful whether the CEO, Chairman or Directors can possibly have a deep commitment to all these disparate charities and causes.

The larger corporations may well have special charity committees or even separate trustees to administer these funds, and it is becoming increasingly commonplace that charities have to 'pitch' competitively to these bodies in order to secure funding, usually of a relatively short-term nature. This is an expensive and time-consuming process for both sides.

All this means that those not inconsiderable sums of money, taken in aggregate, are being spread too thinly. An obvious solution to this problem is to consolidate on both sides. Companies and brands need to effect a strategic realignment between their charitable giving and the main thrust of their marketing strategy and brand building. Charities or voluntary organizations need to become if not monogamous then certainly significantly less promiscuous in their search for funds than they have been hitherto.

This process of rationalization is already beginning and an interesting implication of this emerges when one considers how many truly powerful charity brands there are in the marketplace, and realize that in fact there are relatively few. What this means is that the most desirable charity brands and causes are likely to find major long-term corporate or brand partners and after that it will become progressively harder to achieve powerful CRM relationships, particularly in the areas of mainstream consumer concern.

While by no means suggesting that Visa has focused all its attentions on a single charity to the exclusion of all others, its commitment to the cause of improving the levels of literacy in the USA through its multi-layered 'Read me a story' CRM campaign with the charity Reading Is Fundamental (RIF) is indicative of the enormous benefits of single-mindedness to both sides.

Case History: VISA:
'READ ME A STORY'

Stimulated perhaps by the highly visible programmes run by American Express in the USA, Visa entered the Cause Related Marketing fray in 1997 with its high-profile 'Read me a story' campaign.

The statistics on literacy in the USA are depressing: 38% of children have never been read to, and over 30% of families in America 'live without books'. Astonishingly 40% of fourth graders can not read at the basic level.

Consumer research had shown that 70% of Visa cardholders were interested in 'Read me a story' as a campaign. At the same time the charity involved, Reading Is Fundamental, was rated one of the top 20 most credible charities by Parenting Magazine and one of the 10 charities that 'really helped kids' by the chronicle of philanthropy. Furthermore, and a great attraction as far as Visa marketing was concerned, was that the charity has more than 219 000 volunteers and has been running a nation-wide network of community based projects since 1966. Given the nature of credit card marketing this grassroots contact was to prove extremely useful.

The basic proposition of the Visa 'Read me a story' programme was very simple: the concept was 'use Visa and help a child learn to read'. Visa card usage was encouraged by the offer of Visa making a donation to 'Reading Is Fundamental' every time the card was used. At certain selected merchant locations Visa also undertook to double the donation and as a further dimension Reading Is Fundamental sites could earn free books from Visa by posting point of sale signage thus increasing the visibility of the brand.

In communicating the programme a 30-second TV commercial was made and local market radio promotions were used as well as shopping mall media. In all a $20M advertising budget was deployed

behind the 'Read me a story' campaign, augmented by more than
$4M of cooperative merchant marketing. An example of some of
the print and point of sale materials is illustrated below.

The campaign was augmented by statement inserts to the 50
million Visa card holder base and there were other supporting
elements including a cheque card usage mailing with a Waldenbooks

'Making the point at the point of purchase.'

offer using the 'Read me a story' theme. There was also an activation mailer for credit issuers giving them the incentive to use the card and obtain a donation for the Reading Is Fundamental charity.

Waldenbooks further supported the effort with in-store signage with 'Check up' insert distribution and inclusion within their holiday catalogue and newsletter and also mentioned it in their advertising.

Merchants were enlisted in a big way, being supplied with a wide variety of signage materials, programme kits for managers, the provision of special reading events and the support of a direct mailshot to 1 million small merchants to enlist their support.

The American Academy of Paediatrics was also enlisted with their president being used as an expert spokesperson. Take-ones, signage and guides were offered in 20 000 doctors' premises and the guide was inserted in AAP news. Material such as Visa 'reading prescription pads' were also widely circulated.

United Airlines was also a big supporter, broadcasting a 2-minute in-flight video in November/December and displaying promotional signage in city ticket offices and their Red Carpet Clubs. They also offered Mileage Plus in their November newsletter as part of their frequent flier programme and displayed airport banners and arranged for character appearances from the campaign. Additionally they provided a feature in *Hemispheres Magazine* and 400 tickets for the 'Read me a story' tour.

Public relations support was also very important with Anthony Edwards from the cast of *ER* starring at the opening event in Washington DC. A theatrical performance was created to illustrate the campaign and the top 24 cities in the USA had performances which were given at Reading Is Fundamental sites and in shopping malls. This generated local media tie-ins and produced a major publicity campaign for the cause.

The results from the last quarter of 1997 demonstrated that 'Read me a story' had had a significant impact on Visa's brand image. There was an awareness increase of 7% and an all-time high of 62% achieved for 'best card overall' in the tracking study. There was 20% consumer awareness of the promotion and 64% of those perceived the value of the effort. Advertising had clearly communicated a balanced message of cause and card usage: of those exposed to the advertising 73% understood that Visa card usage helped the 'Read me a story' and Reading Is Fundamental campaign.

In hard business terms the CRM campaign also had an impact. Share of market was up from 65.9% to 66.3% year on year and in November/December Visa sales volume was up 16.9% over 1996 as was transaction volume up 18.9% on the year before.

All in all, it was a highly successful campaign for both Visa and Reading Is Fundamental in the shared 'Territory' of reading. As one of the copylines from the campaign so aptly put it: 'to succeed, kids need to read'. A highly appropriate sentiment, to be seen in the context of the Visa brand with its aspirational values.

Unsurprisingly the campaign has now moved into its second year with a minimum of $5M already having been raised for the Reading Is Fundamental charity. In the long term there is little doubt that the association with the cause of literacy, a fundamental 'enabler', is going to add important 'credo' to a service which is all about facilitating or enabling important financial transactions.

The role of foundations

There are many companies which have set up charitable foundations to handle the monies which they give to good causes. In the UK there are such giants as the Lloyds TSB Foundation which holds 1.5% of the ordinary shares of Lloyds TSB Group, but instead of receiving dividends the foundation receives 1% of the Group's annual Gross Profit. This means that they have in excess of £30 million to distribute annually, making them one of the largest benefactors in the UK.

In the United States of America, the Foundation Center publishes a list of the 50 largest corporate foundations, ranked by total giving. AT&T Foundation heads the list with total grants of nearly $38 million, with Wal-Mart Foundation giving $32.5 million and the Ford Motor Company Fund awarding $29 million in grants.

Historically the creation of these foundations has obviously been highly desirable from the point of view of the charities or voluntary organizations which have been beneficiaries. The money has been guaranteed, as in the case of Lloyds TSB, and has been dispersed by a board of trustees who are completely independent of the original source of the funds.

However, in the changing consumer climate in which customers seek ever greater transparency in the organizations they do business with, and at a time when the public is expecting corporations to declare their position within society and their contribution to the community at large, the existence of these trusts or foundations presents a dilemma.

On the one hand, the foundations are transparent and can be seen to be at a distance from the corporation. But in reality, given the clutter, and the disinclination of consumers to get to grips with complex and perhaps inessential topics, it can be very unclear what the relationship is between a foundation and a corporation, especially if they appear to bear virtually the same name.

The other dilemma – and perhaps a more pressing one from the marketer's point of view – is that if a very large sum of money coming straight out of the company's profits is being devoted to charitable causes, should the corporation not be a beneficiary of that generosity in reputation terms? If consumers are increasingly expecting the companies they do business with to do good works, in effect on their behalf, then how can a company do this if it has to operate, by statute, via a charitable foundation over which it has no influence? The issues raised here are not easy ones to grapple with but there would seem to be four clear options facing companies that find themselves in this situation.

The first of these is to spend time and effort communicating to the trustees of the foundation their vision for the brand in a CRM context. Given the marketer's analysis of the brand 'territory', and from this the sorts of voluntary organizations or causes that will provide a good 'fit' or synergy, do these appeal to the trustees?

The second option is to spend some of the marketing communications budget clarifying the role of the foundation to make it clear that it is a separate but related organization which is doing outstanding work, without being beholden in any way to the profit motive. While theoretically possible this route does seem rather circuitous and unlikely to have any real consumer impact.

The third option, if allowable, is for the foundation to spend a proportion of its own funds on publicizing the good works that it is doing, i.e. to mount in effect a CRM campaign about itself.

The fourth option, which could be alarming, but nevertheless needs to be contemplated, is that of changing the articles of association or legal structure of the company so that a legitimate influence may be brought to bear on the company's charitable foundation.

These four options are not necessary mutually exclusive and it may be that in a particular situation one or two of them may be able to be pursued. The main point is that nowadays customers are expecting companies to be involved in altruistic or higher order activities and they are increasingly demanding to know how the company is actually fulfilling a responsible role within society. If that role is already being fulfilled by proxy through a charitable trust or foundation, then it seems entirely right that the company should gain the credit for the good work that is being done on its behalf.

The 'Chairman's Wife' syndrome

The desire for 'new money' to be accepted by 'old money' is very strong indeed. Despite the fact that this syndrome is mocked, it is deeply embedded in many ways, and enshrined in literature, theatre, musicals and movies.

Each generation of self-made entrepreneurs seems predestined to tread the path again. No matter how much money has been earned how quickly and in what dramatic style, there nearly always seems to be an inferiority complex, which sits as a chip on the shoulder of even the doughtiest new captain of industry. The approval of the people that made the money generations before seems to be of paramount importance to them.

This is despite the often relative penury to which successive generations of many of these famous families have now fallen, having traded for years on the name that was originally made for them. The new billionaire seems oblivious to the self-indulgent way in which many of the established families allow their inheritance to disappear through their own dissolute, disappointing and simply lazy behaviour. It does not seem to reduce the appeal of their approval for the nouveau arriveé.

This desire to rise above 'trade' and to require the trappings of the aristocracy is very strong indeed and has been over the centuries. It is important for the successful capitalist to acquire the veneer of class and culture that old money seems to have by right, or at least by dint of longevity. They quickly learn that an easy way of achieving this goal is simply to buy it. This fits naturally with all their experience of business – if you can buy factory, plant and employees, why can't you simply buy class and peer group approval?

One of the most effective ways of doing this is for the entrepreneur to embark on a parallel career in philanthropy, either personally, or by proxy through his wife. Historically this has meant that the beneficiaries of 'new money' charity have been areas of personal rather than corporate interest, and certainly not those of the consumer. Stereotypically these areas have been sporting in the case of men and the arts in the case of women.

An added dimension is that this social climbing has been justified as a part of the corporate entertainment strategy, with the enjoyment of sponsored activities or events by key customers and business contacts (and their partners of course) being a key criterion of success. To combine this with a charitable dimension has often resulted in the best combination of all – a cultural activity, enjoyed by men and especially women, with a charity aspect – to reflect well on the host benefactor.

This then is what has led to the 'Chairman's Wife' syndrome – the disbursement of a company's charitable donations with social approval, cultural aura and entertainment value being higher on the list of motivations than the needs of ordinary people, let alone the company's customers.

This may be a harsh judgement and there is no denying that many very worthwhile causes have been supported over many years as a result of this approach. But the social climate has changed and the sponsorship of elitist non-functional visual and performing arts, or sporting events that have a mass appeal or are already well funded, must now be seen as less relevant than causes concerned with addressing fundamental social needs in the areas of health, education and the environment.

Where there is a charitable aspect, and this is very often the case with the arts, two objectives can be achieved in one: social standing, by being associated with an intellectual, aesthetic pursuit, and moral sanctity by being seen to 'give something back'.

One of the great attractions, and one that does not escape the successful capitalist, is that sponsorship of these sorts of activities can provide a very useful vehicle for corporate entertainment – much to the frustration of the genuine fan. Given that male dominance still exists at the highest level in these areas it is entirely natural that much of the money has gone for sponsorship at major sporting events. Football, yachting, golf and racing are but a few of the sporting areas which have thus benefited.

However, if corporate entertainment is an objective, then the entrepreneur rapidly discovers that there is a need for male colleagues and clients' partners or wives to be included in the group. This leads to a large corporate presence at certain events, which have a particular appeal to women. It is hardly politically correct to say so nowadays, but any visitor to Henley, Ladies Day at Ascot or Wimbledon can hardly fail to notice the very significant numbers of smartly dressed women in attendance.

This means that these sorts of events and also those involving the arts such as ballet, opera, painting and music have all become great beneficiaries of this tendency to corporate entertainment with an aesthetic or even social climbing aspect.

Thus it is that the 'Chairman's Wife' has become extremely influential in the way in which corporate monies have been dispersed to sponsorship or charitable ends. Very often it is her preference which leads a particular company to sponsor a particular activity. But in the era of increasing scrutiny of corporate behaviour by employees, shareholders, regulatory authority and indeed all the 'stakeholders' involved, does this sponsorship or charitable behaviour stand up to inspection?

The marketer would recognize that in nearly all these sponsorships all that is achieved is simple name awareness and brand recognition. While this may be a valid objective in some cases, it is notable that many of the major sponsorships are taken by brands which clearly have no need of brand recognition or brand awareness. It could be argued that they are doing this to consolidate an already dominant position, but this motive is questionable.

Does a well known company name on a football shirt really do a great deal more for that company other than remind the consumer of its presence at a relatively basic level? There is certainly no potential to say anything more about the brand in the context of a title sponsorship. Is it groundless to suspect that it is also an opportunity for the chief executive or the chairman to realize their personal fantasy as manager of a football club?

If we are in an era of increasing corporate transparency is it right that senior executives of companies should be indulging themselves in this way? Many organizations have instituted policies governing the receipt of gifts or business inducements. More and more of them have very strict policies which eliminate altogether the receipt of even a business lunch. Anything that might be construed as an inducement or a bribe is strictly forbidden. In this context is it appropriate for senior management to be seen to be pursuing their personal passions for particular sports or arts?

The rise of Cause Related Marketing presents companies with a way out of this dilemma. A well constructed programme can provide a genuine opportunity for corporate entertainment, it can also coincide with the core goals of the company and, if the top management's own personal objectives are aligned with the company, it is likely that their interest too can be satisfied by the appropriate CRM campaign.

In all this, the consumer's view must be borne in mind and the research evidence suggests that the arts are relatively low on their lists of priorities. It seems likely therefore that the future of arts fundraising from the corporate sector is not all that rosy unless a community or educational dimension is added. In the far more commercialized and commercially successful sporting sector it may not be an issue. There is enough money being generated from the sale of broadcast rights to make many sports not only financial viable but extremely wealthy, as the latest deal between Rupert Murdoch and Manchester United testifies.

Corporate versus consumer dissonance

As can be seen in the table below from the Research International survey for Business in the Community, the UK consumer certainly has much more down to earth requirements than companies when it comes to corporate giving. They want the money to go towards areas of real human need such as health, education and the environment rather than the arts, which do not even feature on their list, but are high on that of corporates.

The Future Foundation report for British Telecom (BT) reinforces this point. The chart below shows clearly what concerns people. The order is a little different from the BiTC data, but makes broadly the same point. Naturally enough, given people's high degree of self-interest, it is those issues 'closest to home' with which they are most concerned.

For many brand owners this set of priorities is good news because if they are targeting the mass consumer then it helps if the mass consumer

	Social Issue	Consumer Ranking %	Corporate Ranking
1.	Medical / health	68	7
2.	Schools / education	52	1
3.	Environmental	44	4
4.	People with disabilities	41	–
5.	Children's charities	38	3
6.	Poverty / social hardship in UK	37	5
7.	Housing / homeless	33	10
8.	Animal rights & protection	31	11
9.	Alcohol and drug issues	30	–
10.	Community issues	27	–

Source: The Winning Game, Business in the Community / Research International / RMRB Omnibus Survey 1996. Base 1053 respondents

'Customers have different priorities from corporates.'

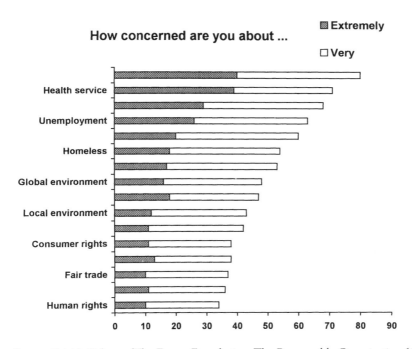

Source: British Telecom/The Future Foundation: The Responsible Organisation 1997

'Closer to home means closer to heart.'

has concerns which are relevant to so many product categories. There are also areas in which there are many professional charities actively at work and there are many causes which need to be championed.

When contrasted with the list of priorities for which consumers perceive companies have responsibility, as set out in the chart below, it is clear that the arts and sports are at the bottom of the pile. This raises serious questions about the level of funding these activities have traditionally received from the corporate sector.

No doubt there will still be a future role for corporate sponsorship of

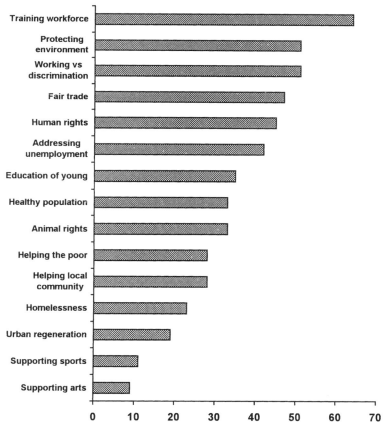

**Level of responsibility companies have for ...
(according to consumer opinion)**

Source: British Telecom/The Future Foundation: The Responsible Organisation 1997

'*What price sports or arts sponsorship?*'

the performing and visual arts such as the ballet, opera, concerts and major art galleries and art exhibitions. Nor is it likely that the names of major non-sporting brands will disappear from football shirts in a hurry, despite the economic realities. Although there was a time when sheer brand name registration could be achieved at a relatively cost-effective price by sports sponsorship, rampant price inflation has taken hold as sport is used as the battering ram to sell consumers pay-per-view and thus it becomes harder and harder to justify.

Both these areas may well still have a role in corporate entertainment and in helping with trade customer relations. The real question is the underlying motivation from corporate involvement in these areas. There must be a nagging doubt in this area. It is too easy to paint a picture of leaders of corporations wanting to use these kinds of activities as a form of spurious intellectual credentials or ego enhancement.

It has become a cliché, but very large numbers of attendees at these prestigious arts occasions, and indeed sporting ones, have no real interest or understanding in the activity on display in front of them. These places are taken at very high prices, thus preventing access by the true aficionados or fans and is something of a scandal.

As we move towards an increasing consumer demand for corporate transparency, and as the shareholder democracy gains momentum with more and more ordinary investors wanting to know the details of the companies in which they put their financial trust, are managed, it seems likely that these kinds of extravagancies will become harder and harder for boards of directors to sustain.

11

Making a Commercial Case for CRM

Marketing is a hard-nosed commercial business. Before any serious brand manager would want to put a single dollar, pound or even euro towards a CRM campaign, he or she will want convincing that that money will be better spent in this way than in the many other channels that can be used to support and develop a brand. Why should precious funds be put towards enhancing a brand's 'spirit' via a Cause Related Marketing campaign as opposed to being invested in more familiar forms of communication with either a thematic image or tactical price message?

The fundamental first question that needs to be asked about the effects of CRM is whether or not the association between a brand and a good cause is likely to influence consumers to favour that particular product or service brand over and above its competitors, all other things being equal.

Fortunately there is a growing body of quantitative and qualitative market research which gives very strong substantiation as to the potential for Cause Related Marketing campaigns to influence buyer behaviour to a far greater degree than more traditional forms of communication. As can be seen from the tables later on, the answer to the question of CRM influence is emphatically 'yes' as far as consumers' claims are concerned.

The second key area of concern to marketers is whether or not Cause Related Marketing, and the sort of values it adds, are those which can actually help sustain a price premium. In the heyday of environmental concern, nearly all research suggested that while consumers were in favour of recycled packaging and other manifestations of 'greenness' in brands, they were not prepared to pay a premium for them, nor were they prepared to accept any diminution in product quality for the sake of environmental protection.

In that context it was not altogether surprising to marketing professionals that products largely based on environmentally friendly platforms, and which have sacrificed degrees of functional performance to do so, have not really succeeded to any great degree in achieving significant brand shares of key markets.

However, the data seem to suggest a rather different situation in the case of Cause Related Marketing. The research on both sides of the Atlantic and in Australia shows that quite significant numbers of consumers say they are prepared to pay a small price premium for brands which are known to support good causes. For brand managers who are fighting an intense and apparently never-ending price war this is extremely good news.

However, this price premium is probably best seen in the consumer's mind not in terms of extra profit to the brand owner, but as a proxy charity payment to the good cause that the consumer would like to support. In effect the brand is being used as an easily accessible, credible and trustworthy 'collection box' on the shelf with no change to its functional properties which might alienate consumers. It is the brand's beliefs which have changed for the better, and thus its total 'performance' has too.

In mature market sectors the battle for growth is by definition largely over and so the long-term war is for relative market share and is usually one of attrition which is won or lost on degrees of customer loyalty. In this context again CRM seems to be a potentially powerful new piece of ammunition. Consumers claim that they will switch brands to those that support the causes of which they approve.

It would seem entirely reasonable to draw the conclusion from these major pieces of quantitative research that there is a very powerful case for Cause Related Marketing to be a very effective tool in the market place. It is pretty clear that brands which have a 'belief' are going to be more convincing than those that do not.

Much of this research has been conducted by a few pioneering organizations. In the USA Cone Communications have commissioned a good deal of work through the well-known research company Roper Starch. In the UK most research has been commissioned by Business in the Community through Research International and BT through the Future

Foundation and Public Attitude Surveys. There has also been valuable work done by Worthington Di Marzio ('Consumers, The Community and Business', and 'The New Bottom Line'), for Cavill + Co. in Australia.

Roper Starch, in the second major survey carried out with Cone Communications, showed very significant levels of claimed brand switching towards brands which espoused good causes. In a relatively mature market such as the USA where the battle for share preoccupies marketers, these are exciting findings.

Some key findings are listed in the tables below:

• Likelihood to switch brands if associated with a good cause, when price and quality are equal	76%
• Likelihood to switch retailers if associated with a good cause, when price and quality are equal	76%

Source: The Cone / Roper Cause-Related Marketing Trends Report 1997

'CRM *becomes a tie-breaker in the purchase decision.*'

These are mirrored in the UK by work carried out by Research International for Business in the Community in 1997:

- 86% of consumers have a more positive image of companies they see doing something to make the world a better place

- 61% of consumers would switch retail outlet if the other were associated with a good cause

- 64% think cause related marketing should be a standard part of the corporate's business

Source: The Winning Game, Business in the Community / Research International 1996

'*Now a major phenomenon in the UK too.*'

Even more exciting from the marketer's point of view, there is evidence that consumers are even prepared to pay a small price premium for products or services which are associated with good causes. This is shown in the Business in the Community research which also reveals that a

- 64% of consumers are willing to pay slightly more for a product associated with a cause – on average 5% more

- 20% of the population is willing to pay 10% more, for the right cause

- 37% of consumers always refuse to buy a product because they **do not** like the company that makes it – and a further 37% say they occasionally refuse to do so

Source: The Winning Game, Business in the Community / Research International 1996

'Premiums and vetos arising.'

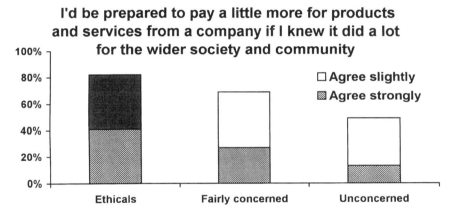

I'd be prepared to pay a little more for products and services from a company if I knew it did a lot for the wider society and community

Source: BT/The Future Foundation: The Responsible Organisation 1997

'Corroborating data from another respected source.'

'negative preference' may well begin to operate as the consumer focus on corporate and brand 'ethics' becomes more widely shared.

Again these findings are reinforced in the survey for BT by the Future Foundation.

Given the great difficulties which face them in the constant battle to maintain margins and fight against the tendency to commodity, this should be music to the brand manager's ears.

However, two cautionary notes must be sounded. Recently a survey commissioned from RSGB research company by the Corporate Edge confirmed that there are still levels of consumer cynicism to overcome in the

UK. The response of the public rather than the charities themselves was felt to be companies' main concern by 70% of respondents, while two-thirds regarded big corporate brand names' involvement with green issues as a cynical marketing ploy.

This scepticism is also matched to a degree among marketing professionals. A survey in May 1998 by Saatchi & Saatchi Cause Connection among 169 marketing directors, managing directors and chief executives of major UK companies showed that about 60% of them were doubtful as to whether consumers would actually behave as they claim they would. This top line finding in response to the key question is set out in the table below.

Question: 61% of consumers (1998 Mintel research for Marketing Week) claim they are more likely to buy products or services which are associated with good causes. Do you believe they will actually do so in practice?

	No.	%
Yes	57	33.7
No	83	49.1
Not sure	29	17.2
Total	169	100

'Already a third of marketers think cause marketing will work.'

There are two main points to be drawn from all these research findings. First, while very positive overall, the consumer is probably right to still be cautious about the motives of companies and brands. There have been too many misleading claims in the past and consumers are increasingly sophisticated in playing the marketing game. They are looking for transparency and integrity and it is only the brands that embark upon CRM campaigns in this spirit that will succeed. The second point is that those marketers who embrace the concept of CRM in the right spirit are very likely to gain competitive advantage while the Doubting Thomases sit on the sidelines.

As can be seen in the case histories there is conclusive proof that those marketers who have embraced the concept have already been big winners in the market place. It is also worth putting some of these consumers' intention to purchase figures into context. The 60% likely to switch recorded by Research International and Roper Starch should be seen against brand switching figures that might be derived from new flavour introductions or new varieties or extra-value packages which typically might be of the order of 10–15%.

Even if one discounts the consumer claims by a factor of four or even five, the likely impact on buyer behaviour is at the very top levels in conventional marketing terms compared to that resulting from the more normal sorts of innovations. All the social and attitudinal trend data suggest that in future considerable numbers of consumers will behave in line with altruistic motives as well as rational product or image based ones. Brands need to acquire the appropriate values to take advantage of this new reality.

Few marketers would question the suggestion that the automotive sector is one of the toughest in which to operate. Whether they are called dealers, retailers or franchisees, and despite the best efforts of GM's Saturn programme in the USA or Daewoo's in the UK, the people who sell cars for a living are a hard-bitten lot. Thus any motor manufacturer who attempts to mount a radical new sort of sales campaign based on the concept of CRM, with its inherent appeal to the generous side of humanity, had better be pretty sure of their ground! BMW did just that.

Case History: BMW: 'THE ULTIMATE DRIVE' (FOR SUSAN G. COMEN BREAST CANCER FOUNDATION)

BMW is a very successful global marque of car positioned as the 'ultimate driving machine'. But historically the brand has been more associated with male drivers than female drivers, and its aggressive sporting image might be seen as a disincentive to purchase among females. In the USA women constitute some 50% of car drivers and thus in order to expand its reach into this market BMW needed to counterbalance its traditional imagery with a more caring profile that might have more appeal to women.

The challenge for any breast cancer charity is to encourage more openness about this disease which is one of the more treatable and curable forms of cancer. Clearly self-inspection and screening are

The Ultimate Driving Machine

'The ultimate drive – against breast cancer.'

vital ingredients in the programme but with the Susan G. Comen Foundation a vital co-priority is to fund proper research to keep up the medical fight against it. In the United States 178 000 women are diagnosed with breast cancer each year, and about 12% of the female population living into old age are faced with it at some point in their lives.

The Susan G. Comen Breast Cancer Foundation is a charity whose mission is to eradicate breast cancer as a life-threatening disease by advancing research, education, screening and treatment. They run a national Freephone service to give help and advice to those women worried about breast cancer, as well as funding research into the disease which still has a 24% mortality rate in the USA.

The way the Cause Related Marketing campaign works is that three fleets of BMW cars tour around from BMW centre to BMW centre during a 4 month period. On special event days, which are widely publicized on a local basis, these particular cars can be test driven with a commitment from BMW of a $1 per mile donation to the charity. At the same events 'local heroes' are lionized, for example someone who has fought breast cancer and won, or a doctor who has worked hard against the disease in the locality.

This test drive strategy is a clever way to get consumers into BMW cars giving dealers the best chance to sell to them. People are pleasantly surprised that they drive the miles, and BMW donates the money, and this creates a 'soft sell' environment. It is obviously very attractive for a prospective purchaser – they will have arrived at the dealership in their own car and have an excellent opportunity to compare and contrast a variety of BMW models with their own vehicle, and feel good for every mile that they drive doing so.

The campaign has been regarded as a considerable success and BMW attribute 400 vehicle sales directly to the promotion. With BMW cars retailing at an average of between $40 000 and $50 000 this is obviously winning the company a very significant amount of revenue, enough to satisfy even the most hardened dealer. Thirty-five thousand people have test-driven a BMW via the programme to date so in the longer term there may well be further sales to come through the system.

At the same time over $1M was raised for the breast cancer charity and the relationship has been consolidated with a 2-year agreement with an objective of raising even more money and involving at least 40 000 people per year. Harder to quantify, but equally important, is the 'softer' imagery that will have been added to the BMW brand personality and the link in people's minds between what might have previously been seen as a hard or masculine image and something as personal as breast cancer with its more relevant appeal to women.

12

Charity or Cause?

Most of the Cause Related Marketing campaigns that have been carried out so far have been in conjunction with a charity. However there have been several which have been 'direct to the cause'. This dichotomy presents an interesting question for marketers. Is it better to partner with a charity or is it more appropriate to go straight to the cause? Is there a third 'hybrid' way of working?

Charity partnership

Starting with the charity partnership approach, there are clearly a number of advantages. First, in many cases, the charity will be a well-known brand or organization in its own right. It will have established its position in the 'market place' for the particular issue with which it is concerned. It will have credentials within, for example, the scientific community and perhaps even the government if it is working in an area of health concern, education, safety or the environment. It will have valuable on-the-ground experience if it is an environmental charity, as will others in different areas if they have local branches with grass roots support, such as the Samaritans in the UK or the battered women's refuges in the USA.

It is also quite likely that the charity will have a well-oiled fundraising machine, which can be partnered very effectively. Their marketing department can also share the task of developing the communication strategy with that of the company or brand management.

Many charities have very significant numbers of volunteers involved with them. For example, in the UK, the Samaritans have 20 355 volunteers. In the case of the NSPCC, in addition to 1500 staff members there are over 3000 fundraising committees, each comprising a minimum of three or four members. In the United States in the Red Cross there are 1.3 million volunteers nation-wide, and this situation repeats itself around the world. The Wesley Mission, one of Australia's largest caring organizations, has 1900 staff and 3500 volunteers.

Clearly there is a distinction to be made between activists and dormant supporters in establishing the real potential within a prospective charity partner. If they exist in large numbers, then these private volunteers and supporters of the charity can be a great resource as in effect a 'sales force' for both the charity and the brand in a partnership situation.

In partnering with a charity, therefore, the client organization or the marketing company is buying into a whole infrastructure, which is potentially extremely useful in developing the CRM campaign for the brand. At the same time, of course, the involvement of the brand and all its resources in terms of marketing muscle is extremely beneficial for the charity. An excellent example of the logistical benefits of such a relationship is the one between British Airways and UNICEF, the United Nations International Children's Emergency Fund.

Case History: BRITISH AIRWAYS: 'CHANGE FOR GOOD' WITH UNICEF

British Airways was re-positioned as 'The World's Favourite Airline' by Saatchi & Saatchi and is a brand that has been built with this positioning and some outstanding advertising to realize it in the consumer's mind. Perhaps one of the most famous images is that from the 'Global' commercial showing a huge army of people holding coloured cards turning into an image of the world through the use of choreography. This key visual from the commercial can be seen on p. 130.

As a global airline, BA by definition flies to all points of the compass and as such takes its passengers to many countries where large proportions of the population live in very poor conditions and often abject poverty. While it is clearly essential that BA continues to provide its passengers with outstanding service in terms of punctuality,

'The world's favourite airline.'

ground handling, in-flight service, quality of seating and entertainment, etc. it is also important that the airline conveys a sense of psychological comfort and well-being.

One of the ways of doing this is through Cause Related Marketing and to this end they have forged a long-term partnership with UNICEF, the international charity which started in 1946 in response to the aftermath of the Second World War.

UNICEF is a charity affiliated to the UN, but it receives no funding from it. It is the only UN-linked charity to be dedicated worldwide to the relief of the hardships facing young people. Its focus on children involves it in many different areas of related work, such as clean water and sanitation, health issues, women's issues, education and nutrition. It takes a long-term approach in tackling these problems along with also providing emergency relief where required. Working in over 160 countries world-wide it has a very good fit with a global player such as BA whose services reach well over 100 countries.

We have all had the experience of returning from a foreign trip

'Small change making a very big difference.'

and having loose change in a foreign currency in our pockets which is useless at home and also often unacceptable to bureaux de change or banks. British Airways and UNICEF have created a wonderful way of capturing these small amounts of money and putting them to excellent use.

Quite simply British Airways enables passengers to deposit foreign currency in envelopes in-flight, collects them and passes them on to UNICEF. The scheme is publicized via an in-flight video, back of seat cards and in-flight announcements. The feedback from the staff as they collect the money and become involved in the campaign is extremely positive. This is a living demonstration of the fact that BA is a caring airline. It is calculated that due to the exposure to the cause in this way, BA has been able to spread the word to over 100 million people who have flown with them. Even better, over £7M has been raised for UNICEF.

BA has also produced television broadcasts showing a child thanking BA for their contribution to the work that UNICEF do, which were aired during the last Christmas period. Apart from this however, due to the direct, physical, practical involvement of passengers and staff in the CRM campaign the communication through mass media such as television has not needed to be extensive, and as such this CRM campaign is one of the most cost effective there is.

Other good examples of such long-term partnerships between companies or brands and charities are as yet hard to identify. Given the relative newness of the concept of Cause Related Marketing there are just not that many case histories where we can see a relationship developing over time.

In the United States the Harley Davidson brand has been a key sponsor of the Muscular Dystrophy Association in that country, having supported them for 18 years. The link is clearly a powerful one in terms of 'Territory' as many victims of the disease can only get around in wheelchairs. This in a stark contrast to a motorcycle, one of the ultimate symbols of mobility.

This counterpoint has also been very relevant to Harley Davidson as an antidote to their 'Hells Angels' imagery and in broadening their customer franchise. However, it would not be true to say that this is a full-blown CRM campaign because Harley Davidson have taken a policy decision not to publicize their relationship actively beyond the considerable awareness generated by public relations and word of mouth, particularly at their massive city rallies.

In the United Kingdom there has been a partnership between Norwich Union and St John Ambulance for a couple of years and there have been relationships between Andrex and the Guide Dogs for the Blind, but neither of these has more than 2 years' history. It is very much to be hoped that as CRM gains momentum more of these partnerships will develop, and for the longer term.

There are however some potential downsides of working with a charity which the marketer and indeed the charity ought to be aware of.

First, there is the question of 'ownership'. In a partnership between two strong brands there is clearly going to be an issue as to who gets the credit for the CRM activity. Is it the brand or is it the charity? Is it clear to the consumer who is actually the prime mover in the action? Research data from the Norwich Union campaign with St John Ambulance (detailed in the case history) shows encouraging levels of awareness for Norwich

Union but awareness of St John Ambulance didn't change or was statistically insignificant.

Another question is that of clarity of policy making: if there are two strong marketing departments how are decisions made? Does the commercial organization and the charity elect one or other of their key people to be the project leader? Is a working party formed perhaps headed by a third party representative, for example from either one or other organizations, PR or advertising agencies or conceivably one that is brought in from outside who has no particular relationship to either party?

These are all important considerations and it is obviously worth resolving these issues as part of the process of developing the relationship in the first place: the advice of professionals working in the field is that the agreement should be negotiated as clearly as any other contract between commercial parties.

Direct to the cause

However, there is another way of approaching CRM and that is for the company or brands to identify a cause or an issue, on the same basis of common 'Territory' as with the charity partner, but the resulting action is for the commercial organization to take on the task itself.

There are some immediately obvious benefits from doing this. First, there does not need to be the management of a relationship with another organization with all that is entailed as has been outlined above. Secondly, when done well, there is absolutely clarity of 'ownership'. In terms of communication of brand names life is much easier – there is only one logo.

It is interesting to note that some of the most successful CRM campaigns so far have been ones where the corporation or brand has taken this approach. In the United States Liz Claiborne, a women's clothing company, identified the issue of domestic violence (primarily against women) as being a cause which it saw as being of powerful relevance to its largely female customer franchise.

The Liz Claiborne case history is one of the best available for practitioners to study and it is detailed fully later in this book. However, it is worth noting at this point that there was no single national branded charity in partnership on this now 8-year-old project, although Liz

Claiborne does work closely with local and regional groups such as the national 'Families Against Violence' coalition in Washington DC.

In the United Kingdom the single best known CRM campaign is that of the Tesco Computers for Schools programme.

This case history has been detailed earlier in the book but it is worth reiterating that Tesco have been running this campaign for 7 years and have helped deliver 34 000 computers to schools in the UK (by the end of 1997) without the need for a formal charity partnership. In the USA, a very similar project has been run in the past by the supermarket Giant where, cash register receipts could be turned in to earn computers for the school of your choice.

Another example in the educational area where the brand is going 'direct' to the cause is that of WHSmith and its initiative in reading for schools.

Case History:
WHSMITH: 'READY STEADY READ'

WHSmith is a very long established and powerful retail chain in the UK. It has 742 outlets, with the newsagent chain John Menzies, as well as owning Europe's largest internet bookseller The Internet Bookshop. They started as newsagents selling newspapers and magazines and early on expanded into books and then into other paper products. From there they went into writing instruments and thence to an increasingly wide range, now as broad as music CDs, tapes, videos and computer software.

However they have had to work hard to maintain their core business in an increasingly competitive market. At the same time specialist bookstores such as Dillons and the recently separated Waterstones, to say nothing of the Internet book marketers such as Amazon.com and the newly arrived Borders with its coffee bar and sofas culture have encroached on their market. Thus it is of great strategic importance that WHSmith reinforce its presence in its core brand values of education, and a Cause Related Marketing campaign has provided them with one element in this fight-back.

What is interesting about this CRM campaign is that it involves working with the Government, and in the context of the Saatchi & Saatchi Cause Connection co-funding initiative with the Department of Health, indicates that the New Labour administration is serious about public/voluntary/private partnership. WHSmith has teamed up with the Department for Education and Employment and the Scottish, Welsh and Northern Irish Offices and entered into a 5-year commitment to provide books for schools in 'difficult' areas of the country, with a specific target of 400 primary schools. The idea is to provide that cohort of pupils with the books they will require for each year of their school career. Thus at the end of the process WHSmith will have provided the complete array of reading materials that are required for each scholastic year in each target school.

WHSMITH GROUP

READY STEADY READ!

PUTTING BOOKS INTO THE
HANDS OF 75,000 CHILDREN

'Reinforcing core values.'

Teachers and children are effectively compiling the ideal list of books and the benefit to them is an increased level of literacy. Of course, as WHSmith is a major supplier of books this is also of long-term benefit to them. The programme will give WHSmith an inside track into what is regarded as good reading for school age children and also provides links between them and the local purchasers of books in the business to business market.

But perhaps most importantly WHSmith are now getting an excellent understanding of which books to market at a retail level and thus to optimize their sales. The scheme also gains them better relations with the Government. It is hard to quantify the precise value of the latter, but any retailer on the scale of WHSmith is inevitably going to be involved with planning applications, mergers & acquisition discussions, and issues such as the national curriculum. There are many Government related issues which have potentially important implications for their business.

The current campaign runs until the year 2001 and there is a joint research programme with the Government in place to assess the scheme and in particular how much levels of literacy will have been improved. It is also interesting to note that, like Tesco, WHSmith has the authority as a brand to go direct to a cause without a charity to control the scheme for them and give them an automatic image lent by the charity's own branding.

In the same vein, SmithKline Beecham have declared from the head of the organization, Jan Leschly, downwards that a fundamental part of their corporate mission is to help eradicate lymphatic filariasis, caused by a parasite carried by mosquitoes and which leads to the dreadful disease elephantiasis. This grotesquely disfiguring illness afflicts literally millions of people every year, and most of them already live in conditions of great poverty.

It is too early in the programme to say definitely, but it seems very likely that because SmithKline Beecham have identified elephantiasis as their cause and are intending to kill it through a cocktail of three drugs, of which they provide one, albendazole, that the 'credit' for the initiative, and hopefully the achievement of the objective, will accrue to them.

Of course it is very probable that they will enlist the help of local agencies in carrying out the programme and no doubt there will be some charities and other voluntary organizations involved. Indeed, they are already cooperating with the World Health Organization, but the point remains that SmithKline Beecham will be seen to be the unequivocal owners of the campaign.

In assessing the 'direct' option there are also some downsides to consider. Clearly the commercial organization is going to have to commit additional resources in setting up effectively an in-house charity. This is not as simple as it might seem. A culture composed of commercial managers and employees used to working in a purely business environment does not necessarily contain the right people. They may lack the necessary altruism or commitment to a non-commercial activity to drive a CRM programme with the burning energy that will be required, often in the face of very difficult conditions.

There is also the cost to consider. Most companies in Westernized economies are busy trying to reduce headcount rather than build it up. Stock markets usually react badly to increases in overheads without a direct increase in revenues and profits to match. Leasing of capital equipment and the outsourcing of many corporate functions has become widespread in an attempt to make balance sheets and cash flows look as good as possible.

Another benefit of working with a charity partner, apart from the obvious ones of expertise and resources is that in some ways it may act as a buffer or an insulator between the corporation or the brand and any potential negative PR that may arise along the way.

Clearly, in developing the relationship any skeletons will have to be taken out of the respective cupboards of commercial company and charity. Alan Andreasen, in 'Profits for Nonprofits: Find a Corporate Partner' (*Harvard Business Review*, November–December 1996), recounts the case of a children's clothing manufacturer who set up a joint campaign against child abuse with a national child welfare foundation. Six weeks into the campaign, the manufacturers were accused by a human rights organization of using sweatshops and child labour to make their clothes in developing countries, and the campaign collapsed.

Even if all such 'skeletons' are avoided, as in any relationship there are bound to be some rocky moments. If in a hypothetical situation there was some negative PR to do with the CRM campaign then the presence of a charity partner to field press enquiries, and, frankly, to take some of the flak, can be of great benefit to the preservation of the corporate or brand reputation.

Another consideration is the relative strength of the brands involved. If the corporation or the brand is a very powerful one and has levels of authority and credibility near the top, then clearly it will have the status, prestige and perceived resources to be able to tackle even the most difficult cause on its own. By the same token, a brand which is slightly weaker in an overall sense, despite its particular strengths within its market or its niche, may find it more credible and more likely to add the desired brand values if it partners with a charity brand which might be seen as stronger in the public eye.

In the case of Tesco and SmithKline Beecham the former is clearly the case. What is interesting about Liz Claiborne is that it is very likely that there would have been charities in America which would have had greater brand awareness than the retailer itself. But in taking the risk of adopting domestic violence as its cause the company rolled the dice and won with a campaign, which has done a significant amount to boost its reputation.

Hybrid

The third option which marketers could consider is a hybrid between the either/or options of partnering with an existing big charity brand or going direct to the cause. This is for a company to identify a very small charity, which nevertheless has a nucleus of talented and committed people, and put its corporate arm and resources around it and help to build it up. Or, in a similar way, to identify a cause, which may as yet not have a formal charity associated with it and actually to stimulate the formation of one in order to become a focus for fundraising, campaigning and, of course, branding. A third option is to partner with a major charity and create a special programme.

Approaching CRM through this hybrid route could give the corporate all the benefits of 'ownership' plus the brand insulation of a separate charity as the interface with the cause.

The case of Dollond & Aitchison, the UK eyewear retailer and charity Help The Aged partnering in a special tailor-made programme called World in Sight, effectively a cause 'sub-brand', is a good example of this 'hybrid' route.

Case History: DOLLOND & AITCHISON: 'WORLD IN SIGHT'

The UK market for eyewear has become intensely competitive in recent years. There are now a number of major chains battling it out for market share in the high street and one of these is Dollond & Aitchison. This retail chain is a long-standing brand and had suffered from a rather old-fashioned and traditional image in contrast to some of the newer players such as SpecSavers, SpecialEyes and

Vision Express, to say nothing of a rejuvenated Boots with its Boots Opticians chain.

Discounting is rife in this market place and retailers have to work extremely hard in order to retain their margins. There is also a tendency for the market to go towards commodity because of the vast number of outlets selling remarkably similar ranges of styles.

Dollond & Aitchison's objectives therefore were to increase customer footfall, improve the price points at which products were sold and continue to refresh its brand image as a contemporary eyewear retailer.

Good vision is one of our most important gifts and it is a highly emotive issue if it becomes impaired in any way. Dollond & Aitchison perceived the potential power of this in developing its Cause Related Marketing campaign in association with Help the Aged. They have been running the campaign for about 7 years now with publicity in-store showing how Dollond & Aitchison customers can help those in developing countries through the scheme called 'World in Sight'.

The idea is that customers should bring their old glasses into Dollond & Aitchison shops to be recycled to other people. The glasses are actually sorted by prisoners, on a voluntary basis, into various classes of prescription and are then distributed to people with sight problems in the Third World. For most of the time the scheme has been running its focus has been directed towards motivating staff and reaffirming Dollond & Aitchison's reputation for work in health areas, in which it has been successful.

This year Dollond & Aitchison decided to rejuvenate the campaign, realizing that they were not getting all that they could out of the scheme in terms of sales, branding and the number of glasses recycled. For a 4-week period they ran a discount offer as a reward on the handing-in of old glasses, supported with an advertising campaign and large direct mail hits. The offer gave £10 off for purchases of glasses up to £99.99, £20 off for purchases between £100 and £199.99 and a full £50 off the asking price for glasses £200 and above. The promotion was a resounding success, and during the promotional period one in six customers actually participated in the campaign.

Rewardingly for Dollond & Aitchison the customers who joined in tended to spend all the money that they had saved by buying more expensive glasses, with a consequent improvement in margin for the retailer. The campaign has been promoted heavily with advertisements in the national press – an example of which is reproduced below – and with posters in the windows of branches, many of which have had a display taking up the whole of the available space.

'A far-sighted campaign for an eyewear retailer.'

The campaign has been very enthusiastically received by staff and again this has boosted the effort. It has been very hard to be precise about the level of sales improvement but it has been judged a success and there is a long-term commitment to use this Cause Related Marketing campaign to increase business, especially during quieter times of the year. It has created positive PR coverage for Dollond & Aitchison and, perhaps equally importantly, more than 750 000 pairs of glasses have been distributed to people who would otherwise have never have been able to afford them – truly the gift of sight.

PART V
Creating a CRM Campaign

Summary

Entering into a CRM campaign is not something to be taken lightly. Given the nature of the commitment that will be required and the degree of involvement of the company at all levels, it is clearly essential that there is 'buy-in' at the top of the corporation. By the same token, identifying an appropriate charity partner or good cause with which to associate the company or brand is a serious business. The search needs to be carried out as thoroughly and professionally as that for any other strategic business partner, and should culminate in a formal agreement or contract governing the relationship.

In doing this the company will be embarking on a process with potentially great benefits for their brand, but also potential risks. The best way to maximize the former and minimize the latter is to ensure that there is the best possible 'fit' between the desired brand values and those which will accrue to it via the association with the chosen charity or cause. Using the technique of identifying shared 'Territories', aided by the creative use of exploratory qualitative research, is an effective way to achieve this synergy.

Ensuring a strong, clear leadership of the CRM campaign is an important contributor to success. The source of responsibility and funding for charitable donations and projects has traditionally been close to the Chairman's or CEO's office, i.e. the Corporate Affairs or Community Relations Departments, and this gives them a valid claim for that leadership. However, given the emerging strategic importance of this area for brands, there are strong arguments for that accountability to be transferred to the usual guardians of the company's branded assets, namely the Marketing Departmental.

In forging a powerful relationship between the company and its charity partner, there are a wide range of means by which that can be achieved and all of which must be systematically explored and exploited to mutual benefit. Areas such as the level of corporate donations, advertising and communications expenditure, engagement of employees and charity supporters in volunteering, third-party support from suppliers or government, benefits in kind, special products and celebrity endorsement can all do their part in constructing a truly rounded and effective CRM campaign.

Clearly a Cause Related Marketing campaign is no different from any other when it comes to the communications planning aspects. The use of exploratory qualitative research and quantitative studies to give clarity on the target audience to be addressed, the key messages to be conveyed and the most appropriate media channels to be used are all familiar marketing disciplines. The use of the 'Temple', the 'Logic Train' and other planning tools can facilitate this process as they do for conventional campaign development.

It is essential that the exposure of a brand's CRM campaign is consonant with the rest of its communications. Consumers are affected by the 'corporate body language' of brands in their use of media and their executional styles. New media such as the Internet also present the marketer with exciting new channels of communication: the standard TV spot or press ad is no longer the only answer.

PR is normally one of the most potent elements of a Cause Related Marketing effort and in order for this to continue to be the case it is essential for the campaign to remain newsworthy. The eight-year-old Liz Claiborne programme to combat domestic violence in the USA is an excellent example of how this can be achieved over time.

Measurement is always a prime factor in any marketing campaign and CRM is no exception. Most of the case histories that currently exist have focused on sales results. This is entirely valid, but only tells part of the story. In one or two cases, there are awareness and attitudinal data which start to explore the impact on the brand in image terms. In the long term this must become an essential part of any proper programme. The results of the Co-op Bank staff survey are a good example of this.

13

Preliminary Stages in Developing a CRM Campaign

There are essentially three key preliminary stages in the development of a CRM campaign. These are listed in order below:

1. Commitment
2. Due diligence
3. Contract negotiation

Understanding the full scope of the mutual value in a CRM relationship is clearly a detailed and potentially demanding exercise. Self-evidently it is not worth going into such detail until it is clear in broad principle that the parties are interested in such a relationship. Only when these preliminary stages have been gone through can the executional processes of establishing the 'Territory' and developing the fully rounded CRM campaign in creative and media planning terms begin with confidence.

It may be that some marketers decide to pursue these preliminary stages in parallel with the executional ones. However, the risk is that a great deal of time and effort may be wasted both internally at the middle management levels, and externally with communications agencies and charities if, for example, top management commitment has not been obtained up-front and is subsequently not forthcoming.

Commitment

As we have seen, the first and most obvious stage in the process is for the corporation or brand owner to commit itself to the idea of Cause Related Marketing. This entails an understanding of the potential benefits of adding 'spirit' to the existing brand values but also some of the implications such as longevity of relationship and allocation of resources.

It is clearly absolutely essential that there be 'buy-in' at the top levels of management of the company. Ideally the chief executive or the chairman should be personally committed to the idea because there is nothing more powerful than leadership from the very top of the organization. However, it is important that there is a broader base of support at board level than simply one individual, no matter how senior. Given that top-level changes seem inevitable in the contemporary management scene it is important for the sake of longevity of the relationship that it should not founder when its sole sponsor departs the company.

Looking at the situation from the perspective of the charity, an almost mirror image process can be envisaged. Many charities, especially the larger, longer established, and more professional ones, have a very valuable brand asset, which they need to protect. They also have a very important cause to promote. They should therefore approach the selection of a potential CRM partner, or, equally, respond to the approaches of potential partners, with some initial caution.

It has become a feature of modern marketing life that many companies' marketing directors change with alarming frequency. The latest data from the UK trade magazine 'Marketing' suggests that the average tenure of the role of marketing director is as short as 18 months. Except in the most disciplined companies and those with the strongest culture, there is a strong tendency for each new incumbent of this vital role to want to stamp his or her own personality on it.

The quickest and most dramatic way of doing this, at least for the gathering of trade press headlines, and perhaps an extra entry on a CV, is to review the communications strategy and the agencies which act on behalf of the client. In far too many cases this leads to a call for a review and resultant changes. These changes are rarely brought about by an objective analysis of the performance of the campaign, which leads to the conclusion that it is ineffective in some degree and needs to be made more efficacious. The brand is therefore subjected to a zigzag path through life with a lack of coherence to its personality and a lack of clarity of positioning in the consumer mind.

There are those who would argue that there is an underlying strategic continuity through these processes and that it is merely an executional change that is being sought. But consumer research usually indicates that the public is much more affected by changes of advertising style and execution, which are taken to be indicative of changes of personality in the brand, and is much less bothered about hidden aspects of 'strategy'.

What all this means from the charities' point of view is that potential partners' history in terms of their brand communications behaviour is likely to be indicative of their future behaviour in a CRM partnership with them – the short termists are likely to remain that way.

The consumer research from Worthington Di Marzio ('Consumers, The Community and Business', The New Bottom Line, for Cavill + Co., Australia, 1997) suggests that one of the key elements in a successful CRM campaign is longevity and continuity. The Worthington Di Marzio survey found that 13% of consumers felt that duration devoted to a cause by a corporate proved the corporate's commitment to that cause, third in importance behind the necessity to show tangible results (25%) and media publicity (23%). Therefore the charity or voluntary organization should beware of marketing companies which look to be habitual quick-fixers and the sort of brands which are in the habit of changing tack every couple of years or so.

Building a relationship is not something to be entered into lightly. There is an enormous investment from both parties. If the relationship gets off on the right foot, i.e. the parties have done a thorough mutual assessment, then they can embark on the process of reciprocal involvement in a way that builds a truly integrated and deep understanding of each other.

The two organizations can become enmeshed in the particular area of joint enterprise and the longer and deeper the ties go between them the more robust the relationship will be. More importantly, the more meaningful the relationship is seen to be by the brand's consumers, and the charity's supporters, the more likely the relationship will go from strength to strength over time. It is very important to avoid the perception in the consumer mind that a CRM relationship is exploitative and this is very hard to avoid if it is a short-term one.

However it would be overly optimistic to think that CRM relationships between organizations can be forever – commercial realities probably prohibit that. Therefore it becomes important to be candid about the respective organizations' objectives and a perceived timescale at the outset, and it is important for each party to manage not only their own but also their public's expectations.

It probably would be better to declare at the outset that a relationship is to last for a finite time period, for example 3 to 5 years, rather than to lead everyone concerned to believe that it is forever and then to terminate prematurely. Setting a medium-term target of this sort still leaves both organizations with the mutual opportunity to extend if the partnership seems to be rewarding.

Another benefit of setting a timescale for the relationship is that it also enables the setting of mutually agreed targets. Consumer research indicates that one of the most powerful dimensions of the communication of a CRM campaign is the public commitment of an organization, with its partner charity, to a goal which it is declaring its intention of achieving. There is clearly nothing wrong with setting the goal within the context of the timescale so that it is both achievable but also credible in brand terms.

There are those who feel that a short-term relationship is of merit but it is our view that short termism has few benefits and many disadvantages. The disadvantages are that it may engender consumer cynicism and it certainly inhibits the development of a full relationship between two organizations. How can a consumer be expected to believe that a brand really believes in something if it is only prepared to vouch for this belief for a year or even less?

It is also interesting to note that one of the main questions that a marketer will ask of an agency when a new creative idea for advertising their brand is presented is how 'campaignable' that idea is likely to be. It is not at all uncommon for a client to require an agency to demonstrate campaignability over a period of 2, 3 or even 5 years. Quite rightly, the marketer wants to see how the brand personality will evolve over time and to ensure that the creative idea is not a one-off which will immediately lead to an apparent change in execution, and therefore an apparent change in strategy, a year or so hence.

By the same token a CRM relationship should be seen as 'campaign-able' and, as in the case of Liz Claiborne and the campaign against domestic violence, an idea that can be developed over time and evolved to maintain its news value and its relevance to different aspects of the cause.

Due diligence

Having made the decision in principle that a brand would benefit from a CRM campaign, there is then the task of identifying likely candidates, either charities or causes. This is a key part of the process and one which should either be given to a clearly defined sub-group within the multi-disciplinary project team or sub-contracted to a specialist communications agency.

The essence of the due diligence process in a CRM context lies in identifying a company or brand and a charity or cause which share enough common ground to make the basis of a long-term and mutually beneficial relationship. The analogy of marriage is often used in the CRM context and it may be useful to keep that in mind during the process of due diligence.

Obviously in marriage the most important criterion is whether or not the two partners are in love and have enough in common with each other to sustain a long-term relationship with its ups and downs. But as those who know about marriages are aware, when one person marries the other they don't just marry that individual, they marry into their respective families, social circles and indeed to a large degree their respective careers.

This is also true of the relationship between a brand and a charity.

There is the core relationship between the two with its dependence on shared goals and visions of the future. But there are also a cluster of third parties and a network of other relationships with which each party inevitably become enmeshed. It is important to understand the ramifications of these 'in-laws' and to ensure that both parties are comfortable with them.

Turning to outside suppliers of services to the marketing department, there are obviously quite a large number of agencies that may be able to help in the process of the identification of potential CRM partners. Advertising, sales promotion, sponsorship, direct marketing, design and public relations agencies are all theoretically useful sources of inspiration. However, as in all relationship building programmes it is essential that the process is managed.

The corporate 'body language', when it comes to negotiations of this sort, can be very influential in whether or not a relationship subsequently comes to fruition. There are few things more off-putting to a potential partner than a series of apparently uncoordinated and random approaches from several different intermediaries all coming within a week or two of each other.

The best advice to the marketing department is to act as 'point man' in the process and ensure that all approaches are made only by the company. The alternative is to mandate the task to one 'lead' agency and make it clear to the other communications agencies retained by the company who it is and who should make the approaches required in the search process. Clearly the criteria for this appointment should be fairly self-evident but it is worth restating the need for a full strategic understanding of the brand and its objectives, and a thorough comprehension of the concept of CRM and the need for strategic 'fit' between company and cause.

In any courtship the person or organization being courted likes to feel that they are special. If there is a sense that a shotgun approach is being used then clearly that sense of 'specialness' cannot be achieved. The best advice is for a great deal of work to be done internally, and in discussion with advising communications agencies, which would result in a very clear brief for the CRM partner and a very short list of desirable candidates.

These should be thoroughly researched with as much background information and data as possible being assembled on each charity. Fortunately, most voluntary organizations are more than happy to provide documentation, leaflets and annual reports to enquirers and this will give a large part of the picture. It is also worth talking to volunteers who support the charity and perhaps even some beneficiaries, on a strictly anonymous basis. There may also be technical aspects to the charity's activity and it is useful to read some of the relevant trade journals in order to gain an understanding of the full extent of their good works.

In the process of developing a CRM relationship a lot of emphasis should be put on the positive side of the equation, namely in assessing the mutual value of the 'assets' that each side can bring to the party. However, an important part in the building of any relationship is understanding the potential down-side.

This process requires a high level of transparency and honesty from both parties. Starting with the charity, it is absolutely essential that the organization's full agenda is visible. It is reasonably often the case that charities have within them some supporters who are well-meaning, but who may harbour differing views about the core issue with which they are engaged.

For example, there have been reports suggesting that the highly respected and long-standing charity in the UK, the RSPCA (Royal Society for the Prevention of Cruelty to Animals), has been targeted by elements of the animal rights movement. This activist grouping has tended to be at odds with the mass of its membership because their private agenda is to move the charity's objectives towards areas which are too radical for many people. Fortunately they have been sidelined.

The Royal Society for the Protection of Birds has, for some time, recognized that some of its million plus members are unclear about the work which they support. A proportion of its members believe the RSPB to be an animal welfare organization, running bird hospitals and protecting garden birds (the bird equivalent of the RSPCA). These members are surprised to discover that the RSPB is a science-based conservation group, heavily involved with influencing national and European government policies. Some members also feel that some of the RSPB's actions to benefit bird conservation (such as the control of red deer to allow regeneration of pinewoods and the killing of foxes and crows on some of its nature reserves) are at odds with the aims of a 'bird protection' organization. Others find it difficult to understand why the RSPB does not oppose sustainable field sports. In response to the confusion over branding, the RSPB is currently working on a 'Mind the Gap' project.

For several years, members of the National Trust have presented motions at Annual General Meetings to ban all hunting on National Trust land. Although these were defeated, in 1994 a members' resolution was passed calling on the council of the National Trust to address issues of animal welfare, and they therefore commissioned a study from Professor Bateson of Cambridge University into the effects of deer hunting on both the land and the animals.

The study revealed that the hunting of deer causes great distress to the animals and as a result, in October 1997, the decision was taken not to renew licences for deer hunting on National Trust land. This issue was a divisive one, setting pro- and anti-hunting lobbies against each other, and several pro-hunting members felt strongly enough to resign from the Trust. The strength of feeling involved is demonstrated by a member's letter to *The Spectator* (29th August 1998) where he refers to resignations in protest at the anti-hunting moves as 'playing into the hands of the loonies'. However the Trust's decision was again upheld overwhelmingly at their AGM in Cardiff in November 1998.

The black and white rights and wrongs in each of these cases can never be ascertained – there are always shades of grey. But what all this means is that the company, or its agent, needs to ask not the first or second, but the third and fourth questions about the deeper philosophical concerns of the charity in order to assess the potential risk for fundamental disagreements and adverse publicity. What is the full range of views contained within the organization? Are there any areas with which the company may be uncomfortable? How does the leadership of the charity see the way forward over the timescale of the CRM programme? Do they anticipate any significant changes in policy?

Turning to the potential 'skeletons' that may lie in the corporate cupboard, it is essential that the company management puts itself in the cynical shoes of an outside observer and inspects their potential list of liabilities.

For example, does support of the particular charity being considered for partnership raise questions about the company's own policies, either towards its employees or towards its suppliers? Look at the damage that seems to have been done to the Nike brand image by the allegations of employing underpaid and underage labour in developing countries.

We referred earlier to the children's clothing company example in *Harvard Business Review*; another volte-face was caused by Oxfam's discovery that the innocent-sounding biscuit brand they were considering a partnership with was owned by a munitions company!

It would obviously be very embarrassing for a major corporation to become involved with an environmental charity and then for it to be exposed as a significant polluter of its own backyard or indeed the globe.

This does not necessarily mean, as Jonathan Porritt and Sara Parkin former Green Party leaders, and now of Forum for the Future have argued, that a given corporate has to be absolutely 100% perfect and squeaky clean before it can make any claims in these sorts of areas. What is absolutely crucial is that there is transparency and a genuine belief, not just in the letter, but in the spirit of the cause. Forum for the Future, a leading proponent of the philosophy of 'sustainability', i.e. the use of replaceable resources in industry, appreciate that in the politics of the real world it is more important for major corporations to be genuinely working towards these kinds of solutions rather than to claim in a facile way that they have already achieved them.

Admitting weaknesses up front can be both disarming of critics and galvanizing for the organization. Having an internal target for housecleaning can be part and parcel of building a deep CRM relationship.

No doubt in this mutual appraisal there will be some issues which are sensitive to either party – it would be very odd if there were not. However, as in a personal relationship, acknowledgement that these issues exist and then a sensible and mature agreement as to how they're going to be addressed is the key to success. In doing this a leaf needs to be taken out of the 'crisis management' book.

It is very useful to act out a 'devil's advocate' role-play with a third-party moderator taking the part of an aggressive investigative journalist in order to test the position statements that the corporation and the charity will make in certain circumstances. In going through this process the relationship and its potential to come to fruition will be tested. But again, surely it is better for it to be tested privately rather than in public once major commitments have been made? Because so much of the value of brands is in their public perception (and in many cases we are clearly talking about two brands – that owned by the company, and that owned by the charity) these practical issues need to be very carefully considered.

The reputation of a brand can so easily be damaged by an embarrassing revelation of the sort outlined above. Fortunately, so far in the history of CRM, there have been very few cases where there has been a public falling out among partners. Apart from the Johnson & Johnson and Arthritis Foundation case in the USA, Sunbeam Corp., a cosmetics company, is suing the American Medical Association after they pulled out of a CRM partnership on skin cancer fearing a conflict of interests.

Sunbeam's view was that a commitment had been made, regardless of whether the AMA was attracting criticism for the partnership.

In a similar area in a comparable but more mature field, namely that of affinity branding in credit cards, there have been high profile legal actions in the United States: for example, that between BJ's Wholesale Club and Beneficial Bank with consequent negative effects on their respective images and customer bases. The moral of the story is clear: 'look before you leap'. Divorce can be a messy and expensive thing and the children, (consumers and others) can be seriously hurt in the process.

Contract negotiation

This process is an important one. Most practitioners agree that it is necessary to have a signed agreement between the company and the charity, which sets out the respective commitments and obligations of each party.

There is clearly the potential for an expensive legal field day in developing these agreements and in an ideal world this should be avoided. One way of doing this is to recognize that these sorts of agreements are in fact very similar to the agreements that advertisers have traditionally had with their advertising agencies and in these agreements there are in reality very few material clauses.

The first of these concerns money and it is important that the company or brand in particular states their financial commitment to the relationship in an unequivocal way. Given that the typical marketing budget is no more than annual in length it may be difficult to give precise figures for more than the first year of the CRM relationship, but it should be possible to give guarantees of minimum spends for a longer time period. It may even be better to have the question of financial support in its many manifestations detailed in a side letter to the contract, which can be reviewed and updated on an annual basis, as marketing budgets are confirmed.

The second key dimension is that of time. The agreement should set out very clearly what the minimum relationship period should be and also provision for notice on either side. With regard to duration, the relative newness of the CRM concept and the paucity of real examples makes it hard to be prescriptive about the optimum period for such a contract. However, in an ideal world it should be for an initial period of at least 2 years and preferably three. Many of the most successful campaigns such as Avon's against breast cancer, Liz Claiborne's against domestic violence and American Express' against hunger have run for 6 years or more in the USA. The best known example of CRM in the UK, namely the Tesco Computers for Schools programme, has now been running for 7 years.

This time period should certainly bridge more than the life span of a single vice president for marketing and thus will militate against the Pavlovian response of a new incumbent to change his or her predecessor's plans. Two to three years will also give the programme enough time to become fully developed and for the relationship to become truly embedded.

Given the complexities of building the relationship and the potential for adverse public relations in the context of a withdrawal, it is recommended that a longer notice period be given than is often found in marketing agreements – at least 6 months and ideally nine. This will give time for either party to exit gracefully and, perhaps more importantly, to develop new partnerships. It is also worth building into the agreement mandatory reviews of the relationship, possibly conducted by an agreed third party, on a regular basis, at least annually and preferably every 6 months.

On balance then, our recommendation would be to go for a relatively simple and straightforward contract; however, there may well be companies with organizational cultures which require much more detailed and specific ones. These more elaborate documents may well give apparent comfort at the time of their negotiation but it is unlikely whether in the real world they will be of much additional benefit. If the relationship breaks down, no amount of legal paperwork is going to repair it.

14

Establishing the 'Territory'

One of the most fundamentally important aspects of brand marketing is defining what Saatchi & Saatchi has termed the 'Territory' in which the brand will sit, that is to say, the 'ground' in which the 'brand's personality' will stand and from which its fully rounded character will develop.

The strongest brands tend to have a clear and simple territory that is easy to see in their communication. For example, Castlemaine XXXX lager own 'Authentic Australian', and Pampers own 'Happy Babies'.

Our belief is that identifying the 'Territory' is fundamental to creating the brand's positioning; once we understand what that is, the rest of the communications programme will follow, as indeed should other fundamentals such as new product development (NPD) and packaging development. In our experience, clear and compelling 'Territories' are fundamental to building powerful and enduring brands and campaigns.

How do we arrive at a 'Territory'?

We arrive at these 'Territories' through a combination of:

1. Understanding *Product Truths*
2. Having *Consumer Insights*
3. Empathising with the *Brand Character*

There are three components to the 'Territory', the Product Truth, the Consumer Insight and the Brand Character. The process of developing a

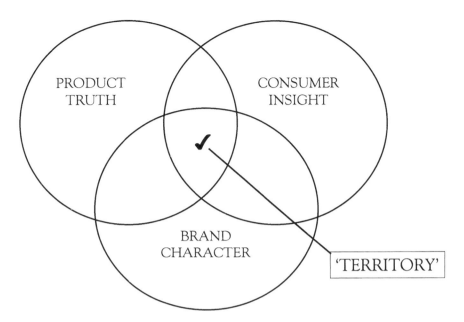

'Territory – a fundamental to positioning.'

'Territory' is of developing and synthesizing a key aspect for each of these three areas.

It is important to recognize that these components of a 'Territory' can come from anywhere and thus it is critical that we are prepared to look everywhere to uncover them.

Product Truth

In the case of Product Truth a huge amount of detective work is required in order genuinely to understand what it is about the product or service that is truly distinctive and on which the rational elements of a claim may be made. As Robin Wight of WCRS has said 'we need to interrogate the product until it confesses to its strengths'. Taken on its own, this is the methodology which leads to the 'USP' and if the process stops there then the type of advertising communication that results tends to be targeted at the left-hand brain and, while compelling in many cases, usually lacks any real emotional reward.

The answer to Product Truth may lie in a pile of data; so it is important to be rigorous in the inspection of all the available quantitative information about the brand. Marketers and their agency should strive to be inventive in the specification of further special analysis or original research in order to unearth revealing patterns of consumer behaviour or attitudinal traits.

Pedantic reviews of competitive activity can be very productive – what language, casting, settings and symbolism are the opposition using? Can an opportunity be seen in something missing in a competitive reel of TV commercials in the context of the team's understanding of the market? Can something important about the product be found that others have overlooked; perhaps by talking to a factory worker; an NPD manager, a salesperson or a customer services executive? Are there sidelights from experience in other markets overseas? How does the product *really* perform against its competition?

Consumer Insight

Achieving a really compelling Consumer Insight is usually just as difficult. While quantitative data needs to be scrutinized and cross-analysed in the search for the needle in the haystack with which a key insight can be stitched together, more often than not qualitative research is the route to gaining the kind of clues that are needed. A chance remark by a respondent in a group discussion or a suggestion made at the end of an in-depth interview can be just the springboard that is needed to a genuinely exciting piece of consumer understanding. Being innovative in the choice of sample and research technique can lead to even greater insight.

For example you can recruit respondents who are regular users and *starve* them of your product category before talking to them. Perhaps in this way you can dig deeper into the psyche of the sector. Talking to *fervent rejectors* of your brand for a change can produce the stark contrasts with the attitudes of brand loyalists from which true insights may spring.

Going beyond the conventional format in the conducting of a focus group can sometimes help a great deal. For example, in a piece of exploratory qualitative research for a watch company, respondents were asked to bring their partner's watch with them as well as their own. They were also asked to swap watches temporarily with other people in the group. The effect of this was striking: it revealed the deep emotions that consumers have about their timepieces and the enormous significance they have for them. Functional, rational values are way down the pecking order in this product category.

In another piece of NPD work for a soap manufacturer the solution to a tricky positioning problem concerning a new product with skin care properties was solved almost before the focus group began. Previously the concept had failed using conventional qualitative research techniques despite its objective performance benefits, so this time a new methodology was used. Respondents were asked to wash their hands before the discussion began and each in turn visited the washroom outside the room in which the focus group was taking place: unbeknown to them a sample of the new product had been placed beside the basin!

One by one each woman left the room to return a few moments later to rejoin the group. The moderators were looking hard at their 'body language', and sure enough each person who had washed their hands was observed to be rubbing their hands together in a pleasurable way. Once everyone had paid their visit to the washroom they were asked about how their hands felt. The opinion was unanimous – wonderfully soft and smooth. However, as soon as the potential new product was referred to as 'soap' the consumers refused to accept that it could have the properties they had just experienced. The realization was clear: the word 'soap' carried with it too much 'baggage' to be capable of being used effectively to describe the new product. The positioning solution was to develop the new language of the 'wash bar' to communicate the skin care benefits.

The relevance of this in creating a CRM campaign is that innovative research methodologies such as these may be invaluable in enabling consumers to reveal their innermost feelings about such personal issues as charity, transparency and ethics. They may also be useful in achieving the sort of creative breakthrough that could become the basis of a great CRM idea for the brand. Juxtaposing a range of charity collecting boxes with the packaging of the brand could produce some enlightening reactions to potential partnerships.

Once the Consumer Insight has been generated the marketer has usually arrived at the basis for the emotional aspects of the brand position and obviously in an ideal world there would be clear linkage already or potentially between the Consumer Insight and the Product Truth.

Brand Character

In the case of a new product development, the Brand Character clearly needs to be created, and given that it is a blank sheet of paper it can be constructed quite precisely to fit Product Truth and Consumer Insight.

However, in the majority of cases the brand already exists, has a complex heritage and contains different strands within its personality, which can be enhanced or suppressed in communication terms. Again the trick is to identify within the Brand Character elements which can be combined with Product Truth and Consumer Insight to create a coherent position.

We know that consumers tend to be anthropomorphic about brands. They can describe inanimate products and services in human terms, talking about their practical abilities, personality attributes and imagery as easily as if they were describing a family member or friend. Whilst the practical and emotional aspects of Brand Character remain fundamentally important to consumers, increasingly they are interested in other 'higher order' values of a brand, for example, its position in the community and society, and its ethics or 'beliefs'.

In expanding and rounding out Brand Character in order to encompass 'beliefs' and form a basis for CRM it is worth asking again the basic questions about the brand. What is there about the history or heritage of the company or brand which is interesting and motivating to its existing or potential customer base? Does it have any national or regional characteristics which connote positive (or negative) thoughts? Is it seen as a 'female' or 'male' brand? Does its packaging or presentation format fit with or contrast against the 'norms' in its market?

Are modernity, innovation and creativity its core strengths or are more traditional values its forte? Is its corporate parentage big and anonymous or small, familial and friendly? Is there an eponymous founder still alive and if so can he or she be used in communication terms? If dead, can he or she be resurrected? Is there something in the brand's past, whether it be a descriptor or image from packaging or advertising, which was dropped for good reason, but whose time has come again? Thorough brand 'archaeology' can reveal hidden assets.

'Territory'

Having defined an area for our brand, which makes a coherent link between the key elements of Product Truth, Consumer Insight and Brand Character, we must always ask ourselves, 'Will owning this "Territory" really build business for the brand? Is it competitive and differentiating? Is it motivating? Is it defensible? Will it really make a difference?'

It is likely that a good brand has already established its 'Territory' in order to market itself successfully. So if the marketer wants to give the brand a 'spirit' via a CRM campaign it is obvious that this must fit with the rest of the personality and be a seamless extension and amplification of it.

Assuming that the brand 'Territory' is clearly identified then the process of developing a Cause Related Marketing campaign and thereby adding a 'Belief System' is to find a charity or a cause whose 'Territory' is the best possible fit with that of the brand.

While the larger charities, which have sophisticated marketing departments, do have a pretty clear idea of who they are and where they are going, many of the small to medium sized voluntary organizations may be less focused. They have often not been through the process of defining their 'Territory' in as rigorous a way as is required in order to produce a satisfactory match with a commercial organization. Many of them may have too many issues on their agenda and a lack of clarity as to what their priorities really are. It is almost certain that a halo effect of the development of CRM is that more and more charities will focus on their own brand personality and come to a better understanding of it and become more effective campaigning organizations as a result.

15

Developing a CRM Concept

Brands are very valuable concepts. Recently VW sold the Rolls-Royce brand name to BMW for £40 000 000. The price did not include any physical assets, only the intellectual property rights to the Rolls-Royce name and logo. This is but the latest in a series of demonstrations of the value of branded assets to companies. Any responsible chief executive will therefore ensure that anything that may affect the corporation's branded assets will be very carefully scrutinized before it is embarked upon.

As an aside it is astonishing how often chief executives allow relatively junior marketing managers to make far-reaching decisions about the communications of their brand's values to their public without recourse to top management approval.

In the case of Cause Related Marketing which is likely to create, in effect, the very 'spirit' of the brand, it is clearly crucial that the most senior managers in the business understand the concept and its potential ramifications for their company and its brands.

Thus the very first step in embarking on developing a Cause Related Marketing relationship is an in-company one. Do the executive board and the chief executive fully understand the concept? Do they believe that, appropriately implemented, it will add relevant new values to the brand? In short, do they have the collective intention to proceed along this new pathway?

Most commentators would agree that the successful CRM campaigns that have been developed so far owe their success in large part to the commitment to the programme from the very highest levels of their companies. This championship by senior management has given the CRM campaign resources, longevity and profile: American Express is a good example of this.

By the same token the involvement of top managers can also accrue further benefits for the brand in gaining for them personally and for their companies valuable public relations exposure in a context which does nothing but good for corporate reputation and perceptions of its wider role within society.

Assuming that there is 'buy-in' to the idea of a Cause Related Marketing relationship within the company, then the process can be embarked upon with a much greater degree of confidence. With senior management leadership it is much more likely that the subsequent process of staff empowerment, enabling them to become 'ambassadors' for the cause with consequent improvement in their *esprit de corps*, will be successfully achieved.

As the section on 'Territory' in the previous chapter shows, a vital first stage is to understand what the brand is about and the ways in which Cause Related Marketing may add further values to it. Most well-run brands will not have too much difficulty in stating these values for their brand and defining the 'Territory'. However, given the relative newness of the CRM concept, it is unlikely that more than a handful of marketers will have actually explored the area in conceptual terms with their consumers. For most professional brand managers this will be an important first step.

Qualitative research would usually be the most appropriate tool for this and focus groups will fit most situations. If however, the target audience is being asked to deal with a sensitive product category or if it is perceived that respondents may be more comfortable discussing the topic on a one-to-one basis, then in-depth interviews may be more valuable.

Clearly the discussion guide which is developed for the moderator to use as an 'agenda' for the focus group needs to be tailored to the particular case. However, it is likely that after the warm up, a general discussion of the brand and its position *vis-à-vis* competitors in the market place can be followed fairly quickly by an exposure to the concept of CRM. This can be done in a number of ways but perhaps most simply and easily by showing examples of concept board versions of some of the better known campaigns. In the UK this would be Tesco's Computer for Schools; in the USA it might be American Express and the 'Charge Against Hunger' campaign.

Professional moderators of focus groups will all have their own particular techniques for eliciting a consumer response, but this area is a prime candidate for the use of projective techniques along the lines of: 'If this brand was a person what sort of person would it be? Would it be kind? Would it be caring? Would it be greedy? Would it be harsh?' and so forth. Or, 'If this brand was a car, what make would it be? What colour?' And 'If this brand were a famous person, a TV or movie star, who would it be?'

Another technique worth considering is the use of cartoons depicting relevant situations to the CRM context with empty speech bubbles representing what the brand and another character might be saying. These will be passed out to each respondent who would be asked to complete the speech bubble for this particular situation. This would be done in private and then the sheets collected for subsequent analysis. Given the human tendency to anthropomorphize, consumers find these techniques enjoyable and they can be very revealing.

Exposures of these concepts should lead naturally on to the discussion of the appropriateness, or not, of this sort of activity for the brand under discussion. The marketing team and their agencies will have already brainstormed some CRM ideas for their particular brand and these can be introduced at this stage. Experience shows that these do not need to be presented in a highly finished form as consumers very quickly grasp the Cause Related Marketing concept.

The purpose of this exercise is not necessarily to find the final answer but more to understand how the 'Territory' of the brand can be enhanced and extended by the addition of a CRM which in turn builds a belief system or credo for the brand.

It may be that some fairly concrete ideas for the CRM relationship emerge from the group discussions or the in-depth interviews. This could be facilitated by examples of charities or causes that the marketing and agency team already considers from its own experience to be likely to be relevant to the brand.

If this is not the case then it is likely that further brainstorming and concept development work will need to be done before a further round of qualitative research. At this point it is worth noting that, in the recruitment process for the in-depth interviews, it would be useful to have a pre-screening question in order to establish whether or not the potential respondent was positive or negative in principle to the idea of products or services becoming involved with charities or good causes. It may also be worth considering innovative methodologies as described earlier with examples from the marketing of watches and wash bars.

Given the extant quantitative data on the subject produced by Roper Starch and Research International it is clear that there is likely to be up to 40% of the population at large who are not well disposed towards the concept *per se*. Work by The Future Foundation in 1997 for BT has also indicated that there are definable segments with varying propensity towards CRM. It would probably be useful, therefore, not to recruit them into the sample, unless of course the brand owner has a specific interest in understanding the behaviour in respect of the brand of those who hold negative attitudes to CRM and, for example, whether they are buyers or non-buyers in general.

If, however, the qualitative research has given some clear guidance on likely routes for developing a CRM relationship then it may be worth-while conducting a simple quantitative survey to check levels of approval of one or two competing concepts. This could be done among the public at large and, if affordable, among the specific target market. This data will also be useful in getting 'buy in' from top management to the eventual proposals for the campaign.

The process described above would be typical of that pursued in the normal development of a communications campaign, and in this sense CRM is no different. It may be that the brand owner does not have the financial resources to commit to even this modest level of market research. In this case the next best thing is to rely on the brand manage-ment team, other colleagues from within the company, including cor-porate affairs and internal communications and personnel, plus their advisors within their professional communications agencies to brainstorm the routes for themselves. Internal focus groups among employees are also surprisingly often accurate indicators of the attitudes of 'genuine' con-sumers, since of course employees are just that away from the work place! Because, in many ways, CRM is such a straightforward concept, informed common sense can easily prevail and produce perfectly valid solutions.

Having confirmed the brand's own 'Territory' and come to a view as to

the related area in CRM terms, the next task is to identify potential partners in the charity world or, as described elsewhere, a specific cause to
deal with directly. An important preparatory step and precursor to this
process is to produce a clear written brief, which summarizes the key
aspects of the brand in relationship to the future CRM campaign.

Perhaps the most efficient way to do this is in the form of a creative
brief. Nearly all advertising agencies have their own format for this but
the common headings are recurrent and would usually include at least the
following:

- Background to the brand and the market
- Objectives of the campaign
- Target audience including demographics and psychographics
- Brand proposition
- Supporting evidence
- The 'desired response'
- Media candidates and budgets
- Production budgets
- Timing
- Mandatories in terms of the use of typefaces, logos and copy lines.

Developing a brief is an art in itself – Saatchi & Saatchi has a 33-page
booklet devoted to this area of expertise alone. While there are clearly
benefits in limiting the brief to perhaps one or two pages of A4, in nearly
all cases it is valuable for this briefing paper to be accompanied by qualitative research debriefs, company reports, examples of competitive products and previous examples of advertising to round out the understanding
of the brand and its values.

Assuming for the moment that the strategic decision has been taken to
find a charity partner for the CRM campaign then the process can be
fairly straightforward but quite easily long-winded. This is simply because
there are so many charities. In the United States there were 637 272
registered charities in 1997. In the UK there are 182 000, in Australia
over 11 000, in Canada 76 000, and so on throughout the world.

The problem therefore is not finding a charity; it is identifying the
right one. To help facilitate this process for clients, Saatchi & Saatchi
Cause Connection has developed an active database of over 100 key UK
charities, each of which has been thoroughly interviewed in order to

gain a deeper understanding of their mission and criteria in a CRM relationship.

Fortunately, in most countries there is the equivalent of a charity commission with which charities have to register in order to operate. These organizations therefore have long contact lists of names and addresses of charities and they can be used as a primary source of information.

Hayley Cavill of Cavill + Co., one of the pioneering spirits in CRM and originator with Worthington Di Marzio of the key quantitative research in Australia, believes very strongly in the importance of sourcing the right charity partner for a client. The process of screening a number of possible alternatives until the best 'fit' is arrived at was central to the creation of the exciting partnership she has facilitated between Kellogg's and Kids Help Line. It's early days in their campaign to enable more children to get advice and support over the phone, but already it has the makings of an excellent case history. It is of particular interest to marketers, given the intense competition that a brand such as Kellogg's faces in so many marketplaces.

The case of Kellogg's in Australia, and the way in which they established the criteria in their search for a charity partner, is a good example of how the comparative professionalism of one charitable organization over others who have as good a theoretical 'strategic fit' can be a decisive factor in influencing partner choice for a major brand owner. The key role of a specialist intermediary in taking the initial brief, refining it in consultation with the client team and playing an important part in partnership 'match-making' is also demonstrated here.

Case History: KELLOGG'S 'KIDS HELP LINE'

Kellogg's first approached Hayley Cavill of Cavill + Co. in 1998 with the brief to develop a CRM programme for them. The brand was having some difficulties in the Australian market because of competition from two very strong brands, one called Sanitarium and the other, Uncle Toby's. Both have strong positionings in the market. Sanitarium has taken a stance with a focus on health and nutrition. Uncle Toby's ads use famous, sexy people and their outdoor lifestyle imagery has created an aspirational vitality for the brand.

In contrast to this opposition Kellogg's didn't have such a strong brand and decided to create a new values-driven position in the market as a counter-attack, with CRM as a key strategic component. Unlike many companies in Australia which had previously carried out the more traditional sort of short-term charity promotion, Kellogg's recognized from the outset the importance of making a long-term commitment to a particular charity, and did not see the role of CRM as a one-off sales promotion.

Kellogg's decided they wanted to choose an appropriate charity, enter into a long-term partnership with them, and budgeted to donate 5 cents per pack, which at their going sales level of 2 million packs a month implied $500 000 a year. Consultancy Cavill + Co. worked with Kellogg's to make the aims of the scheme more tangible and more measurable, and helped to establish some very specific objectives for the partnership. Rather than simply choose a well-known 'household name' charity, Kellogg's conducted research through Cavill + Co. to find one that was not only responding to a real and urgent social need and was pro-active and preventative, but which also was a close fit with the company's own values and appealed to its primary target audience.

From this it became clear that Kellogg's specifically did not want to partner with a charity that was too well known, such as the Salvation Army: they wanted one that would give the brand a greater sense of 'co-ownership' of the joint programme. Because their primary target market was with grocery buyers buying for children it seemed logical that it should ideally be a children's charity. Hayley Cavill then interviewed 15 different children's charities, and based on the response from those charities recommended Kids Help Line. Two of the strong reasons in their favour were that there was a lot of potential for this partnership to develop to mutual benefit, as we shall see later, and the charity clearly had some professional people in-house who could manage the ambitious programme that was envisaged.

Unfortunately many of the other candidate charities did not seem to have the necessary resources or professionalism to match Kellogg's. Responsiveness, or lack of it in many cases, when faced with a short deadline to provide information and indications of the benefits of an association, let down many of Kids Help Line's competitors. In fact when Cavill + Co. went to present the 15 candidate charities to Kellogg's, half of them had not provided any information. They were simply not geared up for a 'pitch' to a corporate of this sort, whereas Kids Help Line already had a list of benefits that they could offer a corporate partner, such as the brand's logo on a leaflet that went into 10 000 schools.

A prime attraction to Kellogg's, given its target audience, was Kids Help Line's status as Australia's only free, 24-hour, confidential and anonymous telephone counselling service for 5–18 year olds. There are 3.6 million young people in Australia between these ages. Every year they make 1.5 million phone calls to Kids Help Line, but only one in two calls have been able to be answered due to lack of funds.

From the charity's perspective a key attraction of Kellogg's for Kids Help Line was that while the service had a particularly high awareness among kids, it was not particularly well known in the mass market. This was due to a lack of advertising spend compared with the likes of World Vision and the Salvation Army. Obviously one of the benefits of aligning with Kellogg's was that it was going to give Kids Help Line significant exposure, thus answering the need to raise both awareness of the service as well as funds as part of a strategy for building community funding support.

However, with that benefit also came a problem. At the time 30 000 children were phoning the Kids Help Line every week but the cost of the paid professional child counsellors meant they could only answer one in three calls. An increase in the awareness of the charity would naturally lead to more phone calls, so it was essential in planning the partnership and the financial commitment that Kellogg's took this key factor into account.

Thus it was that the communications strategy, and the public target for the partnership, emerged out of what might have been regarded as a limiting factor. Kellogg's per pack donation enabled the Kids Help Line counsellor capacity to be increased and thus improve the answer rate by 156 000. Indeed the Kellogg's TV commercials promoting the CRM programme show children ringing up, and getting an engaged phone symbolised by a receiver with a 'blank' handset. Gradually the speaker holes appear on the telephone mouthpiece and then they are answered, all made possible by Kellogg's.

The following key objectives for Kids Help Line were established for the fundraising programme developed around the Kellogg's partnership:

1. Raise significant funds to increase the number of calls Kids Help Line could respond to.
2. Raise awareness of the service among the general community and giving public, as well as awareness of the need for funds.
3. Raise awareness of the service among kids.
4. Raise awareness of issues related to childhood and parenting.
5. Develop opportunities for a licensing and merchandising programme.
6. Develop opportunities for other major corporate partnerships.
7. Establish a donor database for Kids Help Line.

Kellogg's objectives in turn were as follows:

1. Support Kids Help Line in generating donations to fund calls.
2. Enhance consumer perceptions of Kellogg's as a company committed to supporting Australian kids and families.
3. Assume a leadership position in the corporate sector in terms of social responsibility.

In 1998 a sponsorship arrangement was formed with Kellogg Australia that delivered significant funds to answer more calls, raised the profile of Kids Help Line substantially and laid the foundation for building a donor base for the service. Crucially, Kellogg's committed $500 000 in financial contribution in the first year of its support for Kids Help Line. This is one of the largest monetary donations from a single grocery brand to a charity over 12 months in Australian CRM history.

The Kellogg's Kids Help Line partnership was a landmark in Cause Related Marketing consisting of an integrated, multi-faceted campaign that was far more extensive than the typical product promotions conducted in the past. Also vital was that an extensive advertising strategy was put in place to meet both partners' public relations and promotional objectives.

Kellogg's commissioned the creation of two television advertisements. One 30-second advertisement promoted the sponsorship by

Kellogg's and aimed at raising consumer awareness of the specially marked packs. The second advertisement was a 30-second fund-raising Community Service Announcement aimed at generating donations for Kids Help Line from the community.

In parallel Kids Help Line produced a 30-second radio fundraising Community Service Announcement which was distributed to all radio stations nationally. The charity also produced newspaper filler advertisements with a fundraising focus, which were distributed to all newspapers nationally with a request for free space.

Kellogg's commissioned the production of newspaper and magazine advertisements and used their media leverage to secure pro bono spots in major magazine titles and thus encourage even more donations for Kids Help Line. The television, radio, magazine and newspaper Community Service announcements received extended airplay during the promotional period and Kellogg's magazine ads were given an extraordinary run over weeks in high circulation magazine titles which even featured the ad on the inside cover in their own contribution to the cause.

One of the most powerful components of the campaign was delivered by Kellogg's producing 7 million cereal boxes to raise awareness of Kids Help Line. These featured an entire back panel devoted to educating kids about the service and how it could help, as well as a special side panel targeting adults and soliciting donations for Kids Help Line. Families at Australian breakfast tables were perfectly targeted in this way with great synergy with the key eating occasion for the brand, reinforcing the core values and adding an ethical element or 'spirit' in the process.

In coming months a panel of experts on family issues will produce a range of helpful information for parents, which will be promoted on pack. With Kellogg's brands reaching 40% of households nationally this will provide invaluable support to families and achieve an important educational aim for Kids Help Line.

Kellogg's, in conjunction with a major retail supermarket, produced point of sale posters promoting Kids Help Line. They also commissioned the production of 1 million Kids Help Line bookmarks in $2 and $5 denominations, which will be available in supermarkets to raise additional funds for Kids Help Line.

Public relations were a crucial part of the communications strategy. Kellogg's sponsorship of Kids Help Line was launched in Sydney in May 1998 at the Australian Theatre for Young People. Key statistical trends concerning Australian kids were released to heighten media awareness of issues facing kids today. The actual day was the 5th anniversary of the establishment of Kids Help Line as a national service, and thus the partners were able to gain maximum impact by releasing 5-year trends in caller data, which showed a 200% increase in calls related to youth suicide.

July 13th–19th was designated Kids Help Line Week and again a youth welfare issue was chosen as part of their media focus – teenage depression – based on statistics of a 60% increase in calls received at Kids Help Line over the last 5 years related to mental health issues.

Celebrity involvement in the week was secured through the creation of an event, called the 'Kellogg's Beating the Blues Celebrity Photographic Auction'. Twenty leading Australian celebrities were approached to have their photograph taken doing something simple that cheered them up when they were feeling down.

The prints were framed with a message and autograph from each celebrity and auctioned off at a breakfast function at the Museum of Contemporary Art in Sydney on the first day of Kids Help Line Week. Sir William Deane AC KBE, Governor General of Australia and Patron in Chief of Kids Help Line officially launched the breakfast and Kids Help Line Week and several of the celebrities from the photo shoot were at the breakfast adding to its newsworthiness.

With great good fortune the auction led to the recruitment of Kylie Minogue in a special role as Official Ambassador for Kids Help Line. Kids Help Line is the only charity in the world with which the star has taken a formal position, and she has made an ongoing commitment to work with the charity to raise awareness of the service and funds. Her ambassadorship was announced at a State Reception held in her honour by Victorian State Premier Jeff Kennett in July 3rd 1998 in Melbourne. Clearly her involvement represents a major bonus to both brand and charity.

Later in July a separate launch was held at a corporate breakfast in Melbourne with a media release focusing on the issue of teenage depression. Victorian State Governor Sir James Gobbo officially launched the breakfast, which was hosted by Felicity Kennett.

Income for Kids Help Line was generated through activities beyond Kellogg's initial commitment to Kids Help Line in Year 1 of the partnership, through the Celebrity Photographic Auction, the Corporate Breakfast, the advertising campaign soliciting donations and the sale of Kids Help Line Bookmarks nationally. Total income after only 6 months was in excess of $550 000 and continued to rise, which will allow Kids Help Line to answer more than 156 000 additional phone calls over the coming year.

The public relations strategy was highly effective. The twin strategies of using celebrity interest as well as topical youth issues were extremely successful in generating extensive media coverage. The launch generated 13 newspaper articles nationally, including Page 3 of the major Sydney newspaper. It was also covered by national and local television news. Twenty-eight radio interviews were conducted, including the national radio networks. A major magazine for the supermarket trade and suppliers featured the sponsorship launch as their cover story.

The announcement of Kylie Minogue's ambassadorship and the launch of Kids Help Line week generated an enormous media response. Eighty-five newspaper and magazine articles were run nationally including the more major national daily newspapers and in many of the national Sunday papers, as well as a two-page spread in a major national magazine title. Television coverage included all commercial networks news, entertainment programmes and cable television programmes. In the 24 hours following the depression media release, 91 radio interviews and news items went to air nationally. Regional papers still continue to run the 'depression' issue and the Kylie Minogue involvement.

Kellogg's internal commitment to the relationship has been enormous with Jean Louis Gourbin, Area President of Kellogg's taking a position on Kids Help Line's board. Kellogg's Managing Director David Mackay has also taken a personal role in challenging the community and other companies to join Kellogg's in supporting Kids Help Line. Beyond its own commitment to Kids Help Line, Kellogg's has taken an active role in recruiting other corporate partners to the programme such as retailers, media and business partners. As a result of this promotion and the involvement of Kylie Minogue, Kids Help Line is now in negotiation with two other major companies interested in a significant relationship with the service. The charity has also been approached to become the beneficiary of a range of fundraising events over the coming year.

The community response has also been very encouraging. Kellogg's have received a stream of congratulations from customers, the trade and staff for their involvement with Kids Help Line. Feedback has been overwhelmingly positive.

Since the launch of the cereal packs on shelf, 12% of new callers to Kids Help Line have told counsellors that they first heard of the service from the Kellogg's cereal boxes. Around 40% of callers during the promotional period cited television as their source of referral, generated from the Kellogg's ads.

As a key aspect of tracking the performance of the CRM campaign in attitudinal terms, Kellogg's commissioned market research into community awareness of Kids Help Line and perceptions towards both organizations prior to the launch of the campaign. Follow-up research has yielded the following results:

Importance of Charities among Adults

Charity	Quite Important/Very Important %
Kids Help Line	77
Ronald McDonald House	71
Variety Club	56
Starlight Foundation	53

Spontaneous Awareness of Kids Help Line

	Adults	Kids
Wave 2	38%	46%
Wave 3	59%	67%

Kids Help Line has achieved the highest position in perceived importance of charities amongst adults and there have been striking improvements in spontaneous awareness.

Hayley Cavill of Cavill + Co., the consultancy that brokered the partnership says: 'The Kellogg's/Kids Help Line partnership is a wonderful example of a CRM programme that delivers benefit to the brand, the charity and the community. I believe that its success is down to the strategic way that Kellogg's went about finding the right partner – one that enhanced their image and appealed to their prime target audience, rather than choosing one based on a personal contact. CRM relationships formed on a CEO's pet cause do not work. The Kellogg's/Kids Help Line partnership is a shining example of a win–win partnership.'

16

Creating a CRM Campaign

Campaign leadership

It is axiomatic in communications that committees make very poor 'authors'. While it is desirable, indeed essential, to get buy-in from interested parties and for feedback to be obtained through a number of methods, including qualitative consumer research, and soundings from key opinion formers and representatives of other interest groups, great campaigns usually have a single author.

This is no different in the case of the implementation of a CRM campaign. The risk of the 'camel – a horse designed by a committee' syndrome is heightened by the partnership inherent in most CRM campaigns. At the outset it has to be made absolutely clear who is the key decision-maker for the campaign.

This role is not an easy one to fulfil but it is made much more likely to succeed by a clear mandate and clear lines of authority. There are many potentially excellent campaigns which have foundered during the well-known process of being advanced through layers of brand management, all of whom have the power to say 'no' but very few of whom appear to have the power (or the courage) to say 'yes'.

It is most likely that the leader of the team will be a member of the marketing company and its corporate relations, community relations or brand marketing group, if only because they are supplying most of the financial and other resources. This should not however be a *fait accompli* and should be part of the negotiation of the formal agreement between the company and the charity described earlier, especially if the charity 'idea' is the substance of it all, as in Save Our Strength's mission to feed homeless people. If it is agreed that the CRM campaign leadership should fall to the company, then there remains the issue of where that authority should sit in a departmental sense.

Historically the responsibility for charitable donations has traditionally fallen within the corporate affairs or corporate communications departments of companies. Indeed the Saatchi & Saatchi Cause Connection survey of 169 major UK advertisers suggested that 83% of them had separate budgets for this purpose apart from that managed by the marketing department. The survey also revealed that 44% of these budgets were not strategically aligned with the company's brand communications programme – an immediate opportunity for a CRM 'win' in a large number of companies.

The corporate and community affairs functions have traditionally been close, both physically and operationally, to the Chairman's or CEO's office, and thus it could be argued that they are best placed to get the essential endorsement and involvement of top management.

However, if one of the key drivers of CRM is to imbue the brand with a belief system and a 'spirit' then it is obvious that the CRM activity needs to be very closely aligned with the rest of the marketing communications programme. As described elsewhere there are many disciplines which need to be applied to the process of CRM communications campaign development which are the natural domain of the marketers in the company as opposed to those in corporate affairs or corporate communications.

It is also obviously the case that in the past charitable donations have been just that. There has been very little thought given to the idea of publicizing charitable activities over the long term and indeed up until quite recently it has definitely been regarded as 'not the done thing'. However the argument has been made that 'the British consumer is not ready for this' and that 'the American consumer is not interested'. These views may be more deeply ingrained within marketing departments than corporate affairs and community relations, and thus make a wholehearted leadership of a CRM campaign more difficult for them.

On the other hand the role of marketing departments has always been to sell. And now that CRM is going to become part of that selling process it seems to make sense that CRM should become their responsibility.

In all this is the obvious potential for a turf war between these key internal departments and it would be very unfortunate if the greater good of a CRM campaign for the brand would be disrupted or even blocked by the potential for this kind of internecine dispute.

Perhaps a sensible way of resolving the matter is for a representative from corporate affairs or communications to join the project team under the leadership of the senior marketing executive or 'author' with the specific responsibility of managing the relationship with the charity partner involved. This is likely to play to the strengths of corporate affairs and give comfort to the charitable organization that someone who is familiar with the voluntary sector will be one of their primary contacts within the client organization. Meanwhile the marketing department will have the primary responsibility for devising and delivering the CRM campaign itself (in consultation with the charity of course) and in managing all the communications processes and supplying agencies involved in achieving that.

Most marketers today believe that an integrated communications campaign, that is one in which a central idea is about the brand, which is communicated through a variety of different media channels with interpretations appropriate to them, is the most cost effective and persuasive way of developing brand values.

If the CRM campaign's over-riding objective is to add a new layer of brand values in order to create a 'spirit' then the procedure for developing an integrated campaign should be no different from that utilized in producing any other form of brand communication. The creative brief, described earlier, is the jumping off point for the all-important 'Territory' which is the cornerstone of the campaign and the context for the creative idea for the brand.

The key to implementation is to ensure that the integrity of the idea is preserved while its execution through all the media channels to be employed are optimized. This will usually entail the campaign leader or 'author' hiring the specialist skills in a number of fields such as advertising, media planning and buying, public relations, direct marketing and sales promotion.

There are two broadly diverging views of how best to achieve this. On the one hand there is the 'one-stop shop' and on the other there is the 'dream team' approach.

The benefits of the 'one-stop shop' are that all the disciplines required to deliver the brand communication programme, including that required by the CRM campaign, are available within a single agency. There are a number of fairly obvious reasons why this approach is beneficial.

First, there are no turf wars about the division of the budget – all the money ends up at the same place within the group and it does not matter which door it comes in by. The second financial benefit, this time overtly for the client, is the simplicity of invoicing and payment procedures – one company, one bank account. A third operational benefit is that there is only one address to go to for meetings and there is a tighter team of people to talk to.

Beyond all these practical advantages there is a fundamental and over-riding one. This is that one agency is much more likely to be able to retain perspective on the core idea and to maintain its integrity through-out all the different channels. Being by definition on the same team they will support the same strategy and creative interpretation. Saatchi & Saatchi is a good example of an agency committed to the 'one-stop shop' approach, with the company clearly positioned as an 'ideas company' pro-ducing communications that are bigger than just advertisements.

The critics of this approach suggest that it is literally impossible for one agency to contain all the diverse talents that are required in each of these separate and specialized disciplines. Clearly the validity of this needs to be tested by the client in each situation.

The other approach, the cherry-picked 'dream team', has alternative attractions. The client may perceive that a single agency cannot contain all the necessary talent and prefers to shop around within each segment identifying what he or she believes to be the leading company with the skills most appropriate to the brand brief. This means that the client has to do a search through perhaps four or five different areas, conduct pitches and come to decisions about who to work with, with all that that entails in terms of contract and fee negotiations.

Having cherry-picked the 'dream team' the client then has a funda-mental decision to make. Is the organizational and intellectual team client-based (whether that be the corporate or the charity), or is this lead role delegated to one or other of the agencies on the roster that has been created for the project?

The benefits of taking the leadership role for him or herself are clear –

the client pays the pipers and calls the tune. However, given that the total communications function is estimated to occupy perhaps only 10–15% of the average marketing professional's time, this means that a high proportion of the available hours are likely to be spent in administration and coordination of four or five different supplier communications agencies.

The alternative, used by many, is to appoint one of these supplier companies as 'lead agency' for the purposes of the CRM campaign. This can be a very effective way of running the project if it is made absolutely clear to all concerned that this is the way in which it has to be run. The protocol has to be firmly established that the lead agency has the overall strategic and creative mandate from the client and that the role of the other companies is to be in support of that. As the area of CRM has developed a number of specialist agencies have emerged in the field and the client could consider using one or other of them as 'lead'.

There are many communications agencies which belong to the same group and operate independently within it. It can be the case that choosing companies which are members of the same holding company can have benefits in terms of their preparedness to co-operate. Equally, there is anecdotal evidence that this is exactly the reverse of what might be expected. The Omnicom and WPP communications groups are good examples of diversified agencies which operate in this way with cross-referral being a key part of their strategies for delivering integrated communications to their clients.

Apart from the obvious increase in management time and operational skill required in coordinating a number of different companies, there is a bigger philosophical issue at stake. Even if the client takes a very firm lead or alternatively places a very clear mandate with a lead agency there is still the vexed problem of the 'not invented here' syndrome. Different companies in the world of creative communications seem to find it very hard indeed to accept that someone else's creative interpretation is better than their own, or more suitable in a given situation.

Thus the 'dream team' approach has the inherent potential for discord and counter-productive creative disputes. It requires diplomatic and leadership skills of the highest order in order to ensure that the whole is indeed greater than the sum of the individual parts. Without them the 'dream team' could easily become a nightmare!

From practical experience of working in both of these campaign management systems one important over-riding factor can work in favour of success and give the client the sort of solution that is required. This is to use timetabling and deadlines, usually rather tight ones, to force the team to bond together with the common objective of achieving their goal and with the shared attitude that 'nothing is impossible'.

Leveraging the CRM campaign

Having come to an agreement on a CRM partnership in principle, an important precursor to signing a contract governing the relationship is for both parties to be clear on the degree of involvement and how far this should be manifested through their respective organizations. If this is clear from the outset expectations will be managed and a fruitful working relationship is more likely to result.

From the brand owner or corporate perspective there are clearly a number of key assets which can be put at the disposal of the charity or cause at relatively little on-cost to the normal programme of activities. At the same time the charity has valuable communications channels and assets of its own which can benefit the corporate partner in a reciprocal manner.

Many charities, and particularly the larger ones, produce a wide range of communications materials and often significant advertising and communications campaigns. Some have retail outlets and run catalogue-marketing operations. They often have large databases of members or supporters and they can also have quite significant numbers of active volunteers in the field. It may be that they have proprietary rights in established events, which may be broadcast as part of the national calendar. These include the Royal British Legion and Poppy Day, the Variety Club of Great Britain and The Royal Command Performance, and the biennial Red Nose Day in the UK. These national flag days have in many cases enormous heritage and if they were to be linked to a corporate sponsor or brand name this would bring very significant additional publicity to that sponsor.

These areas for mutual collaboration and leveraging of the CRM campaign, particularly in communications, are set out below. In embarking on the negotiation of a relationship between two prospective partners there ought to be an open evaluation of these options and a clear commitment as to which of them is going to be fulfilled and to what level.

This analysis will be valuable to both parties: for the corporation or brand owner it will focus the collective mind on the CRM programme. For the charity it will enable the trustees or the management to appreciate the full potential of the prospective relationship and therefore will become a significant factor in deciding on degrees of exclusivity, or indeed one prospective commercial partner over another.

Below is a bullet point checklist of the areas of evaluation:

- Brand or corporate communications
- Employee communications
- Employee volunteering
- Third parties
- Corporate and employee giving
- Benefits in kind
- Special products
- Celebrity supporters

Brand or corporate communications

Given the overall thesis that CRM is a way of adding new brand value in the third wave of branding and indeed a way of giving brands the added dimension of 'spirit', perhaps the most important area for consideration and negotiation between prospective partners in the relationship is the investment that the corporation or the brand owner intends to make in consumer communication about the CRM campaign.

As we have seen, all the indications are that the consumer is absolutely ready for this new type of communication. It is potentially extremely advantageous for the brand and, of course, the charity, if a proportion of the existing brand communication budget is allocated towards the specific purpose of advertising these values.

The question will immediately spring to the minds of both the marketer's and the charity's managements as to what is an appropriate portion of the advertising communications budget that should be allocated for this purpose. If the experience of a number of practitioners is anything to go by – for example Norwich Union and St John Ambulance – the impact of a TV commercial with a CRM theme is extremely powerful. In many cases it is going to have more influence on consumers than conventional messages about the brand which have to do with the usual rational and emotional values or indeed short-term promotional tactics.

Clearly each brand manager will want to test the likely impact of such a communication before putting it on air or in other media and this can be done in the normal way through both qualitative and quantitative pre-testing.

The more cautious marketers may even want to do a regional test market of the activity to be able to fine-tune it before going national. And as will be detailed elsewhere the results in terms of improved brand awareness and audience involvement, even in as tough a market as financial services, have shown the benefits of the approach to Norwich Union. Visa and American Express have had a similar experience in the United States.

A practical way of looking at CRM budget allocation is in terms of audience delivery. It is clearly relatively easy for the endorsement of support of a charity or cause to be included as a copy line in advertising, point of sale, brochures, packaging and other communications materials. While relatively low in cost these additional communications are worth an enormous amount in extra publicity for the cause. Even the mere dissemination of a telephone number or the charity's Internet address can significantly increase the potential for fundraising.

If the brand has already committed to the charity through these forms of communication then it may be that communicating the theme at a broadcast level will be relatively easily achieved, given the newsworthiness and impact of CRM campaigns. Thus a TV campaign which achieved 70% coverage with an average Opportunity To See (OTS) the commercial of, say, 2.5 times might cost £630 000 (based on a 30-second spot, at an average time of year) in the UK.

Given that among the 50 biggest brands in Britain, as rated by *Marketing Magazine*, Ariel and Persil have adspends of £22 million and £20 million respectively, and Coca-Cola a massive £31 million, such figures for including a CRM dimension do not represent an undue encroachment into the marketing budget. These massive figures are of course dwarfed by the equivalent brand communications budgets in the USA.

The campaign for the Co-op Bank in the UK, which again is set out in more detail in the case history section, suggests that in the UK a spend of £1 800 000 over a period of 18 months has managed to establish a pretty unassailable position for the bank in ethical terms.

By the same token the inclusion of a section in the annual report and accounts detailing the corporate or brand commitment to a charity or cause can be an important addition to the positioning of the brand. It can also be a valuable communications tool to opinion formers in government, the city and the media.

Employee communications and volunteering

It has been said that many failed marketing ploys have only consisted of 'a launch, a lunch and a logo'. To be truly successful a CRM campaign must enlist some of the company's most important stakeholders and potential army of ambassadors for the cause, its employees.

Most companies have a routine communications channel with their employees in the shape of company or departmental meetings, regular newsletters and posters on notice boards. In more and more workplaces the use of log-on screens on the computer network and special sites on the company website are being used as well as video magazines or even more ambitious private TV networks.

Regular mentions and features on the charity and the involvement of the company with it can be a powerful way of spreading the word and enlisting support from often very large numbers of employees who can become advocates for the charity in their daily lives. Many may well have become involved in charity work themselves which relates to what the company and its brand is trying to achieve.

There are other ways of enlisting employee participation. In 1998 Comet, an electrical goods chain, has carried out a staff survey through the mechanism of a self-completion questionnaire inserted in their newsletter which has a circulation to all staff of 7900. Key functions of this questionnaire were to establish what charitable links already exist within the company and to seek staff reactions to some candidate CRM relationships that senior management were considering.

A natural extension of the areas in which the company and its employees can make an added value contribution to the charity and its work is through donated time. Drawing an analogy with the 3M programme allowing 15% of company time to be used by employees for their own projects, companies could consider donating an amount of time per employee per month, or other appropriate time period. Within that time employees, at the company's expense, could volunteer to help the charity with its work.

Goldman Sachs, for example, run a scheme called TeamWorks, whereby in one month in every year, every employee around the world is given a day off to support the local community. Employees usually go out in groups and work with an organization on a particular project. Each region tailor-makes its own projects, but they cover a wide range of causes – children, the elderly or disabled, and the environment.

Quite apart from the practical help that this will obviously be to the charity it will enable employees to gain a much better understanding of what the charity is about and the work that it does in its chosen area of activity. Again it is likely that many employees already do voluntary work for charitable organizations and they may wish to continue to support their own personal favourites. However, if the charity partner is chosen to be a good 'Territorial' fit with the activities of the company or the brand, then it is quite likely that a significant proportion of people will realign themselves towards the favoured charity partner in exactly the same way as the corporation has done at a strategic level.

Third parties

So far we have covered the specific assets that the company itself might bring to the table. But there is another element that needs to be considered in order to come to a full appreciation of the potential of the relationship. This is the area of third parties, which are connected to the corporation.

These will fall into two main categories. The first of these will be suppliers to that company. In a strictly commercial arena decisions taken by major retailers in respect of their policy towards environmental issues have had a direct and immediate cascading effect on suppliers to that retailer. If, for example, a retailer were to make it mandatory that all wood and paper products supplied to them should only come from Forest Stewardship Council (FSC) audited renewable sources then this would have a dramatic knock-on effect on the behaviour of its suppliers.

In the same way, if a company elected to support a particular charity in the ways described above, then it could use moral suasion to encourage its suppliers to join in with the effort. Depending on the scale of the enterprise and the particular relationship it has with these linked companies, the cumulative effect and leverage on the relationship could be very significant indeed. The manner in which American Express and Visa have extended their CRM programmes in partnership with their merchants is a good example of this.

The second area of potentially great significance is that of third parties in the shape of governmental or other state agencies that may be connected in some way to the charity or cause related activity that the commercial partner wishes to support.

In September 1997, following an informal discussion between Marjorie Thompson and Tessa Jowell MP, Minister for Public Health, during which she heard about Cause Connection and the idea of mutually beneficial business and charity links, the Minister said, 'This could be the substance behind New Labour's vision'. From this meeting has sprung one of the most important initiatives in the New Labour strategy of forging partnerships between government, business and the voluntary sector and is indeed one of the key bits of evidence that Prime Minister Blair's 'Third Way' is becoming a reality.

The basic proposition put to the Department of Health (DoH) was that some of the relatively small health promotions budget should be devoted to seeding CRM campaigns focused on key elements in its health agenda.

Thus, the principle of fund matching between government and private sector was given a new impetus through linking to cause marketing and the inclusion of a charity partner. The Department of Health agreed that it would contribute £1 from its budget for every £2 that a corporate or brand sponsor would bring to the table, as long as that corporate partner was deemed appropriate to the health issue concerned. In some cases support will not be financial but in the form of a simple government endorsement, demonstrated, for example, by use of the Department of Health logo.

In the Green Paper (a UK Government consultation paper as opposed to a White Paper, which is the next stage before legislation is drafted) entitled 'Our Healthier Nation' published in February 1998, the Government declared the following priority health areas: heart disease and stroke, accident prevention, cancer and mental health.

Clearly for any charities concerned with any of these key health issues there is a very significant win to be had in the extra funds generated and of course having the resources of government behind the joint effort. The Saatchi & Saatchi Cause Connection initiative divided the government's priority areas into separate and distinct key issues which could be engaged by the three way assembly of the DoH, an appropriate charity and a corporate partner.

The attractions for the Government and the DoH are not just that a particular health advertising campaign is potentially tripled in size, but also because of the scope for the right corporate partner to use its brand positioning, advertising, packaging, distribution and other communications channels to support the health initiative. This could take even more of the promotional costs of DoH health campaigns, for example those entailed in the production and distribution of advisory leaflets, off the Government's balance sheet.

The attraction for the company is that in addition to adding an important layer of ethical or cause-related image value to your brand, there is also the PR benefit of being close to government in an area of high profile policy, i.e. their commitment to public and private sector partnership.

Obviously the attraction for the charity involved is that it will raise their profile, and that of the health cause, significantly. The enlarged campaign should also help generate much-needed funds and lead to real achievements in positive behaviour change through health messages to the target audience via the mainstream channel of a famous brand's communications. It will also help lever the efforts of the volunteer force involved with many charities.

Following on from the Department of Health initiative Saatchi & Saatchi Cause Connection have approached a number of other key government departments and agencies such as the Department of the Environment, Transport and the Regions, the Home Office, the

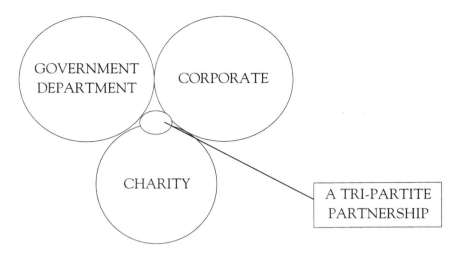

'*Government, commerce and charity in partnership.*'

Department for Education and Employment, the Department of Trade and Industry, and the Office of Science and Technology. It is believed that comparable agreements will be reached with a number of them on the DoH model leading in turn to much wider potential for dynamic tripartite partnerships between government, commerce and charities. As one senior civil servant put it, 'This is really exciting, it's joined up government'.

As the pressure on the Government budget grows due to ageing populations and apparently endless obligations, particularly in the areas of healthcare and education, the Government has to enlist the support of the private sector in order to fulfil public expectations and to make real progress towards its targets. While CRM is at an early stage of its development in this respect, it is potentially a key way in which commercial interests can be served at the same time as and in partnership with the Government's public service agenda. Obviously these tripartite partnerships can never be a substitute for essential state provision, but rather should be seen as primarily for promotional and campaigning activity which the private and voluntary sectors have always been better at. As the Public Health Minister, Tessa Jowell said: 'This is an exciting way of enlisting public, private and voluntary sectors to tackle health inequality. I know that harnessing the creative energy used to promote brands to change health behaviour will improve people's lives and help us meet our health targets.'

Of course charities themselves have their own third-party assets. For example, voluntary organizations involved in any area which requires scientific research are almost always connected to academic institutions because these are the people who carry out the research which they in part fund. Thus there is the potential for extending the relationship and, of course, the awareness of the brand into those institutions which are involved in the process. In the case of institutions like the Great Ormond Street Hospital or the Royal Marsden they have become major charities and causes in their own right. But there are many other institutions of comparable quality which carry out valuable research in areas in which charities are involved but whose teacher/student populations have not yet been involved in any significant way and whose stature and prestige have not been enlisted fully in support of their 'cause'.

Corporate and employee giving

The first and most obvious area to be considered is that of the level of straightforward financial donation. A growing number of companies in the UK subscribe to the Per Cent Club, where the philosophy is a commitment to making a significant contribution to the community, and membership is based on each company donating at least 0.5% of their pre-tax profits to the community.

Blue chip companies in the UK such as Kingfisher, McDonald's and Allied Dunbar Assurance (one of the founder members) have led the way with this. Therefore the priority is to establish whether or not the board of directors feels this is an appropriate amount to be donating, if the company is not doing so already. If the decision is made to give to that level then clearly the CRM charity partner is an immediate beneficiary of that decision.

If the partner corporation were making profits of £100 million per year and agreed to become a member of the 0.5% club in the UK, then this would mean a total donation of £500 000 to the charity. As importantly it would signify a level of commitment indicating that the charity and the cause had truly been taken to the company's or the brand's heart.

As discussed elsewhere it is the rare company that is not already making corporate donations to a range of charities. What is equally rare is the company which has decided to concentrate its giving. If those monies can be refocused on a strategically aligned charity or cause, at no extra cost to the company or brand, then it is an easy win in communication terms.

The second area for consideration is that of personal giving, either in the shape of covenant or payroll giving, as in the UK or via federal matching fund programmes in the USA. On both sides of the Atlantic there are tax benefits to be had, and in the United States for charity giving there are personal tax benefits too.

In the UK the management of the company could make known its commitment to the charity partner and encourage the employees first to participate in payroll giving or in covenanting to the chosen charity, and this may well significantly increase the donations to the funds. It may also be worth considering offering guidelines to board directors and employees alike on the level of giving that might be considered. A quarter of 1% produces an annual donation of £50 for someone earning £20 000 and this is equivalent to less than the price of a pint of beer per week.

Given that the money is deducted at source before the employee sees their pay packet, it is virtually a painless way of giving. This may have its disadvantages, since staff do not see anything tangible and therefore do not develop the 'team spirit' that often results from charitable activities such as sponsored events. However, multiply £50 across a number of employees and this contribution can quickly be of significant benefit to the charity.

Another way that the company could show its leadership in CRM support would be to offer to match the funds raised by employees in this way by a corporate donation. In a hypothetical situation a company with 2000 employees, with an average salary of £30 000, with 50% of them donating via payroll giving and covenanting to the level of a quarter of 1% and then matched by company donations to make up to half of 1% would mean an annual donation to the charity of £150 000.

AT&T run one such scheme, the AT&T Employee Matching Gifts Program for employees both present and retired. The programme provides a dollar-for-dollar match of the tax-deductible portion of individual gifts, between a minimum amount of $25 and a maximum of $10 000 per individual donor. The donations are made to educational, arts or cultural institutions, and no more than $50 000 is given to any one institution in a calendar year.

Benefits in kind

Another important area that needs to be considered in leveraging the relationship is the potential role that the company's product or services may have in generating revenues or even direct benefits for the charity.

In the case of Austin Reed, for example, their programme of giving a donation to Shelter and a discount on a new suit in return for an old suit traded in, is a practical example of where merchandise can be put to good use. The old suits were then donated to Shelter shops to be sold.

The Dollond & Aitchison case history detailed earlier in Chapter 12 is another good example of this.

A similar idea, that of putting the brand or product into direct use, is behind two different three-way partnerships developed between soup companies, supermarkets and charities. In both cases, the scheme was run in the UK in the harsh winter months, when the product, soup, has most appeal for homeless people. The New Covent Garden Soup Company linked with CRISIS, and put money towards the refurbishment of kitchens in CRISIS's open houses, in return the charity connection appeared on the soup cartons. Tesco was connected with the partnership through a straight donation of money for every carton sold during a 6-week period. A very similar three-way partnership was piloted in 1997 between Campbell's soup, ASDA and Shelter.

Perhaps the most exciting and ambitious programme involving a product is that currently being developed and implemented by SmithKline Beecham. As previously mentioned this entails the donation of 45 billion tablets of the drug albendazole.

SmithKline Beecham have been at pains to point out that the product they are donating is not out of date or redundant in any way and is actually of the same quality as the product they sell in the normal way. This is an important point as the integrity of the relationship is assured by these sorts of measures. The 'new lamps for old' promotional technique must be transparent in order to avoid it becoming perceived as a cynical short-term sales generation.

Special products

Another creative interpretation of product usage in promoting a charitable cause is the concept of 'special edition' productions, which are especially created for revenue generating sale. In the context of a charity's own merchandising programme this has been an established practice for many years and indeed a number of charities, e.g. Oxfam, the RSPCA, the National Trust and the World Wide Fund for Nature, have quite large-scale catalogue marketing and/or retail merchandising programmes.

Several UK charities such as Oxfam have substantial retail chains of their own which sell their own manufactured or donated products. Indeed Oxfam is among the top five retailers in the UK by number of shops, and has more outlets in the UK than McDonald's. These chains clearly represent a significant opportunity for partner brands in a CRM campaign to gain extra exposure while communicating their support for the cause.

Many charities also have created 'affinity' credit cards, but whilst these are valuable generators of income and awareness, they do not represent a true CRM partnership between two brands.

In the CRM context the idea is that the partner brand should develop special versions of its own product or service which entail a donation to the charity.

For example, at London Fashion Week '98, Fabris Lane launched one style within their up-market sunglasses range specifically on the platform that purchase would entail a donation of 20% of the price to breast cancer charities. Given the high profile of the Fabris Lane brand within the fashion industry and the support it has from exclusive retailer Harvey Nichols, the impact of this initiative on awareness among opinion-formers could be considerable.

Clearly if a media owner decided to adopt a particular cause which related closely to the 'Territory' of one of its publications or programmes, then the value to the charity of the editorial coverage involved could be absolutely enormous, particularly if sustained over a period of time. The *Daily Mail* newspaper has made enormous gains in circulation in part by a series of carefully targeted reader offers built on a collecting mechanic, and in the year since the death of Diana, Princess of Wales, many of these have been related to her.

Thousands of items of Diana-related merchandise such as candles and CDs have been earned by *Daily Mail* readers through very simple loyalty type promotions. The *Daily Mail* has made donations to the Diana, Princess of Wales Memorial Fund, and therefore the integrity of the system has been preserved. This model can be replicated by other media owners in a way which suits their particular editorial stance and the interest of their readers.

However, there is potential for controversy in this area as the Flora margarine and Diana, Princess of Wales Memorial Fund link demonstrated. This is described in more detail in the Flora case history below. This particular controversy should not put companies nor charities off the idea of product related support for the CRM programme and as is made clear by the SmithKline Beecham global anti-elephantiasis initiative there may be an enormous benefit to be had.

Case History: FLORA:
'THE LONDON MARATHON'

Flora is a leading UK brand of margarine which has had a long-term positioning as a healthier alternative to butter and which has built its business with a primary appeal to women purchasers who wish to 'look after the men in their lives'. This is an area which is hedged about with rules and regulations governing health claims and Flora has been very successful in managing to create an association in consumers' minds that it is indeed a healthier product and may actually help prevent heart disease, without actually directly saying so.

A key plank in their positioning has been the sponsorship of the London Marathon, one of the most famous and widely publicized in the world. Each year Flora and the London Marathon Charitable Trust together choose a charity to be the main beneficiary of the event. This enables the charity to have widespread publicity before the event from Flora as well as the benefit from having a number of dedicated runners raising money for the cause. For Flora the advantage is the link with a well-known charity and an obvious reaffirmation of the connection of their brand to health and a healthy lifestyle.

In 1997 the chosen charity was the British Heart Foundation.

On-pack promotions were used in association with the British Heart Foundation logo appearing on it with offers of sports bags and cuddly toys raising money for the cause.

Flora are very pleased with the results of the association with health and fitness and of course with the fact that approximately £1M has been raised for the British Heart Foundation. The scheme is found to have had little direct impact on sales, but is seen as part of the total marketing effort and the positioning of the brand. There is qualitative evidence that attitudes towards Flora have been improved along relevant dimensions, and certainly there has been very widespread coverage of the London Marathon and Flora's involvement on television and in other news media.

However, one of the most controversial events in the wake of the death of Diana, Princess of Wales has been the Flora promotion of specially printed packs carrying the Diana signature logo of the trust set up for her.

'Diana's margarine?'

While this particular element of the campaign was done with the best of intentions, and indeed £250 000 was donated to the fund/trust as a result, it caused outrage in many sectors of the community. The basic problem was that many consumers and most commentators could not see the necessary connection between Diana and Flora margarine.

The link was formed through Flora's sponsorship of the London Marathon, as the Memorial Fund was the main charity beneficiary for the London Marathon in 1998. Therefore the brand synergy was between Flora and the London Marathon, not Flora and Diana, but this did not translate itself to the consumer. The links were obviously not immediately apparent when the product was on the shelf, and it looked as if it were an exploitative use of her name and memory. It certainly caused a major split between the Spencer family and the Trustees who had made the decision to proceed with the campaign.

This highly publicized controversy is a further reminder of the importance of ensuring that there is shared 'Territory' between the brand, charity or cause, and that that synergy is apparent to the consumer. As this key logic was missing, unfortunately Flora received the brunt of people's resentment and annoyance as a result.

It is interesting to note with the Co-op Bank credit card that if customers wish to support causes like Greenpeace with their affinity card payments, then the rate of interest that the card charges is significantly above the competitive level in the market place. In fact for this particular card the prevailing rate of interest is perhaps 10 points above the best available. This seems to be another confirmation that the consumer is prepared to pay a premium for a brand which supports the cause in which they believe strongly.

Each company or brand involved in the CRM campaign should therefore consider the possibility of an affinity card as a part of their programme, if they do not already have one. This should be approached with some caution given the very large number of credit cards in issue and indeed affinity cards in particular, but given the frequency of use of credit cards it is nevertheless worth considering. Companies which have very large numbers of employees may actually be able to produce a viable customer base to make the development of the tailor-made credit card worthwhile or it may be that the charity has sufficiently large numbers of members or supporters to do the same.

The other consideration in this area is whether the card involved needs to be a credit card. Most of the emphasis has been on this sector because of the profit motive of the underwriting banks. However, the consumer data suggests that increasingly customers are focusing on the convenience benefits of debit cards and indeed the smart cards that are in the process of superseding them. If the motive for using the card from the consumers' perspective is essentially that, i.e. convenience, coupled with a desire to make regular small donations to a charity or good cause, then there is no reason at all why the vehicle associated with the CRM campaign should not be a debit or a smart card, and not necessarily a credit card.

It would also be worth while for the company or brand, particularly if it were involved in retailing, to explore the potential for its own store or loyalty card in a CRM mechanism. If the retail brand has loyalty cards in issue to its customers, whose purpose is to encourage repeat shopping visits, with a view to gaining a higher share of wallet then any other mechanism that works towards this end is beneficial.

If it is true that consumers are looking for 'higher order' reasons for their consuming behaviour then adding a CRM dimension to a multi-card scheme is an attractive idea. If the retail brand establishes a major long-term partnership with a charity or good cause then it makes sense to enable its customer base to contribute via the mechanism of the store loyalty card.

There are two alternative ways of doing this, either as a straight financial donation which can be given instead of the rebate to the customer, or, alternatively, the store card could make a donation of loyalty points to the charity concerned which can then use them for its own purchase of goods and services.

There are other schemes, which belong to 'loyalty villages' such as the Shell Smart Card scheme or the Argos Premier Points scheme in the UK, which might be able to be used in a similar way.

Celebrity supporters

Many charities have famous donors involved with them. Many others have famous patrons, board members or trustees. These celebrities and people of influence are rarely full-time employees of the charity but are often able to devote a surprising proportion of their energies to it.

As Diana, Princess of Wales demonstrated to an extraordinary degree during her lifetime, the impact of a famous patron on the fundraising potential of a charity is absolutely enormous. By the same token, the appropriate association of such a person with a company or a brand could also be very significant.

If the relationship is based on the principles of transparency and integrity described above then there seems no reason why a celebrity patron could not effectively become a supporter of the company or brand. The world famous comedian John Cleese, for example, is personally very committed to the Institute for Family Therapy and is a passionate supporter of its goals and aims. If there were to be a corporate partner with this charity then it seems quite likely that he would be prepared to support events which would be to mutual benefit.

There are many examples of showbusiness stars being prepared to support charities publicly as evidenced by the Reebok 'Human Rights Now!' Tour. Celebrity links to good causes such as Stephen Fry and the Terence Higgins Trust, Princess Anne and Save the Children, Lenny Henry and Comic Relief, Martyn Lewis and YouthNet in the UK, and in the USA, Jerry Lewis and the Muscular Dystrophy Telethon, and Elizabeth Taylor and Elton John with AIDS charities are testament to the power of these associations.

In summary, there are a wide range of ways in which the relationship can be leveraged on behalf of the corporation or the brand in favour of the charity or the cause. Some of these can be achieved simply by refocusing and redirecting expenditure and resources that are already committed to charitable activities. There are others which add significantly more value which entail an on-cost, but one which should be seen as an investment in creating new brand values, or indeed giving the brand a 'spirit'.

17

Crystallizing a CRM Campaign

The Saatchi & Saatchi 'Temple'

Having established the 'Territory' that the brand inhabits and having developed a creative brief for the particular objective of creating a CRM campaign, there is the question of how to ensure that this new strand in the brand's communication campaign should be integrated with, and relate to, the other continuing themes in its portfolio.

As has been said elsewhere, an integrated communications campaign is very much more effective than one which has disparate elements apparently pulling the consumer in different directions. To pursue the anthropomorphic analogy, a brand which falls into this trap is exhibiting signs of confusion.

At Saatchi & Saatchi one of the thinking tools that has been developed is the Saatchi 'Temple'. This very simple but elegant model can give communicators a memorable graphic, which can be used in planning campaign structures.

The top of the Temple is the pediment, and the pediment contains the masterbrand idea. This idea is 'located' in the 'Territory' that has been defined. So in the case of the British Army Recruitment campaign for example, the 'Territory' is 'The Army will bring out the best in you' and the creative idea is 'Be the best' with its executional concept of personal challenge.

Supporting the pediment are the pillars. Each pillar or column represents an important support for the brand idea. Each of these supports

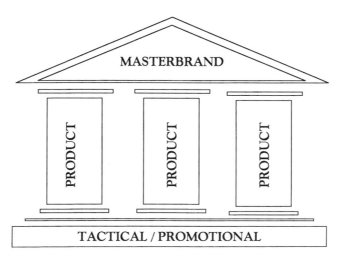

'The masterbrand idea as pediment, with supporting products and services as pillars.'

becomes the basis of an element of communications within the brand's overall campaign. Typically these might represent individual product variants within a brand's range or they might represent individual services in the case of a service brand. There is also the potential for linking particular pillars with segments of the target audience.

Underpinning the pillars are the foundations of the Temple, which are promotional or pricing activities which need to be coherent and supportive, not disruptive, of the whole. How often have we seen promotional campaigns which bear no relationship to the overall theming of the brand and indeed undermine much good work that has been done elsewhere to project the personality? Car dealer advertising is often a prime culprit in this.

Relating the Saatchi 'Temple' to the Cause Related Marketing campaign, it can be seen that the CRM strand becomes one of the pillars alongside other aspects of the brand which may convey rational and emotional benefits. It is clearly essential that the CRM pillar, like the others, supports the masterbrand idea. Using this simple thinking tool helps ensure that all the elements of a brand's campaign are aligned and directed towards achieving the long-term positioning goal. Another useful tool in use at Saatchi & Saatchi is that of the 'Logic Train'.

The 'Logic Train'

The creative process is not a logical, linear rational one, quite the reverse. Jeremy Bullmore has described it as the 'hypothetico-deductive process' in the IPA publication of 1994, 'Advertising costs half as much as you think it does . . ., but do you know which half?' The way the process works is that a hypothesis is put forward and then challenged and knocked down to be replaced by another. It is very much a case of two steps forward, one step back.

Because of the nature of the process it is useful to have thinking tools to help it along the way. In between creative leaps there is the need to rationalize the leap that has been made and to make sure that it ties back into the overall strategy. The Saatchi Logic Train is such a tool for doing this.

The development of a 'Territory' for the brand will have established the basic ground on which the creative idea must stand and in which it must have its roots. The creative brief will be the jumping off point for the leap that needs to be made, usually intuitively, into a creative realization of the strategy. Once a plausible idea has been arrived at, it is very important to make sure that it is indeed a product of the strategy, of the brand and of the various elements which go to make it up.

The model of the 'Temple' can be used in a structural sense to organize the campaign, but the role of the Logic Train is to demonstrate how all the elements actually link together and support each other.

'A great idea is the engine of the strategy.'

The Logic Train is obviously a metaphor, and in the metaphor the train is driven by an engine and it is the idea which provides the horse-power to do so. At the other end of the train there is the guard's van. This can be conceived as containing the problem or the objective that the brand has to achieve in the market place.

Linking either end of the train together are the 'carriages', and the carriages have a dual meaning. They represent passengers, or consumers, who need to be carried along with the idea to its destination and at the same time they represent the supporting evidence which links the idea to the objective or goal.

When the idea is conceived it is placed in the 'engine' box at the bottom of the page. At the top of the page in the guard's van box is written the problem. Between these two poles are a series of carriages and into each of these must be inserted the logic that connects the engine to the guard's van.

The process is therefore one of hypothesizing an idea and seeing how it can be a bridge to the problem or the objective using available evidence from the market data and research that are to hand. The hypothetico-deductive process is to set up the train and then to attempt to de-couple it by challenging all the assumptions that might link one carriage to the next.

The Logic Train technique can be useful in scrutinizing a CRM campaign idea. The brand 'problem' should be placed at the top in the guard's van and the hypothesized idea should be placed in the engine box at the bottom. Finally, the logical steps that connect the one to the other need to be completed in a CRM context.

Very often there are either missing links or missing data or both. The marketer, or the agency involved, needs to resolve these problems by developing new insights through creative thinking or research. The Logic Train diagram is set out below and it can be seen as a very simple analogy, which is extremely useful in practice. This particular one is hypothesized for the Austin Reed/Shelter campaign summarized in the case history that follows.

Case History: AUSTIN REED: 'THE SUIT EXCHANGE'

Austin Reed is a long established UK retailer founded in 1900. The chain comprises 50 outlets and sells clothing for both men and women, although it is best known for the former.

One of the problems facing Austin Reed as a brand is that it has rather a traditional image. It is also associated with more formal and

The Austin Reed 'Logic Train'

Men's fashion is getting younger and more informal. Newer retailers are attracting these customers.

Austin Reed has a rather old-fashioned image and a heritage in more formal men's clothing.

Younger buyers often see the brand as 'not for me' and do not visit whilst shopping for clothes.

In fact, when they actually see the range they are impressed.

Thus the key problem is to get potential buyers over the store threshold to see for themselves.

A powerful dynamic is required to overcome their inertia and the Austin Reed brand image.

Nearly all the target shoppers actually own suits, which they no longer wear, and need to replace with new suits or separates.

These potential buyers cannot help but be aware of the problem of homelessness on city streets.

This is an issue which they can relate to and which has become increasingly high profile.

It scores highly among social concerns of young professional men.

Austin Reed can capitalise on this in partnership with Shelter, the largest charity working to solve the problem.

The Austin Reed 'Suit Exchange'

'A Logic Train driving the campaign.'

structured clothing at a time when fashions have moved away from that mode of dress for many people and when the retailer is being challenged by younger pressure brands such as Next. Thus Austin Reed developed a campaign which would make them a more approachable mainstream brand and give them an image which would appeal to a slightly broader target market.

Meanwhile the issue of homelessness had become increasingly salient in the UK. People sleeping out on the street are still a common sight with around 2000 people out on any one night in England alone.

Particularly in London and in some other major conurbations around the country, salesmen of the *Big Issue* have become an everyday sight on many street corners. This magazine is produced on a professional basis but distributed in a unique way: unemployed and homeless people become effectively franchisees for the *Big Issue* and earn revenue from their sales. Their obvious presence on the streets brought home the issue of homelessness to many who had previously been oblivious to it.

The largest national charity addressing the problem of homelessness and bad housing is Shelter. The attraction for them in partnering with Austin Reed was exactly reciprocal to the motivation of the brand – namely the counterpoint between what was seen as a traditional city 'image' and a charity with a lot of street credibility, using the partnership to gain access to new markets and different audiences.

Another dimension was added because people wearing Austin Reed clothing, archetypally going to their jobs in civilized offices and city centre environments, would see homeless people spending the night on the street and would therefore have the issue high up on their agenda.

The promotion with Austin Reed offered Shelter a chance to raise their profile within the retail sector from which they have not traditionally had support and of course raise £20 000 for their vital work. In addition, the campaign offered Austin Reed customers the chance to support a charity that works to prevent homelessness and to help those people sleeping in office doorways who they may often pass on their way to work.

'Street credibility and help for Shelter too.'

The campaign mechanic was very straightforward: customers were encouraged to bring in their old suits to Austin Reed and to obtain a discount on a new suit. The value of the promotion was very attractive – up to £30 for suits priced under £300 and £50 on suits priced above that. The suits brought in during the programme were passed on to Shelter to sell through their shops up and down the country. These would raise anything between £5 and £25 per suit. In addition a £5 donation from Austin Reed was added to every suit passed to Shelter.

The reaction from staff was extremely positive and reports from Austin Reed suggest that a very large proportion of their employees were completely behind the promotion, and of course in a retail environment having a motivated sales staff is more than half the battle. Feedback from customers was also extremely positive, and there was widespread news coverage, for example on Sky TV, and also within the industry; a great deal of positive word of mouth was generated.

The promotion was deliberately staged for 2 weeks in October 1997 in order to focus attention and motivate customers to act immediately and bring in their old suits. Nevertheless, despite the limited period suit sales were up 53% on the same period in the previous year and this increase was largely attributed to the campaign. Austin Reed's experience of discounts of the level that they were offering through the Suit Exchange predicted a 22% rise in sales for an equivalent scheme. Therefore the association with Shelter more than doubled the effectiveness of a more standard discount offer.

At a qualitative level there were also indications that a broader customer base had been brought into Austin Reed in addition to the more traditional buyer. Reports from the sales floor suggest that over half of all customers buying suits at Austin Reed stores during the 2-week period participated in the scheme.

Perhaps the best indication of sales and public relations success is that the campaign was continued in 1998 but extended to a 4-week time period and widened to include women's suits and also made-to-measure.

From Shelter's point of view the campaign has also been a great success because it has helped them to enter new fundraising markets and of course significant sums of money have been donated to them whilst raising awareness of the issue through advertising.

18

Media Neutrality and Corporate Body Language

There is an overwhelming range of media opportunities facing the communicator nowadays. The explosion in the number of TV channels, first as a result of deregulation and secondly as a result of the move into the digital era, has presented advertisers with an incredible range of choices.

The same sort of process has occurred in printed media with the cost of production steadily falling and the ability to produce high quality niche publications rising in proportion. All the traditional media have become more accessible to advertisers and at the same time a whole new wave of media has come as a result of the Internet and the digital revolution.

In developing the creative idea for the CRM campaign it is important to begin from a 'media neutral' position. That is to say, the marketer and their agents should not start with the predisposition or indeed prejudice that a TV spot is the ideal vehicle to convey the campaign idea. This has been the old way of doing things in the advertising business and has led to accusations, often fairly, that advertising people are elitist in their perception of the communications hierarchy, viewing anything other than the main broadcast and print media as in some way beneath them.

The other communications specialists in their various fields have been relatively slow to exploit this weakness but increasingly agencies in the direct marketing, public relations, sales promotion and sports sponsorship sectors have been able to demonstrate that they have an equal place at the marketing table, due to the power of their communications potential for the brand.

The central CRM idea for the brand should unify the campaign, not a narrow media one. This core idea must come first. Once achieved, it can then be transmitted through the different media chosen for the task.

'Media neutrality' does not mean that media planners and buyers should not be involved in the creative development process. Indeed it is in the spirit of the extended project team described earlier that these specialists should be very much encouraged to participate. If they do, then the detailed media planning which follows will be that much more efficient, as it will be based on a deeper understanding of the CRM idea.

Clearly media planning in the late 1990s is a very complex area. It is the subject of many specialist publications and the focus of activity of dedicated agencies, so we will not explore the process in detail.

However, there are one or two aspects of media planning philosophy which may be useful for the marketer in developing a CRM campaign in particular. The central issue is that of 'corporate body language', i.e. the way that the company goes about its communications activities.

The consumer has become increasingly expert. The general public understands and indeed actively plays the marketing game. They have a broad appreciation of the relative costs of media and production. In focus groups respondents can articulate with perhaps alarming sophistication from the marketer's point of view their critique of TV production values in a commercial. Readers of newspapers understand that a whole page colour is significantly more expensive than a quarter page in black and white. Magazine gatefolds and double page spreads have a well understood stature.

As a result a brand's media usage is a subtle but influential part of its image. At its most simplistic, big successful brands can afford longer TV spots, bigger spaces in the press, more dramatic special build outdoor posters and more exotic locations and dramatic effects in their commercials. Smaller, less powerful brands use smaller spaces, shorter spots and cheaper production values. At a more sophisticated level brands can also score points with the consumer, not just for media choice *per se*, but also for timing and positioning within it.

In the early days of UK Sunday newspaper colour magazine supplements, Sainsbury would only buy the very first double page spread. The fact that their spread was actually one page colour facing a page black and white made this hard to negotiate in the face of other advertisers competing for the same position with genuine double pages in colour. They stuck to their guns and attained leadership status as a result.

Being in the right break of the right TV programme can confer status on a brand. The annual fight for position in the American Super Bowl broadcast is perhaps the most famous example of this. Being first onto a new medium also says something good about a brand, and it is usually a good media buy too as consumers 'trial' the new channel or publication. In 1995 Cheltenham & Gloucester were the first UK savings and mortgage company to list an Internet address in a TV commercial. The fact that at that time very few potential customers had access to the net was irrelevant: being involved early with the hottest new medium since TV was part of C&G's leadership position.

These considerations affect all aspects of a brand's communications. Nowadays consumers expect their brands to advertise themselves. Consumer research shows that if a brand goes quiet or off air for any length of time this tends to raise doubts in the consumer's mind: 'Why isn't it advertising itself? Has the company lost confidence in its product or service? Don't they believe in what they are doing any more?'

All these considerations will of course apply to a brand's Cause Related Marketing campaign. There may be a temptation, for example, to treat the activity as having in some way less importance or stature than the brand's 'main' communications. Marketers and agencies may be tempted to use shorter spot lengths, smaller space sizes, or indeed lower production budgets. This would be a mistake if it looks as though the brand is behaving in a contradictory way: Why is it proud of its rational and emotional benefits and apparently not so firm in its ethical or spiritual beliefs?

In short, the CRM campaign ought to be delivered at the same level of weight and stature as the rest of the brand's communications. If the brand has a cheap and cheerful persona such as a discount retailer then the CRM campaign ought to be delivered in the same spirit. If the brand has a high quality and aspirational character then the CRM campaign needs to fit with that too.

In this context an interesting example of new media thinking and an innovative way of delivering a CRM campaign is provided by the Red Cross HelpAd scheme, as used by the partnership of two major food brands, Anchor and Hovis.

Case History: ANCHOR & HOVIS:
RED CROSS 'HELPADS'

A familiar way of developing a CRM campaign, through on-product promotion, is by exploiting the potential that many products and services have in the available space on their packaging. As part of leveraging the relationship between a company brand and a charity, the brand can include details about the cause or charity it supports on its packaging materials.

This could range from a simple registration of the logo with an indication of support all the way through to an appeal for funds with telephone numbers and Internet addresses. It is important, however, that this is a part of a larger CRM programme rather than constituting the whole campaign in itself, since in isolation it can be seen as boring and one-dimensional, and thus fail to get a message across effectively.

However, an idea originated by Bob Doyle, the Northern Irish community peace campaigner, which was then presented to the Red Cross has taken this concept a stage further with the innovative 'HelpAd' programme. The Red Cross has enormous authority as a charity operating in 169 different countries with 140 million volunteers world-wide. It supports a number of causes in the UK and provides emergency relief to disaster victims and refugees across the globe.

The HelpAd concept is very simple and this is one of its attractions. The HelpAd organization negotiates with a product to enable it to 'sell' some space on its packaging to another product. By careful matching of target audience and communications objectives, HelpAd can provide one brand with almost perfect exposure on another. One of the best examples of this is the arrangement that they made between a range of Hovis breads and the Anchor Spreadable butter brand in 1996.

Anchor and Hovis share a similar purchaser profile and complementary brand values. Anchor Spreadable is a pioneering product, offering 100% pure butter in a spreadable format. At this time, Anchor were looking to attract new users to their Spreadable brand, so the opportunity for Anchor to advertise itself on millions of bread wrappers of a brand with the standing of Hovis was clearly an excellent one.

'HelpAds: an ingenious use of white space for cause marketing.'

As is shown in the illustration above, the HelpAd is clearly identified with its distinctive logo and this makes it clear that Hovis is supporting the HelpAd programme. Anchor places the advertisement of its new product right in front of millions of members of its target audience and in so doing also declares that it supports the HelpAd programme because it has bought the space from HelpAd, which was donated by Hovis in the first place.

The money raised from the sales of this innovative medium went towards the Red Cross funds. In the case of Hovis and Anchor HelpAds the amount of money raised was £100 000, and this is obviously a significant amount of money for the Red Cross.

For Anchor the sales results have been impressive; from the research they have done there are clear indications of increased business from Hovis customers. At the time of the campaign Anchor Butter Spreadable's sales increased by 36% among buyers of the Hovis loaves, and attracted new consumers, increasing its buyer base by 75%.

From the Hovis point of view there was a clear communication to its target audience – 22 million loaves were sold with the Anchor HelpAds on them – and this has improved the perception of the brand among its customers. Hovis also had clear indications of increased sales as a result of the scheme. Ian Greengrass, Brand Manager at Hovis, had this to say:

> Our first HelpAd with Anchor Spreadable Butter was extremely successful and we believe our forthcoming promotions will have similar success. We are certainly committed to the HelpAd scheme and wish it every success for the future.

HelpAd have run a number of similar campaigns for the following products and services: Hovis and Branston Pickle, Hovis and Tropicana, Hovis and Heinz Sandwich Fillers, Tesco White Bread and HP Fruity Sauce, Tesco White Bread and Hellmann's Mayonnaise, Tesco White Potatoes and Homepride Potato Bake Sauce, Shredded Wheat and Marmite, Shredded Wheat and Sun-Pat Peanut Butter, Del Monte Tomato Juice and Tabasco, Bisto Gravy and Wall's Sausages, Quaker Puffed Wheat and Whitworth's Breakfast Booster, Silver Spoon Caster Sugar and Stork Rich Blend Margarine. All of these initiatives generated increased sales, favourable PR and much needed revenue for the Red Cross.

Another key media planning consideration is that of timing. Many marketing plans are conditioned by inherent seasonality in the market and it may be that the CRM campaign should fit in with this natural programme in the brand's life.

However, there is now another timetable to be considered – the charity has one too. Does the partner voluntary organization already have important days in its year plan which are part of its own fundraising and motivational programme for its supporters, such as World Aids Day on 1st December, Breast Cancer Awareness Month in October, or World Mental Health Day on 10th October? Would the brand be better advised to capitalise on that asset rather than slavishly to follow its own traditional seasonality?

There is a third aspect of timing to be thought about which is that of the religious or spiritual calendar. While the pundits may deplore the decline in regular church-going in Western Europe and in some parts of the United States, it will be a very long time before the deep-seated traditions of Christianity will be eroded in the public mind. It does not matter that we have 24-hour shopping and that Sunday as the day of rest is no longer a reality, having succumbed to the pressures of commerce.

There is still a strong residual understanding of the nature of Sunday and this extends to many other important days in the Christian and Jewish calendars such as Easter and Passover. For the foreseeable future these days will be inherently related to higher order thoughts and reflections. It therefore seems sensible for the marketer to acknowledge and, where appropriate, utilize these feelings to support the CRM campaign and to plan media exposure accordingly.

Moving on to the question of creative content, for similar reasons it makes sense for the brand communication to remain coherent in its style. It would be rather odd if a commercial, press ad or other form of communication were to appear which were not in the same visual or aesthetic family as the rest of the brand's presentation to its consumers.

In other markets such as financial services, the argument is sometimes made that a stripped down, very economic form of creative content – rolling titles only on a plain background on TV for example – can reinforce a message of cost efficiency. Similarly it could be argued that a CRM communication should in itself be inexpensive so it is not open to the accusation that the money should have gone to the cause instead of into the pocket of a TV production company.

However, consumer research exploring this issue has shown fairly clearly that while in the hothouse environment of a focus group there are a minority of consumers who will subscribe rationally to this thesis (cheap communications = value for money), the majority of consumers do not. Furthermore, in the real world of communications where people see advertisements in their home, on TV or in newspapers and magazines, they are not thinking with the same kind of rational scrutiny that they might do in a focus group. And in this 'real' viewing situation they are much more susceptible to the overall feeling of brand values that come out of their communications. In this context, cheap advertising = a cheap company.

Turning to the question of communications content, it is obviously the case that each individual campaign will have its own idea, which needs to be conveyed. But general lessons have been learned from the past, for example in attempting to communicate environmental 'green' messages.

The main point is that consumers remain essentially self-concerned. They will always look for the personal benefit coming out of any proposition from a brand. Many environmental communications failed in this respect: they were big on the issue and small on what good it was going to do for the product or service that the consumer was actually going to buy. Too often the reality was that subscribing to an environmental policy meant a diminution in product performance – the example that springs to mind is Ecover, a dishwashing product popularly remembered in its early stages for needing twice as much liquid to be effective.

Assuming that the partner has been chosen well by the brand, there should be a natural relevance in the association between the two in communication terms. However, there is an obvious choice to be made between emphasizing what the brand is doing for the charity or the cause, or what the charity or the cause is doing for the consumer.

Experience suggested by a whole range of case histories would indicate that the consumer is much more motivated by the issues faced by the charity or entailed in tackling the cause, than by the brand trumpeting the commitment to them.

Thus in the commercial for Norwich Union which supports the efforts of St John Ambulance (a charitable organization involved with First Aid training, whose volunteers provide First Aid cover at big events), the main content of the film addresses a First Aid issue. This presents the consumer with the challenge of deciding what the right course of action is when a child swallows some potentially dangerous liquid.

It is clear at the end of the commercial that the solution to this prob-
lem can be provided by participating in a training course run by St John
Ambulance, and that this training is brought to you care of the Norwich
Union, a major insurance company and healthcare cover provider.

The alternative approach, i.e. starting with Norwich Union and talking about its commitment to St John Ambulance and then going on to
give a practical example, would almost certainly have been much less
engaging and looked too much like corporate self-congratulation.

Another lesson to be learned from the wider experience in communications is that the CRM campaign should not fall into the trap of trying
to convey too many messages. The same is true in a TV commercial: one
single-minded proposition clearly and memorably put is infinitely more
effective than a whole series of points strung together in some kind of
loose narrative.

If the creative brief has been developed as described earlier, and if the
company and the charity are absolutely crystal clear about their joint
objective and the criteria by which success or failure will be measured,
then it should be very obvious what the single-minded message of the
CRM campaign is to be.

One of the intriguing aspects of communications is that we may feel
that we have conveyed to our audience that which we intended, but
when the audience is actually asked what they received, in nearly all cases
it is something slightly different.

Thus the pre-testing of advertising before it is finally put into production, with all the expense that this entails, is a very useful stage in the
process. Nowadays the practice is very widespread, and there are many
agencies and research companies who have specialist moderators skilled
in interpreting consumer reactions to rough creative stimulus material
approximating to the finished film, printed poster or other execution.

Because of the sensitivity of Cause Related Marketing activities it is
particularly recommended that qualitative pre-testing be conducted on
the campaign before it is produced and put out into the market. It is also
worth pre-testing the campaign with more than just the brand consumer
target audience.

Clearly there are many other potential stakeholders in the process who
will have a very close interest in how the campaign actually appears. To
this end it is extremely worthwhile conducting focus group research or

in-depth interviews among samples of company employees, the charity supporters and perhaps even key journalists or experts in the field concerned.

While it is highly unlikely that everybody is going to agree about a communication strategy, it would be very useful and indeed essential for the marketer to understand all the dimensions of the communication and the ways in which it will be received by the different audiences involved.

For companies floated on the stock exchange it would also be useful to trail the campaign with the relevant analysts just to make sure that they too are fully on board with the corporate strategy in this area. The Co-op Bank has done this very successfully and perhaps it is more than coincidence that its recent first half 1998 profits were up 21.8% year on year.

Investors in companies obviously look hard at the fundamentals, but they primarily back managements. Thus a company with strong leadership and a clear idea of where it is going and how it is going to get there is very reassuring. As the 'City' becomes more concerned with the social stance of companies – now the influential Sainsbury Pension Fund is reviewing its policy in favour of more 'ethical' investments – those that have a clearly defined stance will benefit. This will not be an altruistic view, but a commercial one based on the notion that in any downturn, companies which stand for something more that just their narrow business interests will retain the favour of their consumers when tougher times see off their fair-weather friends.

Maintaining newsworthiness

Public relations is one of the most powerful tools in the communications armoury. Because the primary role of PR is to create editorial or third-party endorsement of a brand it is a subtle art but nevertheless a professional and quantifiable activity.

Most PR practitioners agree that the value of editorial is infinitely more influential than paid-for communication because of the objective authority that it carries. That is to say, a piece of editorial which fills a quarter of a page in a newspaper is deemed to have far more value to the company than it would have if it had been paid for as an advertisement.

Public relations has developed many aspects to its activities over the last 20 years so that the product offer now ranges from all types of media relations to lobbying and crisis management, with employee and investor relations, sponsorship, specialist publishing and conference and exhibition organizing in between. And many of these specialisms will be relevant to a company or a brand and used in the case of developing a CRM programme.

If the overriding objective of PR is to give a brand or corporation the oxygen of publicity in order to ensure that it continues to live and breathe vigorously, then among the key fuels for the fire are newsworthy events. Regular press releases, conferences and seminars, which generate coverage, will all result from a genuinely dynamic and evolving campaign.

It is simply no good if the CRM programme is just constituted by a logo, a launch and a lunch. If that is all there is to it then there might be some minor coverage on day one but after that the journalists will lose interest. Thus the PR function has a key role to play in developing the CRM programme. In many companies it may well be that someone from the PR department is designated as the leader or 'author' of the campaign, particularly if public relations in preference to advertising appears to be one of the dominant communications channels. However the two should not be seen as mutually exclusive, and it could be said that there has been too much reliance on PR alone.

But what ways are there to ensure that the CRM campaign remains newsworthy? Liz Claiborne's support for the campaign against domestic violence, which is now in its eighth year in the United States, gives a great insight into this. Liz Claiborne has treated the issue of domestic violence as if it were a 'brand' and they have invested in it accordingly.

What this has meant in practice is that they have considered on a step-by-step basis all the different target audiences that are in some way connected to the problem of domestic violence or violence within relationships. Thus they have reiterated the campaign through the different sexes, age groups and familial relationships. By packaging up these individual segments and making them the focus of the campaign over a particular time period they have created newsworthiness because the story has appealed to a different section of the news media. In doing this they also used other on-campus 'media' such as university and college courses, and classroom education to reach their target audiences. This process is described in much more detail in the case history.

Another tried and tested device in generating news coverage is that of the survey. Typically a brand will conduct a small-scale, but statistically significant quantitative survey using a series of questions which are usually designed to elicit the answers that are going to serve the PR needs of the brand. Clearly in the case of CRM it could be disastrous to fix the research in this way.

However, the basic idea of using market research surveys, particularly in areas of charitable activity or in relationship to causes which the consuming public feels strongly about, can be very powerful indeed. This power is enhanced by the fact that there is relatively little market research conducted in many of these areas, simply because there has so far appeared to be no commercial interest in doing so.

Thus there is a dual benefit for the brand in conducting this research: first, it will create news coverage and secondly, it will shed further light on the very issue that the CRM campaign is seeking to highlight.

Perhaps the most effective way of maintaining newsworthiness in a CRM campaign is if there is genuine commitment to it at the highest levels of the company or brand management. Key individuals must be prepared to make themselves available to the media and demonstrate in those interviews a personal passion and conviction for the cause which they espouse.

Given that the media would expect a CEO or senior manager to be almost exclusively and conventionally focused on their company or industry, the impact of a powerfully held view on a topic outside this area can be considerable. How often would the CEO of a leading telephone call handling company be asked to speak at a conference or dinner outside the narrow confines of his or her industry? If they were also committed to a major CRM campaign in favour of the improvement of hearing in young children, it might be a very different matter. They would have something really important to believe in and it would show.

A case in point would be the acres of positive news coverage that Anita Roddick created for The Body Shop. Indeed, she built her brand without the aid of advertising but with PR alone. Hopefully more and more corporate leaders will follow the example of entrepreneurs such as Ben & Jerry of ice cream fame, whose altruism is part and parcel of their business activity.

Binding all this together and underpinning the continuing newsworthiness of the CRM campaign is the fundamental element that drives it, namely the public commitment of the company, in partnership with the charity or direct to the cause, to a measurable target that is going to be achieved in a declared timescale. There is something very compelling about a very simple definable objective and then a regular series of published steps along the way. The fascination with charts, league tables and ratings of all sorts confirms that people are avid followers of teams on their way to achieving public goals.

In exactly the same way that mortgage companies publish regular surveys on house prices or financial institutions interest rates, the brand can publish regular reports on its progress towards achieving its CRM goal. If this becomes a recurrent theme in the company's communications then it will make very compelling listening and reading for the target audience.

19

CRM and the Digital Revolution

The UK, Western Europe and the United States are teetering on the brink of the digital revolution. This switch over from analogue to digital technologies is having widespread implications for broadcast media, telephony and communications via the Internet.

This presents the marketer with opportunities and threats, as we shall see. Taken positively it offers enormous potential for richer communication between a brand and its customers. It is particularly suited to conveying more detailed information in an interesting and user-friendly manner than the extreme cost and time length of traditional TV spots could ever allow. Cause Related Marketing campaigns are clearly a prime candidate for this.

The consumer is not at all concerned about the technologies involved and the bewildering references to band widths and bauds, portals, html, transactional banners, search engine optimization, log files or cookies, because as usual all they are really concerned about is 'what's in it for me?' In the case of the digital revolution 'what's in it for them' means three main things.

First, there is an enormously increased potential for signal transmissions to be received, meaning an explosion in television and radio channels with a massive widening of choice and an improvement in the quality of the transmissions, which will lead to better sound and better pictures.

Secondly, there is a dramatic convergence of technologies, meaning that devices which combine portability with computing and audio or video telephony, and the ability to make remote connections with the Internet will become commonplace.

Thirdly, and perhaps most importantly, there will be interactivity with the potential for the 'couch potato' to turn into the 'couch commando' – a demanding, pro-active consumer. For the first time the viewer or listener will be able to answer back in an incredibly easy and efficient manner. Many organizations are grappling with the complexities of this in a technical sense, as indeed they are with its possible benefits and applications in the marketing arena.

The main threat to brands in this new environment is that of 'dis-intermediation'. Put simply, this means cutting out the middleman. Ironically for the major multiple retailers and indeed the global brand owners, they may both be facing a very powerful new challenge to their authority, just when it appeared that they had achieved an incomparable ascendancy.

The Internet enables an ordinary consumer to compare prices and shop direct across an ever-growing range of product fields. While marketers enthuse about the potential of the World Wide Web to enable them to indulge in their new passion for 'one to one marketing' many of them are privately much more fearful of the threat that it represents to their business in its traditional distribution channels.

A whole new type of company is emerging via the Internet of which Amazon, CDnow and Peapod are some of the best known. These are virtual businesses with no shops but potentially perfect distribution, and they are growing fast.

There are two big questions which many companies are facing as a result of the potential for the customer to 'go direct'. If they are retailers they have to explain to themselves why anyone would bother to continue to visit one of their traditional outlets with all the potential hassle that that usually involves. Why get involved in driving, parking, queues, variability of service, out of stocks and repeated loading and unloading? Alternatively customers can view the merchandise on screen, read the consumer reports and then order immediately by credit card for easy home delivery. What could be simpler? Heavy, frequently bought, low interest product categories which have tendencies to commodity are prime candidates for being bought 'direct', as are 'intangibles' such as financial services and products which can themselves be digitized such as music and games.

Assuming the retailer is stuck with thousands of square feet of physical selling space what is the added brand value that is going to continue to motivate people to make a visit when such a convenient alternative exists? Shopping will have to be increasingly presented as a leisure activity in order to continue to attract people to stores. Skills in creating 'retail theatre' will become much more highly valued with the creative use of 3D and interactive technologies leading the way.

If the company is a brand marketer why should a customer who can instantly compare prices and specifications on screen and also refer to consumer guides remain loyal, especially if there's a premium being asked? How is that brand going to sustain its emotional or image advantages over the competition especially if it is being compared with another well-known manufacturer brand or retailer brand offering a lower price?

For both types of companies there is the added problem of how consumers will 'search' the web, given the bewildering scale of the Internet and the countless search engines and multi-engine search tools available. How is a brand asked for in the first place?

Clearly more powerful brand values are going to be needed on this new playing field in cyberspace. If practical, rational attributes can be compared with ruthless objectivity, and if differentiating emotional and psychological imagery is harder to convey in the aesthetic of the website, then perhaps a new sort of brand belief or 'ethic', which can be powerfully conveyed in words alone, could be a very useful thing.

At this early stage, with only a few trials to go on, it is hard to predict the future, but most of the observers believe that the 'layering' of media is going to be one of the key facets of the future interaction between consumers and media owners. Digital broadcasting licences are being sold as so-called 'multiplexes' which means that the licensee is permitted to transmit a spectrum of material ranging from text, through graphics to sound and moving pictures.

The practical implication of this is that a viewer watching a TV programme can press a button on the remote control or click on an icon as if with a mouse and bring up additional information relating to what is already on screen. This information could be in the form of text or in the shape of additional video information.

If, for example, there was a conventional TV commercial for a car on screen, and the viewer wished to see more extended test drives or details of the interior of the car, i.e. more visual information than could have been contained in a 60-second TV commercial, then the system can enable the viewer to do just that. The extra footage could be delivered straight to a video recorder or could be requested on a time shift basis for later transmission. Alternatively the viewer could decide to request additional information or brochures about the car and this could be automatically requested by clicking on the appropriate icon. This could be extended to requesting a test drive or even dialling a telephone number to a dealership to discuss a price with a sales person.

Obviously this wonderful new 'layered' media world will also be able to be used to convey much more information about the company and its brands. Indeed there are already huge numbers of examples of this being done on the web. Consumers are also becoming more and more accustomed to expecting this sort of depth and transparency. Thus the opportunities for exploiting the Internet to expose and explain a CRM strategy are very exciting. Avon's website is an excellent example of how well it can be done.

Clearly there are many issues surrounding the practicalities of all this and the degree to which consumers will behave in this way with what is still essentially regarded as a leisure pleasure medium: the term 'couch potato' indicates the general passivity of the viewing mode.

One thing that does seem likely is that broadcasters will be very keen to persuade their advertisers to exploit and users to explore these 'layers' in order to justify the cost of setting up the technology in the first place. They will seek to demonstrate that they have added overall value to the medium from the advertiser's point of view and will also want to prove that the sales of products will be accelerated and made more cost-efficient by the integration of these various layers of communication.

To this end, it is likely that broadcasters and advertisers will want to find ways to encourage consumers actually to behave in the way that they would like.

There seem to be two main methods in which this can be done from either the advertiser or the media owner perspective. From the advertiser perspective it is clearly possible to offer financial incentives to encourage certain sorts of consumer interactivity. The incentives could be in the form of rebates or coupons or other promotional mechanisms.

From the media owner's point of view it is also desirable to derive with financial tools the 'right' sort of behaviour from the viewer. If, for example, that broadcaster is involved in the pay per view servicing, it would be possible for viewers to earn points worth discounts off future pay per view events as a reward for interacting with the medium and its advertisers.

If these mechanisms are put in place for commercial reasons, then there is no reason at all why they should not be exploited for Cause Related Marketing reasons. It seems very likely that either broadcasters or commercial organizations will seek ways of rewarding their consumers in the most cost-effective way possible – giving away money in terms of discounts or coupons can be a very expensive business.

An alternative way to motivate consumers and to reinforce appropriate brand values is for the advertiser or the broadcaster to agree to donate small amounts of money to a specified charity or good cause. As with other CRM programmes, the consumer will be able to support a good cause through the channel of a brand, whether it be a product or service or indeed a broadcast one.

Clearly the TV broadcaster has a fantastic 'in kind' benefit to bring to any charity or cause that it chooses to support – namely airtime which can be used by the charity to make appeals direct to the public and to explain its mission overall.

The complex nature of the challenges faced by marketers and traditional broadcasters alike in the emerging on-line world is illustrated by the burgeoning growth on new Internet media such as banners and site sponsorship. One of the obvious factors about cyberspace which differentiates it from the more traditional media is that currently there is an enormous surplus of advertising space available compared with the number of marketers who are prepared to pay for it. This means that very large numbers of 'hits' or impressions are available at really low prices and also that the operators of many sites feel able to donate free space to charities or good causes.

The benefit for the site owners in doing this is that it enables them to fill their various advertising locations, such as the banners at the headers of pages, and demonstrate how they work, thus giving potential advertisers a better understanding of the possibilities of the medium. At the same time they are clearly supporting good causes and in that way are adding appropriate values to their Internet media brands.

The benefit for the charity involved is that, given the nature of the medium, it is possible for there to be hypertext links between the banner donated free on a particular site through to the charity's own website where the consumer can gain much more information about its activities. They can also make donations, volunteer to help and in general discover more about the good cause that it supports or the issue it deals with. If this is well organized the charity can raise additional funds, enlist new supporters and, perhaps most importantly, galvanize action on a broad front remarkably easily and cost effectively.

Perhaps the biggest donor so far has been Yahoo, which is one of the most popular Internet search services, which guide novices and veterans alike through the Byzantine structure of cyberspace. David Filo, cofounder of Yahoo, pledged $2 000 000 worth of free advertising to charities at the President's Summit for America's Future held in Philadelphia in April 1997. The money is going to go to two groups – Youth Service America, which works to get young people involved in volunteering in community service, and an educational programme designed to improve the lives of children which is being run by the Benton foundation.

Perhaps inspired by Yahoo's generosity, a number of other Internet players have begun to provide free advertising to charities and emerging brands, such as AltaVista, Lycos and Infoseek. Microsoft, as you might expect, has also committed five million free impressions worth an estimated $250 000. America Online, or AOL, has said that it will give up to 5% of its advertising slots to charities.

Intermediaries are also getting involved in a constructive and motivating way. For example, the Advertising Council, which is a non-profit organization based in New York, is extending its help to charities in giving information to their various publics by moving beyond traditional media such as television, radio and print into the Internet. They have made slogans such as 'friends don't let friends drive drunk' and 'a mind is a terrible thing to waste' famous in terrestrial media, and now these sorts of messages are being made available to companies with their own sites. The address below can be used to access this information:

The Advertising Council
261 Madison Avenue
New York NY 10016
Tel: (212) 922 1500
www.adcouncil.org/

The potential scale of this is truly mind-boggling. AltaVista, another of the Internet search engines or services, receives in excess of 30 million 'hits' each day. Recently they have promoted the National Fatherhood Initiative (actually without the charity's prior knowledge) and the first that the charity realized of its sponsorship was when its own site which had been getting about 200 'hits' per day suddenly jumped to more than 3000.

The National Fatherhood Initiative's president Wade Horne reports that those who found their way to the charity's website not only gained more information, they made donations and signed up as members on-line. Ancillary merchandise such as books have also seen a significant increase in volume sales.

Important players in the World Wide Web have clearly adopted CRM – perhaps they are leading where more traditional broadcasters and brand marketers will follow. Certainly the Internet is now a prime consideration in developing an integrated communications campaign for a brand and its 'cause' and may well prove to be one of the most dynamic and creative forums for its expression, engendering practical support from increasingly interactive consumers.

20

Measurement

As with any marketing communications programme it is important to set up at the outset the criteria for success and then the tools to measure whether or not that success has been achieved.

Most brands have assessments of one sort or another in position to measure their performance towards their stated goals and a CRM campaign should be no different. Perhaps the extra dimensions of a CRM campaign, however, will require a wider range of tools to create effective measurement – simply because there are so many different stakeholders in the outcome.

The IPA (the Institute of Practitioners in Advertising) in the UK, the trade body for the advertising and communications industry, is regarded world-wide as an authority on the measurement of effectiveness.

In 1980 it held the inaugural competition in the continuing series of IPA advertising effectiveness awards. The original goal as set out in the first volume of winning papers, Advertising Works 1, was stated as follows:

> In the advertising business we all know that the ultimate test of any advertising campaign is the sales result to which it contributes. Sadly this hard truth is not always well acknowledged outside the agency world where the accountability of advertising is held in some doubt.

The Institute of Practitioners in Advertising is now setting out to remedy this situation with a unique competitive award scheme that will be based solely on the assessment of the *effects* of advertising campaigns in any media. It will aim to achieve three things:

1. A better understanding of the crucial role advertising plays in marketing.
2. Closer analysis of advertising effectiveness and improved methods of evaluation.
3. A clear demonstration that advertising can be proven to work, against measurable criteria.

Of the criteria for assessment, they wrote,

> . . . It is hoped that the measurement criteria will be as 'hard' as possible, involving behavioural evidence such as sales, rather than attitude or awareness shifts, unless such indications really are the most relevant.

Nine volumes (with an imminent tenth) of Advertising Works later, the IPA has assembled over 160 case histories which have won prizes in the competitions. Altogether, 611 cases have been entered so far, and all of these, including those which have not won prizes and therefore have not been published in paper form in the 'Advertising Works' series, have been logged in an IPA database. This is available through the IPA and copies of individual case histories can then be ordered from them, but a more limited version can be accessed via the Internet on the IPA site at the following address: http://www.ipa.co.uk

Perhaps in part because of the impact of the Co-op Bank case history, written by Sarah Ryder of the agency Partners BDDH, which was a winner in 1994, the organizing committee widened the remit of the awards for the 1998 competition.

In the supporting publication *Guide to Entrants*, published for it, the IPA makes it clear that they are looking for evidence of the effects of advertising across a much wider spectrum than before. Whereas the focus had been almost entirely on the contribution of advertising to increased profitability – with some stunning examples of this being recorded, such as the £400 million profits over 15 years in the case of BMW or the £297 million overall advertising-generated income over two years in the case of BT, both winners in recent years – other issues are now deemed to be very important too.

The IPA guidelines ask authors of entries to consider the impact of advertising communications on all the stakeholders involved in a company or brand. The judges are now looking for effects on such diverse audiences as the employees of the company, the company's investors and commentators, trade partners and suppliers, and local government and legislators. In doing so there is an inherent assumption that employee morale, for example may be materially improved by the right sort of brand communication.

In moving to this more holistic approach to the assessment of the impact of a brand communications campaign the IPA is doing two things. First, it is acknowledging that most marketers nowadays strive to produce an integrated communications campaign in which various strands are deliberately and strategically interlinked rather than looking at the particular role of advertising in isolation from other communications activities. Secondly the IPA is also acknowledging the 'higher order' as a powerful new factor in the impact of brand communications.

It is very likely therefore that over the next few competitions the IPA will be in receipt of many more cases where Cause Related Marketing campaigns are at the centre of the case history. If these future entries are anything like the calibre of the case for the Co-op Bank then they will demonstrate that the communications campaign has not simply helped sell more products, it will have actually shaped the fundamental nature of the company for which it is produced, and entail a vital change in strategic direction to the benefit of a very wide number of stakeholders.

It is likely that the same types of measures will be taken – quantitative consumer surveys to track attitudes and behaviour, syndicated surveys to demonstrate product distribution and rates of sale, qualitative research to indicate underlying reasons for shifts in consumer behaviour, and so forth. What will be different, however, are the stakeholder groups that will be sampled: not just customers and employees, but investors, government agencies, suppliers and even pressure group campaigners, critics and activists.

PART VI
Getting Down To It

Summary

Brand Spirit contains many examples and case histories of CRM in action and these have been deliberately interspersed throughout the text in order to illustrate particular points. Hopefully this has enabled the practical experience of professional marketers to bring the theory to life.

This section of the book is solely comprised of two detailed cases, either of which could have been used as excellent demonstrations of so many of the key aspects involved in conceiving, creating and delivering a successful CRM campaign. Both the Liz Claiborne and Norwich Union programmes show the importance and benefits of commitment at all levels of the organization. The 'Territorial' fit between the brands and the causes they have supported is tight. The level of budgetary support has ensured that due 'credit' has accrued to them, while also widening public awareness of, and involvement in, important issues. Exploratory research has been key to creating striking communications and the variety of media used has been considerable.

The main difference between the cases is one of scale and duration. Liz Claiborne's campaign against domestic violence is nation-wide and of long standing. Norwich Union's programmme to encourage First Aid training is regional and of a test nature. Hopefully therefore they demonstrate the spectrum of circumstances that a marketer may face.

21

Implementing CRM on a Grand Scale

Of all the cases we have reviewed for *Brand Spirit* the one prepared for Liz Claiborne by New York agency Patrice Tanaka & Company, Inc. is the one that has impressed us most. The origins of the campaign nearly 10 years ago, in which successive iterations of the basic theme of combating domestic violence have been communicated to various target audiences, is an excellent example of how to keep a CRM programme newsworthy.

We have therefore produced the following very detailed case history as an example of 'CRM on a grand scale'. This chapter has relied heavily on the presentation by Maria Kalligeros, Executive Vice President and Associate Creative Director of Patrice Tanaka & Company, Inc. at the Learning in Business CRM Conference sponsored by Saatchi & Saatchi Cause Connection and the *Independent* newspaper in May 1998. There has of course been considerable input from Liz Claiborne executives in all of this.

Case History: Liz Claiborne: 'Women's work campaign against domestic violence'

In the spring of 1991 Patrice Tanaka & Company, Inc., a New York based marketing PR agency, was engaged in talks with a high-level marketing executive at Liz Claiborne, Inc. (LC) about a possible marketing and public relations programme. At the time the Liz Claiborne retail chain was 15 years old, was not advertising and was looking for something to reinvigorate its brand: something that would strengthen the bond between LC and its customers, enhance corporate reputation and ultimately drive profitability.

GET THE FACTS

GET INVOLVED

WOMEN'S **WORK** ▲ LIZ CLAIBORNE

END FAMILY VIOLENCE

'Taking the high ground with a contentious issue.'

In researching programme possibilities, they were struck by the findings of a 1989 poll conducted by Opinion Research Corporation for *Fortune* magazine which showed that 89% of adults felt that a company's reputation often determines which products they will buy. Commenting on the survey findings, the publication *California Business* wrote that:

> Companies involved in social issues are considered more sensitive to their customers . . .

The Patrice Tanaka agency was aware that the technique of linking a company, brand or product to a social cause had increased dramatically in the previous decade and had evolved into a long-term positioning and marketing strategy. In their view, companies faced an increasingly challenging and competitive marketplace. Differentiation had become more and more difficult. And, at least in the States, many brands have been forced into price-cutting. Product parity is a problem and many companies cannot beat their competition through advertising alone.

Long-term customer loyalty has become critical to building a brand's market share, driving top line sales and delivering bottom line profitability: tying into the customer's concerns via compelling issues seemed likely to create significant gains in terms of long-term brand loyalty. CRM is no longer merely a short-term fix – it is a significant and undeniably important corporate strategy and necessary tool in the marketing arsenal that customers have come to expect, and indeed almost take for granted.

The agency felt confident that a sincere, *long-term,* issues-based campaign would add to Liz Claiborne's corporate reputation and provide a variety of opportunities for the customer and *the employees* to interact with the brand.

They established the following criteria for identifying an appropriate vehicle for Liz Claiborne, Inc.:

- It had to be *specific* to women, that is it had to address issues of particular concern to women – LC's core constituency;
- The client had to be able to establish a proprietary stake in the cause. The cause had to be one that people would come to identify almost exclusively with LC;
- It had to address a newsworthy issue capable of garnering coverage for LC in fashion publications – a critical media segment which tends to under-represent apparel marketers with broad market appeal;
- LC's support for the cause had to involve communities at the grass roots level to generate consumer good-will.

As part of their research, an audit was conducted of the many potential issues with which the company could align:

- Environmentalism
- Volunteerism
- Breast cancer
- Domestic violence

Although it initially scared everyone involved in the analysis, domestic violence awareness fitted all the criteria they had established:

- It was perceived to be an issue of particular interest to women;
- No other major corporation was involved in the issue and LC could establish a proprietary stake;
- It certainly would be newsworthy if a $2 billion women's fashion apparel company aligned itself with what up to that point had been an un-sexy, 'hot potato' issue (remember this was 1991 – way before the O.J. Simpson murder trial); and
- It could have many grassroots components via tie-ins with local shelter and advocacy groups.

Yet they still had some trepidation. To allay any lingering doubts about the strength and validity of a domestic violence awareness campaign, they conducted a national survey commissioned on behalf of LC which revealed that 93% of American women believed that domestic violence is a problem in America. The percentage was even higher (96%) among LC's customers. Those same customers said they would have a positive opinion of a company conducting an awareness campaign about the issue (91%) compared with 86% of *all* the women surveyed.

These findings led them to develop a programme called 'Women's Work' which has proved to be a long-term success for the company on a variety of levels.

Statistics

Aside from the marketing aspects of the issue they were also bowled over by the grim statistics:

- In the USA, a woman is beaten every 12 seconds.
- Domestic violence affects every strata of society.
- It respects no financial borders, recognizes no ethnic boundaries.
- And the violence spills into American streets: statistics reveal that children raised in violent homes are 74% more likely to commit assault.

The agency knew that the quality of all American lives continues to be compromised by this issue. It was therefore important for the company to have an *emotional* tie to any issue it aligned with. The company leaders and employees must have a connection to the issue; the issue must resonate within the company culture. And domestic violence did resonate within Liz Claiborne.

Programme

Their programme began in 1991 with a strategy of building awareness of domestic violence and has included many initiatives over the years, such as:

- Public service announcement campaigns on television, radio, billboards and bus shelters.

- Surveys of the general public comparing men's and women's views of the subject, as well as those of relevant audiences such as CEOs and college students.
- An annual charity shopping day that occurs every October at all Liz Claiborne stores nation-wide.

Ten per cent of the day's sales benefit local domestic violence organizations. The same charities receive proceeds from the sale of commemorative products such as t-shirts and jewellery featuring the campaign's tagline. These fundraising objects are also sold through a toll-free 800 number.

Over the years they've developed and distributed for free at least 500 000 domestic violence awareness posters and one quarter of a million educational brochures to social service organizations nation-wide. And they have carried out numerous mailings to business leaders, government officials, celebrities, and the medical and legal communities in an effort to create awareness among influential individuals.

Charity partners

They have partnered with local domestic violence agencies in each of LC's operating regions, which receive the proceeds from their charity shopping days, and on a national level with the Family Violence Prevention Fund, the pre-eminent national advocacy and education group.

They have chosen their charity partners carefully because they are the voice of authority with which LC's corporate reputation is linked. (Domestic violence is a very fractured community.) It is important to find partners who understand the time sensitivities and nuances of a corporate partnership. It is also contingent on the corporation to understand that the charity partner is often an under-financed group with a great deal of credibility and knowledge, but not necessarily the staff to get things done as quickly as one would want. Sensitivity and diplomacy are key ingredients in these relationships.

For a CRM campaign to be successful, the company must manage *everyone's* expectations: be very clear at the outset as to what precisely is expected from each side. Corporate partners should be prepared to help fund extra staff the charity may have to hire to complete the project. A letter of agreement with a clear timetable and an outline of responsibilities are also a very good idea.

Each year the programme evolves in response to society's perception of abuse. And each year Patrice Tanaka & Co. develop a newsworthy programme that positions Liz Claiborne as an innovative, forward-thinking company.

1992–1993

In the first two years of the programme, the company commissioned a variety of emerging and well-known American artists to collaborate with its local charity partners to create images that LC then displayed on billboards and bus shelters throughout San Francisco, Boston and Miami.

Of course, they had to make absolutely sure that, if the billboards were to increase awareness and demand for counselling, those services would be in place. So LC provided funding in each market for local initiatives, such as for hotline numbers, and encouraged other large local companies to do the same.

In addition, they rallied other local businesses to the cause by hosting CEO breakfasts, wherein LC's CEO invited other top executives in the area to a discussion as to why this issue was important at Liz Claiborne, how it impacts the bottom line, why they should become involved. They were positioning LC as a model for public–private partnerships and encouraging other companies to follow that lead. It is very important in any CRM programme to make sure you're not only creating a programme with *sizzle* (in other words a flashy, high-profile project), but that you also provide the *steak* – sincere grass-roots programmes or donations that make meaningful change.

1994 – CEO survey

In 1994, Liz Claiborne commissioned a survey conducted by Roper Starch World-wide to probe corporate leaders on their awareness of the problem, and sense of corporate accountability. One hundred companies were selected at random from the current list of the Fortune 1000.

The results are telling:

- 57% of the business leaders polled considered domestic violence a major social problem;
- 33% said domestic violence affects their balance sheet and a startling 40% were personally aware of employees in their company who had been affected by domestic violence;
- 66% agreed that a company's financial performance would benefit from addressing the issue among its employees;
- A loss of productivity, decreased attendance and rising health care costs were all identified as areas where domestic violence drags down bottom line performance.

Yet for all this, unfortunately only 12% of those surveyed say that corporations should play a major role in addressing the issue. A striking 96% of the 100 senior executives polled felt DV should be addressed primarily by the family. These results were merchandized to media nation-wide and received significant coverage for LC, particularly in the business press.

Simpson murder – evolution from awareness to education and prevention

It was about this time that the Simpson murder took place, forever changing the landscape of the domestic violence issue in the USA. It took this one event to do more for domestic violence awareness than 20 years of advocacy had done.

People were suddenly talking about domestic violence. In-depth coverage of the trial and the issue ran on the news every morning, noon and night of the week. While the LC strategy had been one of awareness building at the outset, it now evolved to embrace education and prevention.

1995

In an effort to reach young men and women as they begin to make critical life decisions about relationships, Liz Claiborne sponsored a pilot programme of campus workshops designed to teach students how to communicate effectively and avoid abusive situations. Called 'Relationships in the real world', they partnered with local domestic violence agency prevention organizations in three cities – St Louis, Seattle and Minneapolis – to offer students a workshop that addressed a spectrum of behaviour found in both healthy and unhealthy relationships. The programme included discussions of emotional, verbal and physical abuse as well as acquaintance rape. The response from the students was overwhelmingly positive.

Liz Claiborne commissioned another survey from Roper Starch polling college students on their awareness of, their attitudes towards, and their familiarity with the issue of domestic violence. The results of this survey were as striking as those from the CEO survey and these, too, were released to the media:

- Of college students 75% considered domestic violence a major problem in American society – only violent crime and Aids ranked higher.
- Six out of 10 reported they personally knew friends, relatives or someone else close to them who had been affected by domestic violence.
- Of those surveyed, 97% believed the family should be in the fore-front of addressing this problem. However, probably in contrast to previous generations, 89% do not think it is solely a family matter. Many think that domestic violence service organizations, the court system and police have meaningful roles to play, too.

The sheer number of college students – tomorrow's leaders – who realize the enormity of this issue, encourages hope for the future.

1996

This year was a major turning point for the programme – Liz Claiborne broke completely new ground on the issue. Patrice Tanaka & Co.'s idea was to reposition domestic violence as a men's issue and point out the need for male leadership in an area where, until now, there has been precious little male initiative. As partners, they sought out Northeastern University's Center for the Study of Sport in Society and the College Football Association. Together they created a series of television public service announcements addressing the issue of relationship violence that appeared at col-lege football games and on television network and cable affiliates nation-wide, including MTV, VHI and PBS. The Public Service Announcements spoke directly to men about breaking the code of silence surrounding relationship violence and went beyond simply raising awareness of abuse by proactively discouraging men from participating in relationship violence or tolerating it in others.

A key to focusing men's attention on this issue was the use of high-profile college football student athletes as role models. By using these 'icons of masculinity' they made it safe for other men to speak out on the issue. The spots targeted bystanders and batterers in the hope that societal pressure and a lack of tolerance would help put an end to violent behaviour, particularly between intimate partners.

1997

In 1997, Liz Claiborne continued this cutting-edge approach to the issue of domestic violence by distributing a series of public service announcements featuring male celebrity recording artists. Again these high-profile male musicians deliver a message directly to men about:

- Breaking the code of silence surrounding domestic violence;
- Applying peer pressure to abusers; and
- Getting 'bystanders' to speak out on the issue.

They selected recording artists representing different genres of the music industry: All-4-One, Backstreet Boys, Clint Black, Coolio, Kenny Loggins, Richard Marx and Travis Tritt all took part.

Their goal was to raise awareness that relationship abuse is not just a women's issue, that men must also be proactive in ending domestic violence. It was felt that the best way to reach men with this message was through other men, and these PSAs encouraged male leadership in this area. This approach very clearly positions LC as an innovative, forward-thinking company.

Employees

Employees are another facet of the CRM programme which is very important in reinforcing further the company's position as a corporate leader in domestic violence. 'Education and Prevention' is an ongoing employee assistance programme that year-round and around the clock provides off-site, confidential assistance in coping with family matters, and drug, alcohol and financial crises. Hundreds of calls have been fielded, referring employees in crisis to appropriate local community and health organizations.

Additionally, the company has held a series of family communication and family stress seminars offered in both English and Spanish at its various corporate headquarters and distribution facilities. Discussions are led by professionals trained in counselling and clinical psychology. In the first cycle, well over 1000 employees attended, learning about:

- What causes communication breakdowns;
- How to identify the warning signs in a relationship;
- What to do if domestic violence arises; and ultimately
- How to improve communications and family relations.

The human resources and security departments at Liz Claiborne also work very closely on special domestic violence policies for employees. For instance, should an employee at the New Jersey corporate offices feel threatened, Liz Claiborne will provide:

- A special reserved parking space near the front entrance;
- A security escort to and from the building; and
- In addition, Liz Claiborne has installed panic buttons at reception desks on all floors.

Above all, the company provides an environment of support that encourages employees to seek help, an environment in which supervisors support employees trying to find their way out of abusive situations, and enlightened managers urge employees to take full advantage of the internal programme.

Involvement from the top

It is important to note that their programme has always had full involvement from the very top of the organization, which they believe has been key to its success. In fact, a top Liz Claiborne executive serves on President Clinton's Advisory Council on Violence Against Women organized by Secretary of Health and

Human Services Donna Shalala and Attorney General Janet Reno. The LC executive represents what companies can and should do to help end domestic abuse. Find an advocate within the corporation – someone who is relatively close to the top. It will make the process of approval easier; it will also bring sincerity and truth to the programme. A company really has to buy into an issue in order for a CRM programme to work. Consumers can always smell a fake. It would be better not to attempt a programme than to attempt an insincere one.

Results

These results give an idea of the scope of the Liz Claiborne Women's Work programme. It is ambitious, and their goals are far ranging. They measure results in a variety of quantitative and qualitative ways:

- Combined media impressions generated via publicity and PSA airings to date total over 700 million. Ad equivalency totals $10 million and PR equivalency totals nearly $30 million.
- National coverage has included: 'The Today Show', 'MTV News', 'Sally Jesse Raphael Show', 'Live With Regis & Kathie Lee', *The Wall Street Journal*, *The New York Times* and various Internet mentions, including a chat on Compuserve's Women's Wire.
- Magazine coverage has included *Vogue*, *Glamour*, *Self*, *Women's Day*, *Harper's Bazaar*, *Elle*, etc. all key publications for the brand.
- Local market coverage included: *Los Angeles Times*, *Chicago Tribune*, *Atlanta Journal and Constitution*, *Dallas Morning News*, *Boston Globe*, *Houston Chronicle*, *San Jose Mercury News*, 'Today in New York', and other local network affiliate news programmes.
- They have donated more than $500 000 in funds for local and national domestic violence organizations. An additional $400 000 has been raised for domestic violence charities from other organizations and companies, like department stores, in the communities in which they work.
- The programme has received widespread recognition. 'Influentials' responded with letters congratulating LC for taking such a strong stand on the issue of domestic violence. The programme received awards from prominent organizations and LC spokespeople have

been invited to speak on the issue at universities, judicial conferences, national and local fundraisers, awards events and marketing seminars.

- LC received further recognition when its CEO was invited to the White House Rose Garden for a ceremony celebrating the passage of the 1996 Crime Bill in Congress and again to speak at a White House press conference with Vice President Al Gore on workplace violence.
- Liz Claiborne, Inc. has received hundreds of letters of thanks and commendations from customers, domestic violence service providers, politicians, other CEOs, the police, doctors, lawyers and judges for their efforts on behalf of the domestic violence issue.

The success of the WOMEN'S WORK programme has encouraged Liz Claiborne, Inc. to continue its commitment to cause-related marketing in 1998 and hopefully beyond. These results link directly back to their original objective: building brand loyalty, adding value and reinforcing corporate reputation. Liz Claiborne is perceived as a responsible caring company. Consumers appreciate the programme and feel that the company understands the issues that affect them. They feel better about spending their money on LC products. And it certainly has been a terrific way for the brand to differentiate itself in a very competitive retail marketplace.

These benefits have accrued to Liz Claiborne because of their long-term commitment to a single issue, a willingness and flexibility to evolve with that issue and, frankly, the courage and foresight to embark on this course in the first place.

22

Implementing CRM on a Smaller Scale

Not all companies may feel able to embark straight away on a national CRM campaign of the scale of Liz Claiborne's in the USA. It may therefore be helpful to marketers to have another detailed case history to look at where the campaign was tested regionally.

This example is based closely on the paper entered for the 1998 IPA Advertising Effectiveness Awards and we are indebted to Craig Mawdsley of Saatchi & Saatchi the author, and client Thomas Cowper Johnson of Norwich Union for their permission to use it as the basis for this chapter.

Case History: Norwich Union and St John Ambulance: 'No-one protects more'

The financial services market place in the UK, and the insurance sector in particular, are tough ones to operate in. Consumers are cynical about insurance companies and it is hard to change the brand image of long-standing institutions such as Norwich Union. Stories of advertising effectiveness are rare in a world where differentiation between insurance providers is so hard to create in consumers' eyes and so much of insurance is sold through intermediaries. Exercising direct influence on the end users is difficult when they very often do not make their own decision about which brand to shortlist as the intermediary or broker largely selects them on their behalf.

While Norwich Union has performed well over the years in this difficult environment and is a company that is often shortlisted for

pensions, investment and life insurance products, it faces new challenges to its position. Quite apart from the dominance of the
Prudential, the company which is best known and scores highest on
all image dimensions, there are new entrants to the market which
bring with them much greater consumer friendliness as part of their
brand reputation.

Virgin, Marks & Spencer and the major supermarkets such as
Tesco and Sainsbury are all entering the financial services arena.
Virgin in particular, with its David versus Goliath positioning, has
been a particularly aggressive player. The highly successful telesales
car insurance operator, Direct Line, has succeeded in growing very
quickly, and although not being in direct competition with Norwich
Union, has shown how well a strong brand can cut through the
swathe of assorted insurance companies. Direct Line has managed
to create a much more tangible sense of brand through its direct
relationship with the customer. It is this increased brand differentiation that is vital in the sometimes 'anonymous' insurance
market.

In 1994 Saatchi & Saatchi worked with Norwich Union to define
a new brand positioning. A thorough-going review of the market led
the agency to believe that there was a major opportunity to own
the unclaimed high ground of insurance. When choosing between
companies, people look for size, reputation, track record and consistency of performance. They seek the benefits of peace of mind,
reassurance and trust in the institution.

The hypothesis, which was later confirmed by qualitative research,
was that these were all generic factors that any insurance company
could provide but the important differentiator is how well *protected*
consumers feel. This 'Territory' of protection had not been occupied
but represented the high ground of the market – a brand with the
size and stature of Norwich Union was one of the few that could
claim it as their own.

Validated in research, this positioning was expressed in the
powerful copyline 'no-one protects more'. But the challenge still
remained as to how to translate this potentially powerful brand
positioning into meaningful communication to the consumer. How
could people be engaged with an advertising message for an insur-

ance company when the products are perceived as 'distress purchases' and often associated with the most unpleasant and unfortunate times in life?

Furthermore, how could Norwich Union be differentiated from other insurance companies which had also enjoyed a generally good reputation when consumers had little or no interest in the sector?

The breakthrough came with the realization that Cause Related Marketing could offer a solution. A wider opportunity also presented itself in the CRM context in that often it is an 'add-on' to an overall advertising communication effort rather than the prime focus of the brand's advertising. The new approach would replace the more traditional corporate brand advertising and generate the brand positioning through the use of television to communicate the Cause Related Marketing message. Television was obviously ideal due to its mass reach but also because of its ability to carry an emotionally involving story.

Both client and agency had realized that if there was this powerfully strong tendency to 'turn off' when presented with insurance advertising, a different approach was needed, one that would in some way get 'under the radar' of consumer inertia and disinterest. It seemed likely that if the final communication device looked like a conventional insurance advertisement it would be 'screened out' by today's 'expert consumer'.

To create the link with protection it was very important to find the right cause to support. To focus the idea generation process a number of criteria were defined which any cause would have to meet:

- Does it communicate a 'protection' message?
- Does it involve and interest people?
- Will it get millions to 'think better of Norwich Union'?
- How affordable is it?
- Does it avoid cynical interpretation?
- Does it say Norwich Union is contributing actively, not just talking?

Over 100 ideas were generated and reduced to a short list of 10 using the above criteria. Qualitative research then revealed some potential pitfalls in some of the possible areas. Ideas where it appeared that Norwich Union was being positioned as doing the job of government or local authority fell down because it was perceived that Norwich Union might be 'papering over the cracks' of the welfare state.

Ideas such as safer playgrounds and safer car parks were ruled out because of the potential controversy surrounding them (accidents, haunts of muggers, etc) and also because they might remind people to think of the inadequacies of their local authority rather than giving Norwich Union the credit.

There were other ideas, which Norwich Union did not seem to have the right to be talking about and were beyond the remit, or perceived expertise of an insurance company.

Campaigns on stress did not fare well as a result of this nor did the idea of providing information on 'practical parenting'. It was clear that when an insurance company seemed to campaign to change behaviour it infringed the arm's-length relationship people seek to maintain with them. A successful initiative would be one that offered a service people could make use of if they choose to, rather than saddling them with a sense of obligation or duty. Initiatives that seem to have broader applicability across society were better received than those that only seemed to benefit the individual, as in the case of stress reduction or heart checks.

In the age of the 'expert consumer' respondents began to relish spotting the 'catch' and could almost always figure out a way in which they thought Norwich Union would benefit. When they could devise a commercial motive behind the good works, the company would gain little or no credit as a result. Safer playgrounds and safer car parks were cynically seen as ways to reduce claims made on insurance policies. Heart checks could be a tool to catch the names and addresses and increase life insurance premiums for those most at risk. Clearly any campaign that aroused these sorts of reactions could run the risk of reinforcing the already negative perceptions of insurance companies in the market and of Norwich Union in particular.

The most powerful idea that emerged during this qualitative research and developmental phase was that of offering free First Aid courses and advertising their availability. This was eventually chosen for a number reasons: reinforcement of the brand positioning of protection, obvious benefit to the community and the potential to produce powerful engaging advertising. However, what proved to be more important than anything else was the factor christened the 'Valid Advertising Component'. Saatchi & Saatchi discovered that the power of the advertising method was reduced when its only role was to promote the involvement of the company in funding the cause. A 'Valid Advertising Component' gives you a legitimate reason to produce advertising about the cause, beyond 'blowing your own trumpet'.

In this case, the validity of the advertising was derived from the need to encourage the people to sign up for courses. Thus the advertising message would be directly relevant to the thousands who signed up, but be seen by millions 'over their shoulders'.

Norwich Union was applauded for helping to recruit people for the cause via a compelling advertising message. This was how the First Aid idea helped Norwich Union to get its message 'under the radar' while still exploiting all the benefits of the mass communication medium of TV. The storyboard of the TV commercial is set out on the next page.

The objectives of the advertising were straightforward – to contribute to the welfare of the community by increasing the knowledge of First Aid and increase the propensity to choose Norwich Union by being seen to do this. The formal objectives were as follows:

- Achieve awareness and salience for Norwich Union
- To associate Norwich Union with protection
- To generate warmth/liking/approval for Norwich Union so that they would become the preferred choice of insurance company
- To have people recognize the importance of First Aid training
- To call the number to go on a course

The campaign ran in two bursts, one in 1996 and one in 1997, but the communications strategy was much wider than TV advertising alone. All those people who called the phone number on screen were sent a booking form with joint Norwich Union/St John branding. Those who attended a course were trained by First

Voice Over (female): What would you do if your child swallowed white spirit?

Member of public 1: 'Don't let her have anything to drink.'

Voice Over (female): Make sure you know what to do in a crisis. Norwich Union are offering 5000 free First Aid courses run by the St. John Ambulance in your area.

Phone no. and St. John logo appear over image of child.

Copy on black background: Wrong.

Member of public 2: 'I'd turn her upside-down and shake-em upside down.'

Copy on black background: Wrong.

Member of public 5: 'I'd give her a glass of water and take her straight to hospital.'

Member of public 3: 'I can't remember.'

Member of public 4: 'Make the child sick – stick my fingers down her throat.'

Copy on black background: This can kill.

Voice Over: Norwich Union. No-one protects more.

'Norwich Union – real evidence of "protection".'

Aiders wearing Norwich Union First Aid T-shirts. Those who completed the course were given a Norwich Union/St John certificate and a jointly branded First Aid booklet. Those who could not attend were simply sent a booklet. The whole initiative was designed to create a much more tangible and complete sense of the brand than would have been possible with advertising alone.

The results have been excellent in a number of areas. A significant increase in spontaneous brand awareness with Norwich Union was achieved, in comparison to the areas of the country where the campaign did not run. Advertising recognition was huge, at the level of 81% among all adults against an industry 'norm' of approximately 50%. Of adults who had seen the advertising 87% agreed that it had caused them to 'think more about the needs of people to know about First Aid'.

Clearly associating Norwich Union with 'protection' was a key objective and the results here were most encouraging, with more consumers rating Norwich Union for 'offering insurance that gives better protection' than before. After being informed that Norwich Union had sponsored the advertising, 94% of adults said they 'approved of Norwich Union offering First Aid courses and advertising them'.

It was clear that the initiative did not arouse any suspicion as to the motives of the institution. Perhaps most importantly preference towards Norwich Union was increased significantly in the short term among ABC1s, the core target audience. Other manifestations of success were that in the first stage of activity 5000 places were offered and the media spend in fact generated 7229 calls at a cost per response of £23.23. In the end 4638 places were booked and 3222 people actually attended courses.

Overall some 12974 people were touched by the campaign and therefore effectively became potential ambassadors for the Norwich Union brand. These results were clearly enhanced by the large amount of free PR coverage that the campaign generated. As a subset of the campaign over 400 Norwich Union staff were trained in First Aid as part of the campaign and 15500 First Aid booklets distributed: 'no-one protects more' was made real for all stakeholders in the company.

At the same time St John Ambulance has been a major beneficiary of the campaign. Their mission, as an organization, is to widen
the knowledge of First Aid and given that nearly 13 000 people
received First Aid training as a direct result of the advertising, this
was a significant achievement for them to say nothing of the 30 000
First Aid booklets that were distributed. For each of the people
trained Norwich Union donated £3 to St John Ambulance and
underwrote all the training costs – a major commitment. Obviously
the profile of St John Ambulance was raised significantly through the
television advertising. The equipment used during the courses was
subsequently donated by Norwich Union following the campaign
and was worth over £25 000 to the charity.

Overall this case is a good example of how sensitive use of
exploratory qualitative research in a complex market area helped
the client and agency develop an appropriate CRM campaign to the
genuine mutual benefit of brand and cause.

PART VII
CRM's Past and Future

Summary

This final part of the book has the purpose of convincing the reader (if that is still needed) that Cause Related Marketing is not just a fad that will bloom and die within a decade or so. It does this by starting with a discussion of the concept of charity in a religious context and reminds us how deeply ingrained it is in our culture, despite society's increasingly secular nature.

It then goes on to give an overview of the historical development of charitable giving by companies. It traces the evolution from individual entrepreneurial initiatives through to the establishment of company towns such as Bournville and Pullman, and major charitable foundations such as those created by Carnegie, Getty and Mellon.

It will then show how the strengthening of central government and the welfare state in the UK tended to reduce the philanthropic role of the private sector as key responsibilities were taken over by the state. This led to the post-war period in the UK during which sponsorship of the arts and a relatively diffuse disbursement of charitable donations through corporate affairs departments became the norm – the 'Chairman's Wife' syndrome.

Meanwhile in the USA, where state authorities have taken much less of a role in welfare, the corporate sector has had a continuing involvement in 'good works'. Coming right up to date we have the 'stakeholder' politics of Clinton and Blair. These are heavily conditioned by the realities of the burgeoning costs of welfare programmes and the growing burden of ageing populations, leading to the need for public and private partnership in many areas traditionally viewed as being the responsibility of the state.

At the same time popular anticipation of the new Millennium is leading many to consider 'higher order' issues and the role of companies in society, as evidenced in special consumer research commissioned by Saatchi & Saatchi. In practical terms this is being manifested by contemporary philanthropic gestures of enormous scale by the likes of Ted Turner, Roberto Goizuita, Michael Eisner, Bill Gates, Tom Monaghan and Peter Lampl.

In a way Cause Related Marketing can be seen as a contemporary means of continuing to fulfil a deep-seated need for philanthropy at both a corporate and personal level. Thus its future will reflect its past with a few visionary leaders demonstrating by their words and deeds that highly competitive and entrepreneurial commercial activity is not at all incompatible with altruistic and charitable behaviour. Indeed these apparently irreconcilable forces can be harnessed to be mutually beneficial and help millions of people in the process.

23

Charity Culture

Cause Related Marketing is a commercial activity, but it can only exist within a cultural and social context in which the concept and practice of charity is deeply embedded. Given that some may feel that we are moving into an increasingly secular era, perhaps it is worth reminding ourselves how long-standing the idea of charity is and how it has persisted through the ages.

One of the earliest manifestations of the institutionalization of charity is in the Jewish religion. The tenth commandment 'Thou shall not covet', is obviously a warning sign that you may have enough, but enough may not seem enough, so you look at what others have and envy them. This commandment recognizes that this tendency to be greedy is built into human nature, so puts a boundary there in forbidding it. On the positive side, the summary of the Jewish law in the words 'love God, love your neighbour', gives strength to the belief that we are part of a society (despite Margaret Thatcher's famous assertion to the contrary); we are in a community, and that human beings are by nature gregarious. As such we need some kind of regulatory system, almost from self-interest, which balances out inequalities.

Perhaps this answers the puzzle as to why people should help other people at all. Clearly there seems to be a strongly in-built characteristic in many, if not most human beings actually to be charitable, and they do not all maximize their own particular circumstances at the expense of others. This may be explained in a Darwinian sense in that much charity comes down to subtly but nevertheless importantly self-interested acts.

People are being charitable to one another because they are in a community with them, and they can see that there is an end benefit if the society as a whole is more coherent, less disrupted and more secure. It is ultimately just another aspect of self-preservation and self-advancement, but one that flies under the flags of altruism and charity. The Biblical phrase 'Do unto others as you would have them do unto you', known as the Golden Rule, expresses the sentiment well. This was the key theme of the Victorian Charles Kingsley's children's book *The Water Babies*, with its wonderful character 'Mrs Do As You Would Be Done By'.

Jesus strongly encouraged charity in the Christian tradition. Perhaps the parable of the Good Samaritan in St Luke, chapter 10 is the most famous example of His teaching. This story illustrates how the religious people, the Priest in one case and the Levi in the other, walk by on the other side of the road, avoiding the beaten up victim. The Samaritan, who was not actually expected to inherit all the benefits of a Jewish heaven, was the one who cared for the person so badly down on his luck.

The other famous parable, which relates to charity, is the one about the right attitude to and use of wealth. Jesus is speaking after he has been interviewed by a rich young man who asks him how he should get into the Kingdom of Heaven. Jesus says, 'Keep the law' and the young man replies 'We have kept all the law' and then Jesus finds out that the thing that really matters to him is not getting into Heaven, but his great riches. Hence His dictum 'It is easier for a camel to pass through the eye of a needle than for a rich man to enter the kingdom of God' (Mark 10:25, New English Bible translation).

But perhaps Jesus' most powerful commendation of the ideal of reciprocity in our dealings with other people are the words in the Lord's Prayer, 'Forgive us our sins as we forgive those who sin against us'.

This religious teaching was closely linked to the financial support of the institution that provided it in the first place. In Jewish history, which is also mirrored in the Muslim tradition, the instrument of charity was the tithe. The tithe was built into Mosaic law as a way of keeping the religious system going and maintaining the priestly caste which was not required to work, but was expected to provide religious services and all that that would entail. The tithe would be in the form of money or in-kind, animals or crops for example, and this was subsequently brought into the Christian tradition with the whole medieval church system based upon it.

Thus you can still find tithe barns in the UK, where goods in kind would be brought by the community to the priest in charge.

These tithes were built into the law of the land and right up until this century this was the way the church was financed: it was effectively a tax. Before the Reformation, pre Henry VIII, the Church was the major landowner in the country and there was an elaborate system of rents, tithes and exactions on people, which then kept all the monastic and church institutions going. Of course what they received in return in addition to religious services were others such as education and health, because the church was the repository and provider of all those special skills at that time.

Today, while no longer enshrined in the law, the Church of England, the Baptists, Methodists and the newer 'house church' movement are still very much reliant on funding by tithe. The Church of England guideline to every member of the congregation is to give 10% of their net disposable income, i.e. after tax and major overheads like mortgage and utilities. These tithes are closely monitored by means of the parish's electoral roll and each church is 'targeted' according to a formula for potential income based on the overall population of the parish, and its social groupings.

Another form of charity is that of giving 'alms' which goes right back to early Judeo-Christian times where people's needs were not being met either by family or by government or institutions. So individuals, either because of their conscience or their religious duty, gave alms, as they were called, to the poor. This became formalized and the disadvantaged would look particularly to large post-Reformational or post-Tudor families in England, as sources of money. Begging itself became institutionalized.

Almshouses were a more permanent form of care for those who were in extreme poverty and they could be accessed by old retainers of families or as work places for other individuals. Again, in the era preceding large companies or interventionist state institutions, they were often founded by wealthy families and in a sense were precursors of the Victorian era 'Company Town'.

In all this there is a strong motivation for Christians to express their concern or compassion for other human beings in practical ways and this need not necessarily be towards people they know directly, or in any particular expectation of a reciprocal response. It is simply in the understanding of humanity and of how the human psyche functions that a

Christian would expect to express their compassion or empathy for fellow human beings in ways that are not just self-rewarding.

The key word that captures all this is the Greek one for love that is used in the original Christian scriptures: 'agape'. This expresses the idea that love is not just about what someone can get out of a relationship, but is a 'self-giving' love which is based in forgetting yourself and focusing on the needs of others.

It is in this original sense that it is used in the great passage from St Paul's letter to the Corinthians, chapter 13, 'And now abideth faith, hope and charity, these three; but the greatest of these is charity'. This passage has more recently been translated with the word 'love' used instead of 'charity' and as a result is often used nowadays as a reading at marriages to endorse the mutual feelings of the wedded couple.

Thus that which Jesus regarded as the greatest virtue, 'agape', can no longer be expressed in English with its narrowed meanings, where both 'charity' and 'love' are used in a literally exclusive way: we use 'love' to express a feeling towards a limited and specific number of people. We use 'charity' to express giving to other people. However, in Jesus' teaching, the greatest virtue is a fusion of the two, charity and love, combining empathy and self-sacrifice in 'self-giving love'. In this sense the reality of Christ on the cross can be regarded as the ultimate act of charity.

Present figures suggest that while there was a sharp decline in church attendance during the 1960s and 1970s in both the UK and the USA, the curve has now flattened. The presence of the church in society has reached something like a stable level, and any continuing decline is being attributed to less regular attendance rather than a complete abandonment of the church. Indeed, in the USA, attendance is actually on the increase in some denominations, such as the Episcopal Church, which estimates the increase at 2% over recent years. The Judeo-Christian heritage is deeply embedded in Western culture and its legacy will be with us until well into the next century and beyond. If 'do as you would be done by' is also a basic survival mechanism for the human species, then it seems likely that charity or 'self-giving love' is here to stay.

24

Victorian Paternalism to 20th Century Philanthropy

The Victorian era, which consolidated and capitalized upon the Industrial Revolution, laid the foundations for the greatest empire of modern times. Curiously the key drivers of this imperialistic movement were in a sense contradictory: grasping ambition and a deep sense of guilt.

On the one hand the headlong rush into the industrial age was signified by enormous and perhaps even vicious exploitation by one minority group of the majority of working people. By and large the labouring classes were treated very badly in terms of their employment conditions. Great fortunes were built on the backs of the masses both at home and abroad. While this exploitation later gave rise to revolutionary, populist movements and ultimately the emergence of Marxism and Maoism, in the meantime a cowed population created huge wealth for the few on a scale previously unthought of.

Within this economic imperialism was another, more personal, driver: the urge for self-improvement. This was the great era of intellectual discovery and invention, which have subsequently changed the course of history. The invention of steam power, the mechanization of production, electricity and many others all contributed to the creation of the British Empire and dominance of the Victorian era. And of course they powered the emergence of the next dominant economy, the United States of America.

But this drive for self-improvement also led to a very acute sense of the need for personal advancement and people were very concerned with their position in society. The niceties of the divisions between the classes and their sub-classes became the obsession of the majority of people, especially the emergent middle classes. Fine distinctions between the classes, the divide that separated 'trade' from the 'professions', and these from the 'gentry' were all-important. As the 'meritocracy' grew to compete with the historical ruling classes, based on the land-owning aristocracy whose prizes had been simply purchased or earned on the battlefield rather than in industry and commerce, the mannered voices of snobbery and elitism were pervasive.

At the same time, and almost in direct contradiction to this, was the sense of Victorian guilt: the quite widespread feeling that all this material wealth and gain had not been truly deserved. This was the era of almost universal attendance at church. Indeed the pecking order in the pews was as important as the placement at a social occasion. People who were rapacious capitalists during the week became church going, God-fearing, altruistic individuals seeking to enter the Kingdom of Heaven on a Sunday.

It is not too fanciful to imagine that these acts of religious expiation were a direct attempt to counterbalance the exploitation of their workforces at the factory. It is a short move from this point to the widespread and extraordinary acts of charity and philanthropy that so marked the era.

At the same time we should not forget the basic human desire to overcome mortality. There seems to be a strong urge, particularly among the successful and the powerful, to 'leave something behind'; entrepreneurs, millionaires, politicians and others in the limelight have an overwhelming impulse to leave some earthly testament to their lifetime's achievement.

In the United States, the UK and most other Western European nations there is the legacy of the 19th and early 20th century giants of industry. The names of Guggenheim, Getty, Mellon and Carnegie resonate in history. In the UK perhaps the most significant memorial patrons were Queen Victoria and Prince Albert. Their legacies, particularly in terms of physical monuments such as museums, galleries or statuary, are still a key part of the cultural landscape.

Possibly the most famous example of a philanthropist who built a monument to himself is that of Andrew Carnegie, then one of the wealthiest people in the world. Born in Dunfermline, Scotland in 1835, the son of a weaver, he went to the United States in 1848 and settled in Allegheney, Pennsylvania. At just 13 years of age he went to work as a bobbin boy in a cotton mill but moved rapidly through a succession of jobs with Western Union on the Pennsylvania Railroad.

In 1865 he resigned to establish his own business and eventually founded the Carnegie Steel Company which launched the steel industry in Pittsburgh. At the age of 65 he ended up selling the company to J.P. Morgan for $400M, equivalent to almost $5.1 billion today, and devoted the rest of his life to philanthropy.

His main mission in life was spurred by the idea that the rich have a moral obligation to give away their fortunes. A famous quote from his book *The Gospel of Wealth*, reads as follows:

This, then, is held to be the duty of the man of wealth: first, to set an example of modest unostentatious living, shunning display: to provide moderately for the legitimate wants of those dependent upon him; and, after doing so to consider all surplus revenues which come to him simply as trust funds which he has strictly bound as a matter of duty to administer in the manner which, in his judgement, is best calculated to produce the most beneficial results for the community.

Carnegie set about disposing of his fortune through many personal gifts, and via the establishment of a trust. His most significant achievement was to create free public libraries. This was spurred by the desire to make available to everyone a means of self-education and when he started there were but a few public libraries in the world. In 1881 he began to promote his idea, and he and the Carnegie Corporation subsequently spent over $56M to build 2509 libraries throughout the English-speaking world. In total, during his lifetime, Carnegie gave away over $350M.

This tendency has continued during this century. President Mitterrand of France will probably be best remembered for the I.M. Pei glass pyramid in the courtyard of the Louvre or the new Bibliotheque Nationale de France. His specific achievements as a political leader will be long forgotten while the impressive physical reality of these extraordinary, often controversial, structures will long survive.

But perhaps nowadays monuments in stone are less important than ones in reputation. Relatively recently *Fortune* magazine, the chronicler of the super-wealthy, has begun to publish a league table of the most generous people in the world. This has become a public club to which many multi-millionaires or billionaires would like to belong. This is their monument.

Ted Turner has donated $1 billion to the United Nations and Bill Gates has donated $200M to the Gates Library Foundation with the objective of ensuring Internet access for all public libraries in the United States. Michael Eisner of Disney fame has appropriately given $89M to underprivileged children. Similarly the late Roberto Goizuita of Coca-Cola donated $38M to underprivileged families.

For most people these are unimaginable sums of money. But while the critic may say that they represent a relatively small proportion of the total wealth of the individual concerned, nevertheless these donations represent a great boon to the beneficiaries involved.

In quite a few of the most significant cases it is obvious that the donation relates relatively closely to the business interests of the donor concerned. Ted Turner's $1 billion to the United Nations clearly related to his CNN network. Bill Gates' donation to the Gates Library Foundation clearly relates to his software computing business. Eisner's donation to underprivileged children clearly connects to his role at Disney and Roberto Goizuita's donation had a close connection with the core target audience for Coca-Cola. McDonald's heiress Joan Kroc has donated $80 million to The Salvation Army, the largest single contribution in its 118 years.

Most recently, in a move on which he comments in language that would not have been unfamiliar to a Victorian plutocrat, Thomas Monaghan the Domino's Pizza billionaire has divested himself of most of his enormous fortune. Reportedly it was his reading of C.S. Lewis's book, *Mere Christianity*, that crystallized his decision. As he reached Lewis's thoughts on 'the great sin' – pride – Tom Monaghan reflected guiltily on his own situation and said: 'I lay awake virtually all night. I realized I had more pride than any person I knew.'

Now Domino's Pizza has been sold for $1 billion, and the Sikorsky helicopter, the corporate jet, the Rolls, the Bentley and the company yacht 'Domino Effect' have all been disposed of. It is expected that the money will be devoted to the establishment of Catholic schools across the USA in one of the biggest acts of personal philanthropy this century.

Another very recent decision, which will benefit education, this time in the UK, has been made by financial services tycoon, Peter Lampl. His fortune was made in the US through his Sutton Company, a private equity and investment management firm. He attributes much of his success to his educational grounding at state-funded Reigate Grammar School, from where he managed to get a place at Corpus Christi College, Oxford.

His belief is that the Labour Government's abolition of direct-grant grammar schools in 1977 was a mistake which has led to many gifted pupils from the state education sector not fulfilling their full potential. The recent action by the New Labour Government in abolishing the £130 million p.a. assisted places scheme which had benefited 40 000 pupils has consolidated the actions of its predecessor in 1977. Accordingly Lampl has pledged to commit up to £40 million to a 'Millennium Project' to open up the top 100 independent private schools to talented state-educated children by subsidising their fees.

Thus, at the highest level of personal and financial achievement, it can be seen that many very successful people still need non-materialistic rewards in life, and that for them the best possible use for their money is an altruistic one. If this is already happening to the degree that it is among these entrepreneurial figures, then perhaps we may see an increasing trend towards the same ideal among a wider spectrum of wealthy individuals and of course at the corporate level through modern Cause Related Marketing.

25

The Company Town

We have seen that very often the desire for self-preservation after death, the personal challenge to mortality, results in the individual desiring to create some kind of physical monument to him- or herself. This was particularly true in the Victorian era and one of the fascinating aspects of this period is the way in which the wanting to create a physical monument extended quite naturally into the notion of the 'company town'.

It seems that the emerging capitalist entrepreneur realized that an exploited workforce may not be as productive as one that was cared for. This introduced the idea of protecting the workforce from the worst excesses of labour exploitation and an appreciation that employees who were better looked after could actually benefit the enterprise and the owner, in improved productivity and quality of output over time.

The Industrial Revolution had introduced fundamental changes to the habits of British society and brought into very sharp focus the issue of corporate social responsibility. There had been a significant shift from farming the land to working in industries such as mining, textiles and iron manufacturing. The late 18th century saw the extensive migration of people from the country to the town and saw the growth of great cities such as Birmingham, Bradford, Cardiff and Manchester. Indeed by the end of the 19th century over half of the population of Britain were living in towns – a dramatic transformation from what had previously been an essentially rural economy.

But in the process this significant migration broke the previously established links between the individual and the community. The semi-feudal structure of the relationship between the land owner and their tenants or workers was lost. In the new environment the mobility of labour, the shift in ownership patterns and population pressure reduced the sense of 'responsibility for others' which had categorized older, rural communities in which people may have lived their whole lives and travelled not more than 10 miles in any direction.

Naturally enough, the new entrepreneurs were very keen to resist government interference and legislation and this led to many of the worst excesses of child labour and the exploitation of female employees. However, this was counterbalanced by increasing concern about issues caused by industrialization and its impact on their environment, public health and the welfare of workers. Legislation such as the Public Health Act of 1848 grew directly from the concerns of those observers who sought to require or persuade the new entrepreneurs and their firms to adopt a more responsible attitude to the needs of their workers and the communities in which they operated.

Another important catalyst for change was the growth of Methodism towards the end of the 18th century. This paved the way for those who 'saw the contrast between equality before God and inequality before man' as being one of the major dilemmas of the age and as a fundamental basis for criticism of the prevailing social and political order. The Methodist church, founded by John Wesley and his brother Charles, became one of the great social reforming institutions. The two of them campaigned against the slave trade, pioneered the public education system, and were very much involved in care for the poor and prison reform.

Religion played a further significant part in the evolution of the 'company town' through the Quaker movement. This was another non-conformist religion and as such any of its followers were not permitted to enter the universities, which in the 19th century were closely linked with the established church. Thus, as a result, any Quakers were effectively barred from entry into the professions and indeed their pacifist principles precluded the military as a possible career. This meant that the energies and talents of Quaker families were inevitably directed towards business and the transformation of industry and society in whatever country to which they resided.

The list of families, many of which are 'brands' today, affected in this manner by their religious beliefs and directed towards a reforming zeal reads like a roll call of British industrial society. Amongst them are the Barclay banking family, the Cadburys, the Clarks shoe dynasty, the Derbys of Coalbrooke, the founders of the British iron industry, the Frys of Bristol, the Hanburys in bringing tinplate to Wales, Samson Lloyd of Birmingham, the founder of Lloyds Bank, the Pilkingtons in glassmaking, the Rowntrees and Terrys of York and the cotton and tobacco families such as Wills and Players.

In some cases these individual personal beliefs were related to the types of products and services that they actually provided. It is part of the Cadbury legend that John Cadbury's life-long involvement with the Temperance Society led him to believe that alcohol was a social evil and that it was part of his responsibility to provide the masses with an alternative. In delivering to them tea, coffee, cocoa and chocolate as an alternative to alcohol he genuinely believed that he was involved in alleviating one of the many causes of poverty and deprivation among working people.

A logical extension for some of these right-thinking entrepreneurs was to expand their involvement in their workers' lives beyond the work place itself. The idea of actually providing proper accommodation for the work force was a revolutionary one, and to augment this with shopping facilities, schools and hospitals was really quite extraordinary.

The Cadbury brothers were among those to set the standards in this area, and their creation of the town of Bournville, which still thrives today, was something of a template for the company town. The enlightened attitude towards their employees began with the factory itself, when the Cadbury brothers made the decision to build their new factory in the country rather than in the industrial quarter of Birmingham. They decided to include in the plans properly heated dressing rooms, gardens, swimming pools and extensive sports fields. Young employees were also encouraged to attend night school.

However, to reform working practices comprehensively, George Cadbury recognized that improving the housing conditions of workers was necessary, and in 1895 he bought 120 acres near to the works and began to build houses for his work force in line with the ideals of the embryo Garden City movement. Since the beginning of this century, the Bournville Village has been managed by a trust independent of the Cadbury business, which ensures that any revenue goes towards the extension of the estate and the promotion of housing reform.

The same sort of approach was taken by many entrepreneurs in the United States, such as the Peabody Coal Company in Kentucky and West Virginia, but thankfully few of them ended up with the problems experienced by the Pullman Railroad Cars Company. Perhaps this was a very early example of what goes wrong when a company's total corporate behaviour is not properly aligned.

The Pullman town was outside Chicago, and as in many other 'company towns' most of the residents were employed by Pullman and patronized company-run stores, churches and schools. However, the company became involved in a vicious attempt to break a strike. This involved political machinations at the highest level, deals and counter deals with unions, government officials and company owners. It has become famous as an example of how the company town can go wrong, and it is where the expression 'Big Brother is watching you' came from.

While the company town may not exist today as it did in the last century, there are signs that the same basic instincts and urges are at work. Nowadays corporations are increasingly concerned about the welfare of their employees. Again there is the mix of altruism and self-interest. The package of benefits that an employee might receive from a particular employer becomes part of a selling proposition of the organization to its staff. Very significant amounts of money, time and effort are spent in providing such things as pensions, health insurance, gyms and recreational facilities, crèches and other forms of non-financial rewards or benefits in kind. Perhaps the roots of this trend in modern times in the UK can be traced back to Daisy Marks, the formidable wife of the founder of Marks & Spencer. She introduced staff canteens and on-site hairdressing on the argument that well-fed, well-presented employees were good for business.

Some organizations actually formalize their input into their employees through the form of institutions. The McDonald's Hamburger University in Oakport, Illinois is a famous example of this, where employees can return at various stages in their training.

In the United Kingdom, Unipart have set up a university for their employees, the Unipart 'U'. The 'U' is physically an integral part of the company, since employees enter the building of the headquarters in Oxford through the 'U', and it is the first thing seen by visitors. Opened in 1993, it offers 260 courses run by Unipart managers and staff. The chief executive is heavily involved and employees begin with certain set courses which everyone completes, and then move on to courses which are relevant to the particular job they are doing. If they have the inclination, they can move on to further courses, which they feel might benefit them in some way. Each employee agrees a personal development plan and learning objectives before beginning the course, which also forms the basis for post-course and ongoing reviews, and the reports from the management suggest that the benefits to the company in terms of improved quality and production innovation are very significant.

Other employers make great efforts to enhance the quality of life that employees' experience while working for them. Given that homeworking is not yet by any means universal, the physical environment that employees experience on a day-by-day basis at their office, or place of work, has a very significant impact upon them. Companies like Microsoft and Nike have developed the concept of the 'corporate campus' where the place of work has more of the structure of a university or college, with the dress code and atmosphere to match, than the more traditional more formal place of work.

While it would be wrong to describe these corporate campuses as 'company towns', because by and large they do not provide furnished accommodation for staff (while they do provide virtually everything else), the sentiment remains the same. A happy, fulfilled, content and relaxed employee is likely to be more loyal, more productive and better value for the employer overall.

In a related area, it is interesting to note that McDonald's, perhaps one of the strongest global cultures in commercial terms, started 25 years ago to create 'Ronald McDonald Houses'. These houses provide home-from-home accommodation for families of children with serious, often long-term illnesses requiring extended hospital care. There are three in the UK in London, Liverpool and Glasgow, and by the end of 1996 there were 182 world-wide.

This is a very powerful piece of CRM marketing on behalf of McDonald's, and blends some aspects of the 'company town' in terms of physical environment with some of the best aspects of company foundations. Perhaps the only puzzle is why McDonald's have not communicated more aggressively what they are doing in this area; particularly since they state as a part of their policy that one of their central business principles is to support the communities in which they operate, and to aim for

McDonald's to 'become synonymous' with helping young people in need. Such links can surely only come through more targeted and public communication.

The recent law suit in the UK, which cost them at least $10M in legal fees and ended in a fudged result which left them looking blameworthy, even though they were not on all accounts, bar two, might perhaps have been mitigated by a greater understanding of the good work that McDonald's do in terms of the Ronald McDonald Houses.

In Germany the concept of the 'Social Firm' is well developed and this is another contemporary manifestation of the 'company town' idea. In this case the 'Social Firm' is one which is essentially created for the employment of people with a disability, perhaps mental or physical, or other disadvantage in the labour market. It will draw a significant proportion of its employees from this category of person and as such the company uses its own business activities and production of goods and services to pursue its social mission.

There are also companies such as Café Direct, which have built their market position in coffee on the concept of fair trade and making a direct connection between properly paid producers and end customers. 'Divine' chocolate, marketed on the basis of a 'fair deal for cocoa growers', and stocked by Tesco, operates in a similar manner.

In all these innovative activities we can see a relationship with human behaviour going back centuries. Commercial enterprises will continue to see real benefits in helping ensure a harmonious balance between the stronger and weaker in society and in structuring themselves to deliver the optimum blend of self-interested altruism to their communities. The upsurge in interest in Cause Related Marketing is another manifestation of this deep-seated factor in the human economy.

26

'Nanny State' to 'Stakeholder Society'

The state and government organizations have progressively involved themselves more in the structure of UK society and through the late 19th and early 20th centuries, a series of legislative changes were made which increased the genuine financial democratization of the country. Income tax was first introduced in Britain during the Napoleonic Wars, although it was not fixed as a permanent part of the tax system until 1842 with Peel's reforms. The next major stage in progressive income tax came effectively through Lloyd George's 1909 'People's Budget', which included a proposed 'supertax' on incomes over £5000 (£150 000 in today's money).

At the time this was a revolutionary and highly controversial move. It was the first time that the idea that the more you had, the more you should give back was enshrined in the Statute Book.

The second landmark in the history of governmental intervention in the economy was the formation of the welfare state with the passing of the National Health Service Bill in November 1946 – the National Health Service finally came into being on 5th July 1948.

The Second World War had thrown the classes together as never before. The reality of the commonality of man was revealed in the stresses and strains of warfare and the Blitz. The surprise majority of the Labour Party in the post-war election of 1945, against widespread expectation that the victorious wartime leader, Winston Churchill, would deliver a majority to his Conservative Party, was confirmation of a fundamental shift in national mood.

There was a strong social, almost utopian desire, for the state to minister to the people literally from the cradle to the grave. The idea of the National Health Service, widespread extension of the state education system and the development of social housing were all manifestations of this desire.

Since their foundation in viciously competitive environments, great industries such as the railways, power generation, power distribution, mining and even air transport had progressively amalgamated through the capitalistic mergers and acquisitions to create if not monopolies then oligopolies. The new development was that these great industries should be taken into public ownership through the State. Thus in the years following the war, major tranches of the British industrial landscape became nationalized. The Bank of England was first, in March 1946, followed by coal and cable and wireless in 1947. Railways and electricity followed suit a year later, gas in 1949, while the nationalization of iron and steel did not take effect until near the end of Labour's term of government in 1951.

For two perhaps three decades in the post-war period in the UK the mixed economy flourished overall despite its 'boom and bust' cyclical nature. But by the time of the arrival of Margaret Thatcher in 1975 as the radical free-marketeer leader of the Conservative Party it had become clear that this economy had not truly succeeded. The nationalized industries had become ossified and excessively bureaucratic. Union power had a perceived stranglehold over industrial relations and productivity was sliding inexorably downwards. The 3-day week in 1974 under Ted Heath had been a watershed in the national understanding of how near the brink the 'Nanny State' had brought those in its charge. Meanwhile British management had become notorious for its short-termism, intransigence and lack of investment in R&D.

With the ascendancy of the state in the affairs of society during the post-war period, this also had an impact on the psyche of corporate Britain. Companies believed that they had very limited social responsibilities as far as society at large was concerned. Given the aggressive and often confrontational nature of labour relations, the idea of embracing their employees in a total relationship as in the days of the company town was far from the agenda of most board rooms: they were more likely to be focused on the next round of pay negotiations.

This period, from a corporate giving point of view, was one typified by private indeed almost anonymous corporate philanthropy and at the same time this marked the heyday of the sponsorship of the arts and those activities which might be deemed to be an early manifestation of corporate entertainment. The 'Chairman's Wife' was definitely in the ascendant.

Thus without being overly simplistic one can see that there is a reciprocal relationship between the corporate and the governmental sector depending on the prevailing political climate. In Victorian England with rampant capitalism exploding in every quarter and a relatively non-involved government the duty for care fell to a much greater degree to those captains of industry whose consciences were pricked to do so. On the other hand in the post-Second World War period with the government increasingly enmeshed in every aspect of society the corporate sector felt able to retreat and leave large scale good works to Government. Fortunately there had always been a strong charitable sector in Britain.

One of the legacies of the Thatcherite attack on the nationalized industries has been a significant roll-back in the level of involvement of the state in industry and society. The New Labour government has accepted that there are limits on the degree to which the 'Nanny State' can extend. There is an acknowledgement from them too that the boundaries must be pulled back and more emphasis put on partnership with the private sector.

One of the fundamental drivers of this is the ageing of the population in the UK and the realization that there are simply not the funds to meet the needs of the welfare state for an increasing proportion of the population who are aged 50 or more with an apparently ever increasing life expectancy.

Out of this has been born the Blair notion of the 'Third Way' in politics. While there is still a lot of debate about this idea, and in particular its robustness, it is obvious where it has come from. On the one hand a comprehensive welfare state is perceived as too expensive to be affordable, on the other hand there is a strong motivation to continue to guarantee certain basic social rights in the areas of housing, health and education.

Thus the idea of a greater integration of the private or commercial sector and government, with the citizenry, has formed the basis of the 'Third

Way'. Stimulated by books such as Will Hutton's *The State We're In* with its notion of 'The Stakeholder Society', politicians have become increasingly interested in the idea that all parties in the economy should share in providing the solution to these fundamental welfare problems.

In the United States there has been a rather different evolution, but interestingly it has ended up in much the same place. The younger, less mature economy of the United States bridged from a mirror image of the driving capitalist expansion of the Victorian era in Great Britain almost without a pause straight through to the corporate state, with a relatively low commitment or indeed requirement for welfare.

Indeed, as a percentage of total GDP the amount of British Governmental monies spent on all welfare programmes combined (including health, housing, education and welfare) is 25%. This places the UK 13th out of 19 industrialized countries, where the average spending is almost 30%, below all the Scandinavian countries, the Netherlands, France, Austria, Italy, Germany, New Zealand, Spain and Canada, but above Ireland, Australia, Portugal, the USA, Greece and Japan.

The sheer growth in the US economy, almost unhalted apart from the Depression of the late 1930s, for the whole of the 20th century may have obviated the need for government welfare on the scale of the United Kingdom. Overall the cost of living has been lower and the wage level significantly higher. There has also been very extensive philanthropy on behalf of the major corporations and this has continued in a more or less unbroken trend through the post-war period whereas in the UK, as we have seen, it has tended to be rather more counter-cyclical to the level of government involvement.

However, the problems of an ageing population have hit the United States too, and it is interesting that in their recent utterances on the subject, President Clinton and Prime Minister Tony Blair have struck remarkably similar notes, i.e. the need for greater partnership and collaboration between government and business.

If indeed we are entering the 'Third Way' in politics both in the UK and in the USA then this is further reinforcement of the basic concept of Cause Related Marketing and the underlying social, corporate and governmental trends which have led us to it. The broad themes of charity, enlightened self-interest and corporate philanthropy which have recurred throughout the centuries are coalescing in a more cohesive way than ever before.

There is an increasing sense of the interconnectedness of institutions and people. Companies are realizing that they play such a significant role in people's lives, not just their direct employees but all the stakeholders with whom they are involved, to say nothing of society and the economy at large. Their globalized scale is becoming so influential that they simply have to take a leadership stance.

It is a cliché, but nevertheless worth repeating, that the world's top corporations have as much if not more influence on the reality of everyday life than any single national government. With this power comes awesome responsibility.

In the UK the New Labour government under Tony Blair has launched its own 'New Deal', an ambitious programme designed to get the young unemployed into short-term training situations within companies with a view to secure longer-term employment with them. Employers are being encouraged to make places available for the New Deal scheme and the government is subsidising those places by paying the employer £60 per head, per week, in order to give them the incentive to do so.

While there has been the inevitable complaint that employers are taking on 'slave labour', and are not really providing genuine training or indeed a prospect of long-term employment, the scheme has to be applauded. This is because it is encouraging companies to play their part in helping solve the problem of youth unemployment. The Prime Minister also unveiled early in 1999 a major new scheme ONE20 calling on people to get involved in their community through giving time, not just their money, to help solve society's problems.

In the United States, Bill Clinton has asked the corporate sector for more volunteers and in the same way Tony Blair is trying to enlist the support of corporations in joint ventures with government in areas of welfare and social concern.

With these developments at the macro-economic level it means that Cause Related Marketing is likely to flourish at the micro one in future.

27

The Millennium Effect

The phenomenon of 'New Year's resolutions' is very well known. On both sides of the Atlantic and in many countries New Year's Eve is an important time of celebration. The origins of this festival go all the way back to pagan festivals intended to encourage new life to appear at the darkest point of the year.

In different places it is celebrated in different ways but one of the key common themes is that of renewal. Although completely artificial in a way, there is a widespread sense that as one year comes to a close a line can be drawn and a New Year can start, almost as if with a clean sheet of paper.

The Scots celebrate Hogmanay and for many north of the border this celebration is more important than Christmas itself. The tradition of 'first-footing' is an important part of the festival. It originated in the belief that if the first person to cross the threshold in the new year is a tall dark stranger carrying a lump of coal (symbolizing warmth) and salt (symbolizing wealth), and a piece of cake or bread to ensure the host did not go hungry or thirsty, the house and its occupants would have good luck for the year, hence the present custom where neighbours and friends are visited very early on the 1st January, with revellers carrying lumps of coal and tots of whisky. The Robert Burns song 'Auld Lang Syne' ('Old Long Ago') is very much associated with the New Year's festival around the world.

Should auld acquaintance be forgot,
And never brought to mind?
Should auld acquaintance be forgot,
And days o' lang syne?

Source: Robert Burns, HarperCollins

The implication of these famous, but largely misunderstood words is quite clear: New Year's Eve is a time to remember the past and old friends and acquaintances, but to look forward to the future and build on those past foundations.

Marketers have often attempted to capitalize on the notion of New Year's resolutions and financial services companies in particular have been able to encourage people to review their financial situation and to set things up for the year ahead. At the personal level individuals will often draw up a budget for the year ahead including plans for any holidays, investments in their home, even moving house, and so forth. The turn of the year does seem to be an appropriate time for this process of stocktaking and forward planning.

What's intriguing about this situation as we move towards the new Millennium is the evidence that suggests that society as a whole may be thinking on the same lines, but on a much broader and fundamental one about the way we live and the way we do our business. A survey conducted by Saatchi & Saatchi in 1997 asked consumers their views on the new Millennium, how they were personally planning for it and what their expectations were.

As can be seen from the table opposite, there is a widespread expectation among UK consumers that corporate behaviour is going to have to change as we go in to the 21st century. Consumers are expecting companies to become much more socially responsible and socially aware. They are looking to see them demonstrate a greater sense of responsibility to the wider community in which these companies operate and in particular areas of concern, such as the environment, which the consumer would very much like to be addressed with renewed vigour. Research done by Saatchi & Saatchi and RSL Research in 1997 with a sample of 1085 adults delivered some interesting findings (see table on p. 273).

What this data may indicate is the idea that there is the potential

	Agree strongly
I think that the coming Millennium will be an opportunity to reflect on the issues facing mankind	65%
The beginning of the new Millennium will be a time for this country to reflect and set a new direction	64%
I think that business and Corporations will need to take issues like social responsibility and the environment more seriously in the new Millennium	72%

Source: Saatchi & Saatchi/RSL Research

'New Millennium, new resolution.'

for a massive series of 'New Year's resolutions' which will actually be tantamount to 21st century resolutions. While there will no doubt be enormous public celebration of the new Millennium it also seems likely that personal agendas will be reviewed and extended to the corporate level.

What this means for the corporation or brand that wants to add a powerful belief system to its personality, or indeed create 'brand spirit', is that the period in the run up to and the immediate aftermath of the new Millennium provides a very powerful opportunity to do so. All the evidence suggests that the consumer is very much predisposed to hear these messages and to favour the companies or brands that send them.

Some commentators are already predicting a global 'morning after the night before' as far as the world-wide economy is concerned. There is an expectation that as we approach the new Millennium the enthusiasm for the closing of one century and the excitement of opening up another new, fresher one will be enough to buoy up the world-wide economy.

But there is the spectre of the Millennium bug, which threatens to disrupt so many of the world's computer systems with possible disastrous results. There is also perhaps the sense that the economic boom of the late 1990s really will have run out of steam and in fact might have ended earlier had it not been for the supporting effect of widespread enthusiasm as the century closes. Indeed, there are now serious tremors in Asia and Russia. Thus it could be that there will be a severe economic downturn at the beginning of the new century with tough consequences for all aspects of the economy and inevitably for brands.

Certainly economist David Hackett Fischer, in his recent book *The Great Wave*, feels that this is the case. He identifies four great price revolutions in the 14th, 17th, late 18th and early 19th centuries, and the one we are in now at the end of the 20th century. These successive waves are characterized by rising prices, falling real wages, rising returns on capital and growing gaps between rich and poor. So far they have only been brought back to the equilibrium of comparative price stability by cataclysmic events such as the Black Death, the European crises and the Napoleonic Wars. Who knows what will end this one? Fischer also notes that 'the penultimate stage of every price revolution was . . . a period of desperate search for spiritual values'.

His thesis would seem to be confirmed by the extraordinary growth of interest in 'alternative' thinking of all sorts, whether it be medical, spiritual or religious. The quite stunning charitable donations being made by individuals as recorded in the Forbes 'Most Generous' league table – itself an interesting *fin de siècle* counterpoint to its long-standing Fortune 500 listing, are also indicative. It is also confirmed by the enormous expansion of Cause Related Marketing.

Thus, it should be of enormous benefit for brands to have embraced the idea of Cause Related Marketing and taken early steps to build new 'spiritual' values into their brand propositions against harder times ahead. It seems likely that if consumers are forced to make tough choices in a harsher economic climate in the early part of the new Millennium they may well favour brands which seem to have set their house in order. Those that seem to be aligned more appropriately to the new era with its ethical, caring and responsible attitudes should benefit.

When if not now? Whom if not I?

Bertrand Russell

Index

Index compiled by Annette Musker